ALL ABOARD!

A journey on the Trans-Mongolian Railway and through Eastern Europe

By Carrie Riseley

For Maria
Who was more adventurous than me
But whose illness prevented her from doing all she wanted to do
And seeing all she wanted to see

Table of Contents

Preface

Come on a journey across the world with me. See stretching grasslands 100km wide; hear the music of ice by a beach; smell some rousing local cuisine. Ten countries, tens of thousands of kilometres, and a whole lot of adventure.

I love travelling and have always kept a journal to record my experiences. After receiving some good feedback on my writing, I decided to edit some of my extensive volumes of travel journal notebooks into a book to publish. I hope you'll have a great time travelling with me, seeing what I saw and feeling what I felt.

I particularly enjoyed learning about the history of the places I travelled through and how its impacts are still felt today. All the countries I travelled through were communist countries in the 20th century, and several were also subjected to Nazi occupation and the horrors of the Holocaust. Joining the dots between what I'd learned growing up in the West and the reality for those in the East was eye-opening.

This book is a casual record written through my eyes only. I wrote down facts about the places I was travelling through as I learned them along the way, but I could never hope to manage - and nor have I ever aspired to - unassailable political or historical analysis of the places I visited. I have simply recorded what I saw and learned along with my thoughts on it. One of the most important things I have learned is that we *all* (even those much more expert than me) view and understand things through the lens of our own upbringing and experiences. This book is written through the lens of a young Australian travelling through Mongolia, Russia and eastern Europe in the 2010s. It is a snapshot of that place in that time as it was seen by me. I hope you'll enjoy the journey.

Carrie Riseley
Hobart, Tasmania
July 2021

The beginning

The Trans-Siberian Railway runs 9,289km from Vladivostok to Moscow; the Trans-Mongolian is the same line from Lake Baikal westwards, but from Lake Baikal it splits off to the south, running through Mongolia to Beijing. Mongolia sounded romantic and fascinating to me. I was intrigued by stories from a friend who had taken this journey and told me that in Mongolia people live in yurts with TVs and fridges in them and suburban fences around them. This I had to see. I booked my rail journey from Beijing to St Petersburg: 7,900 kilometres, one fifth of the circumference of the earth.

I'd been to Beijing before and hadn't liked it much, so I spent two days escaping the city before boarding the train. This is my travel journal.

4th of May, 9:45am:

I'm now on a bus from Beijing to Miyun, hoping I can get from there to the Great Wall without being ripped off too badly. As usual, I have under-budgeted for China. The first time I went to China, I borrowed an old guidebook from the library which said, "The Chinese view it as their patriotic duty to rip foreigners off." I later attended a seminar in my hometown about Chinese business culture, and basically, if you don't know how to haggle effectively and politely, you're stuffed. Which is why I always under budget for China.

So far, however, my experiences have been positive. I came out of Customs at 11:30pm last night, precisely 20 minutes after the airport train stopped running. Found a bus, and missed my stop because for some reason when the bus stopped the driver was yelling, "Ruha," instead of "Dongzhimen". I wasn't too worried at the time because it was only the first stop, but a couple of minutes later I realised that the sign at the airport had said that Dongzhimen *was* the first stop. I asked first another passenger and then the driver and they both replied in Chinese, but they both shook their heads and pointed behind them, as in: "No, Dongzhimen was back there!"

But he'd said, "Ruha!" at that stop! I wonder whether "ruha" actually means, "Oi foreigner, didn't you want to get off here?" He did say it twice.

So there I was at nearly midnight stuck on a bus in a strange city going further and further away from my hostel. I swore loudly.

I was really lucky, though. The driver was kind enough at the end of his route to turn around and take me back to Dongzhimen! So that was positive experience number one – nice bus driver. And he did not ask for an extra payment to do this!

Then when I got off the bus I had to find where I was on the map so I could start following my hostel's directions. I asked a man at a bus stop, and he told me what road we were on and what direction it was going – all in Chinese, but I could understand the hand gestures and he seemed friendly. Positive experience number 2. Also, fortunately I can read the characters for "east" and "west" and they were marked on the road signs - otherwise I wouldn't have understood what he was saying about the directions.

I felt completely safe, even though it was after midnight (closer to 1am at this stage) and I was carrying all my stuff. There were people around and lights and no-one was looking at me funny. Did not get lost. Met a foreigner right at the end who walked me right into the hostel. Win.

I'd known all along that the hostel had 24-hour reception, otherwise I would have been a lot more stressed out!

It's been a while since my last trip and I'd forgotten about those little, *Shit! Where am I? What do I do?* experiences you have while travelling. I freaked out very slightly at the start when I swore on the bus, but after that I just found it invigorating!

<u>4:45pm:</u>

My taxi ride from Miyun to Jinshanling was expensive, but totally worth it to spend three amazing hours hiking on the Great Wall. The start at Jinshanling was a bit touristy, but the people lessened as I went on. The unrestored section further along was extra charming, but I liked seeing the restored bit too, because that's what it was meant to be like when it was built and used. There's incredible mountain scenery, with the wall snaking its way through as far as the eye can see. Even smog looks beautiful from the Great Wall.

One of the steepest parts of the unrestored section had steps going straight up: literally if I put my hand out I'd touch the steps ahead of me without having to bend over. There was a guard tower at the top and there was an old man sitting in its doorway. He was wearing darkish green old-style workers' clothing and a striking army green engine driver hat with a big red communist star on the front of it, and he was smoking a pipe. It was amazing to see, high above the Great Wall, being firmly reminded that I was in China; possibly even China fifty years ago – Mao's China. Then, when I finally got up the steps and walked past him, he said, "Coca Cola! Ice water! Coffee! Beer!"

Always a land of contrasts.

In the taxi on the way back, I got the front seat view of all the vehicles driving straight at me as we drove on the wrong side of the road to overtake all the trucks, and felt every acceleration and brake as the driver prepared to overtake and then decided that car coming towards us was too close after all – or, in one case, when he pulled out to go around a line of about six cars and two or three trucks *which were going around a corner at the time.* He got halfway through and then suddenly had to brake and swerve back into the middle of the line when, between two trucks around the corner up ahead, he spotted a car coming straight at us!

Well, at least he was watching ahead. So was I, believe me, and I saw it too and was quite relieved when we suddenly swerved back onto the right side of the road...

A traffic scenario I was flabbergasted by on a previous trip, vehicles ending up three abreast in two lanes because one's decided giving way is for wimps and it's just going to push right between the oncoming vehicle (and/or truck) and the vehicle it's overtaking, happened at least four times in an approximately one-hour journey. One of those times it was us doing the overtaking and squishing between a truck and a car.

Fortunately for me, that previous experience I had meant that it didn't bother me. I expected it. I took a sharp intake of breath a couple of times, but nothing more. I understand now that it's just how they drive here. They do look up ahead and are prepared to slow down or swerve quite often without incident.

I also expected the driver to make three mobile phone calls – *make* them, not receive them, so he had to spend a lot of time with the phone on the steering wheel scrolling through his contacts list first. I didn't react, other than a subtle roll of my eyes.

I did complain loudly when he started smoking, though. But he didn't stop; he just wound the window down.

5th of May, 8:03pm:

Today I went to collect my train ticket! My travel agent had given me written instructions to go to Room 801 of the CITS Building in Dong Cheng District. CITS stands for China International Travel Services, which, it turns out, is the biggest travel agency in the whole wide world. The first office I passed on the eighth floor was Hawaiian Airlines, and then there were lots of "inbound travel" offices in various corridors. Room 801 was labelled something like, "Inbound Travel – Spanish and Portuguese-Speaking Nations". I walked in, and they said, "Hola!" to me! I explained what I wanted, and it turned out I was in completely the wrong office.

Fortunately, there was a nice lady called Amanda there who spoke English as well as Spanish, and she proceeded to take me to at least three other offices desperately trying to find someone who could help me. First she took me to her boss, who phoned the number written next to the CITS address on my travel documents and found it went to an office on the seventh floor. We went to two offices on the seventh floor before finding out it was the wrong phone number!

I was getting worried that my ticket had been lost, which would have been an enormous disaster! However, though the facial expressions of the people Amanda was talking to (in Chinese) indicated they didn't have a clue what she was talking about, they all seemed to have ideas on where we should go next. They were pointing toward other offices and nodding, so I didn't worry too much. Amanda and her colleagues seemed determined to get to the bottom of it.

The man from office number three (four, if you count Room 801) took us to Room 701, which was the office for inbound travel for Oceania and/or some English-speaking countries or something (I'd stopped reading the signs by this stage). Finally, my train ticket appeared! I thanked Amanda and the man from office number three and they left. Two men from Room 701 told me about my ticket, how to get to the station in the morning etc., and checked my passport number.

The ticket doesn't say my name, only my passport number! They told me that this was normal. They couldn't tell me anything else because the woman who'd issued my ticket, someone called Diana, was out to lunch - as, indeed, was almost everybody else. The main reason why it had taken so long to find the right office was that each room had only one or two people in it, and scores of empty desks!

After that I had lunch at a restaurant which had a spectacular English picture menu offering things like:

- Mushroom and rape
- Husband and wife lung slice
- Starch bath chap
- Long in tomato burn beans
- Pan wan MAO blood flourishing
- Tofu pudding intestine
- A knot in the soup
- Hand bag food
- Pickled duck blood

Then I went to the 798 Art District, which was just incredible. It's in a disused electronics factory/industrial district, and it's enormous! I was wandering down numerous laneways in several directions for two hours before I got back to somewhere I'd seen before, and even then there were still scores of unseen laneways and galleries left to explore. I loved the art, but more than that I loved the location. Derelict buildings, some with bits clearly missing; huge pipes just above street level ducting something or other through the site; bunched up wires; many layers of grime. This was all coloured somewhere from dusty grey to deep brown and musky red, but it was interspersed with brightly coloured splashes of green vines and art in all the colours of the rainbow.

And the shapes. Tall, round smoke stacks; winding pipes; sawtooth-roofed factory buildings. I spent hours taking photos of the architecture, let alone the art! I saw one art gallery whose upper level went right up into two of the triangular sections of factory roof, which was made using that age-old Roman method of setting concrete between wooden boxing. I could see the grain of the wood – I could even see bits of wood – in this dark grey industrial concrete. The art in that gallery was amazing too – by someone called Cao Yong.

I'm intrigued by industrial architecture of bygone eras, particularly derelict buildings, as there's something about the grime and the just so slightly tumble-down nature of it that's endearingly mysterious and interesting to me. I would even say it's beautiful. But the Chinese artists seemed to appreciate it for an entirely different reason. It's an artists' community, so you would think they would be a sub-culture, a counter culture, expressing non-mainstream ideas in creative ways because they're artists, right?

Not really... There was a huge array of militaristic art and lots of communist stuff, including some propaganda postcards I really hoped were satirical but may not have been. They said things like, "Make money is the highest glory!" - OK, not very communist, but representative of Chinese "communism" today. The communist stuff was all meant to look cool; the red star and khaki was a design feature of many of the products in the shops; there was a communist panda and other cutesy stuff that looked quite conventional; and then there was a lot of industrial stuff glorifying cars, planes and trains. There's the wing of an enormous military jet in the main courtyard...

The themes were just so different from any art I have ever seen in the West. Back home, if you see military art it'll usually be hauntingly tragic, showing the horrors of war, not just some soldier on guard looking cool. Kitschy things with cute pandas and car number plates are practically mainstream now - they're not arty. The factory itself was being somehow celebrated, and even the very talented artworks of Cao Yong were so mainstream. They were celebrating nationalistic beliefs. He did one of the USA showing Mt Rushmore, the Statue of Liberty, man on the moon, Iwojima and some fire-fighters raising the US flag at Ground Zero; and an enormous Chinese one showing the Great Wall, Tian'anmen Gate, the Terracotta Warriors, a famous waterfall, a giant Buddha: all the famous stuff that only represents the cultural majority. And, in the mountains in the background, the Potala Palace and Mt Everest, which are Tibetan, not Chinese! It's amazing art - the execution is incredible - but it's just so... mainstream. It's propaganda, actually. That word popped into my head many times while I was there.

6th of May, 8:45am:

I'd been told that on the Trans-Mongolian Railway the toilets are always locked when the train is in a station, and I hadn't really considered the reason why... It's because they tip straight out onto the tracks! There's a chute and a hole – you can see it through the bowl.

Well, here I am, 45 minutes into my 7,900km journey. I'm in a second-class cabin, which is pretty cramped with four beds, but fortunately there are only three of us in here: me and an American couple called Angie and Esra.

Industry really is booming in China - you see it everywhere. Buildings being built, rocks piled, cement laid, dust and rubbish strewn... waste laid... I haven't seen anything beautiful apart from the mountains. The mountains are great. But they're covered in smog.

11:50am:

We're going through an industrial city now – the only settlement the train's stopped at so far – and it's so full of contrasts of old and new, tradition and progress, with progress clearly winning out. The smaller towns we've passed have been full of traditional hutongs: many small one-storey houses arranged in rows along laneways, built in brick with reddish brown tiles, all ochre-coloured and grimy. In the same area, you'll see a handful of (usually derelict) traditional houses, behind them an old grimy apartment building that's still being lived in, and behind that rows and rows of new apartment buildings - some so new they shine - and on the horizon more being built. I got a photo of a grimy old apartment building and a shiny white shopping centre behind it with a huge TV screen on the wall, and another of workers on the endless arid farm fields with a row of concrete pillars running through them, being built through this farmland. From the shape of the row, I'd say it's going to be a highway or railway flyover of some kind. Quite close to the ground, running through the farmland.

And oh, there's so much rubbish.

Still plenty of people employed in agriculture, though - and it's manual labour agriculture. I'd imagine the industrialisation just isn't reaching the poor. They don't even seem to have horses.

<u>2:50pm:</u>

The landscape has changed a fair bit. Flatter, with rolling hills on the horizon rather than mountains. Less people. Less smog, but it's still there on the horizon. There are still factories.

The traditional architecture changed a couple of hours back. The roofs became pointy and the blocks of apartments became less. And the villages look dirtier and more ramshackle.

And even here, they're building flyovers.

Ah, another city with apartment buildings being built. They're shiny and new and there are so many of them. And there are billboards and flyovers. Still a few hutongs though. This city is called Jining. The train station is new.

According to Esra's map, we are in the Inner Mongolia Autonomous Region. That means part of Mongolia is in China. I doubt it's autonomous – they call Tibet an Autonomous Region too. Esra's guidebook says Mongolians are only 15% of the population now, and China has made them assimilate and abandon their nomadic lifestyle. But we have seen Mongol script on the train station signs because they have been allowed to keep their language.

I was excited to see the book mention that we could see Mongol shepherds tending their flocks – we did see some shepherds, very close to the train!

9:50pm:

I watched the sun set over the Gobi Desert. It was magical. I guess we're still in the desert now – we're in a border town called Erlian, on the Chinese side. China and Mongolia have a different rail gauge, so right now we're in a big industrial shed where they literally swap the wheels over!! And we're on the train while they do it! They've finished – wait, have they? We're so confused. The train is still shaking everywhere, and we have no idea if we have wheels or not!

The grasslands were pretty majestic: fairly flat but with little hilly bumps, green and brown, with the odd ramshackle village and some of those shepherds the guidebook mentioned. I'd been worried about getting bored while I was on the train, but I had no problems at all. I had an endless parade of fascinating stuff right outside the window. I literally spent 12 hours today looking out the window. More, if you count the two hours I just spent watching the wheels being changed. Even when I was talking to Angie and Esra or writing in here, I was always looking out the window too. I'm loving this journey.

Dinner was the same as lunch: Chinese two-minute noodles and bok choy in yesterday's takeaway container with hot water from the urn at the end of the carriage. As I was eating, sand appeared at the side of the tracks. Just a little bit at the start - barely noticeable. The sun got lower and lower, gently wrapped in thin cotton wool clouds that were making it glow in a softer, more muffled way. Then I realised that the whole air was muffled; that is to say, everything was a bit blurry. I thought we'd come into some low cloud or fog, but it was actually sand blowing around!

And so I watched the sunset over the Gobi Desert. I couldn't see the desert clearly because of the light, but it was certainly sandy and flat and it went all the way to the horizon. It wasn't sand dunes but flat sand covered in scores of tussocks of grass, exactly like the sand at the edge of beaches.

Changing the bogies

When I came back into my cabin after sitting on a little seat in the corridor watching the last rays of light fade, I found that a departure card and a customs card had appeared for me. I filled them in, put my boots on and attempted to get my belongings in order, but soon gave up and decided to simply hope that we didn't have to take all our stuff off the train.

We arrived at Erlian Station at around 8:30pm, and I stepped into the corridor with my hand luggage only. Our carriage's conductor quickly ushered me right back into the cabin, pointing out a woman in a military uniform who was now standing at the door of the next cabin, checking the passport of the Mongolian woman inside. I put my stuff back in the cabin - evidently we would have our passport check right here on the train!

The woman took my passport and departure card, asked my name and looked at my face. Then she did the same thing with Angie and Esra. When she opened Esra's passport, he was on the floor getting something out of his bag. She said, "What is your name? Please remove your glasses." This is a perfectly reasonable thing for a passport officer to request, but it seemed odd because I never thought I'd hear it requested of a man kneeling on the floor of a cabin!

Then she took our passports away. I did not enjoy this, but I had been warned it would happen. The passport officer left the carriage. We were left looking out onto the platform, from which what I will call communist music was blaring from loudspeakers: proud, patriotic ceremonial/marching music – I recall hearing similar stuff on Vietnamese trains. We watched various uniformed officers and guards (of which there are so many in China and they are always *so* young) marching, walking and running about – or, in one case, balancing on a stone paver at the edge of a garden bed! Told you they were young.

They were lining up in twos in front of an older officer who would ask them something and they would respond, and then he would send them running onward as the next two ran into their place. This continued for a couple of minutes until I saw one of the more experienced-looking (but still young) officers putting an enormous stack of passports into a bag and moving towards the station building. I noticed an Australian/Norwegian couple I'd been talking to at Beijing Station this morning walking along the platform behind him, which let me know it was OK for us to get off the train.

I got off, and was finally able to see the train's full length. It's… long! 10 or 14 cars, maybe? I took photos, and an engine driver deliberately scared me by pulling his horn. I know it was deliberate: he was looking right at me when he pulled it and he smiled when I jumped. Then there was an announcement saying that we would be at this station "for some time" and that we were welcome to go inside and use the loo, rest and, under the announcer's encouragement, shop.

I found the shop on the upper floor. I'd been wishing I'd brought more snacks and getting jealous of Angie and Esra for having lots of them – and good Chinese ones, too, like chilli tofu. Fortunately, there were plenty in the duty-free shop! Small packets were only three yuan each, so I grabbed a few and a packet of preserved eggs, and a cold beer.

Aha! I've just been handed a Mongolian Arrival Card! At 12:23am.

12:29am:

That moment when you realise you don't know what country you're in...
Mongolia. We're in Mongolia!!

12:56am:

Still waiting for our passports back.

After making my purchases I walked back out of the station building and
immediately noticed that the train was half as long as it used to be. I quickly
got back on, as I knew they were taking bits of train away to have the
wheels changed, and I didn't want to miss that.

Our bit of train (the first bit, numbering about six carriages I think) rolled
into an industrial shed that had two open tracks in the middle with red
lifting mechanisms positioned about ten metres apart all the way along
both sides of both tracks. They were pretty modest-looking: just a red
metal pillar with a control panel beneath it and a rubber hydraulic thingy
inside. At the edge of the shed there were lots and lots of train wheel
chassis. These are called bogies, and we were about to go through "the
changing of the bogies".

There was much shuddering and shunting that sounded like a
rollercoaster and felt like a dodgem car or an earthquake. We didn't really
know what was going on until we saw the other half of our train pull in on
the track next to us. After a good ten to fifteen minutes of hearing them
being shunted around but seeing nothing visibly moving on their train, and
workers moving around but not doing anything visibly much, eventually I
became aware that the carriage in front of the one next to us had been
separated and was now several feet in the air, with its wheels sitting
disconnected below it. I went to the end of our carriage to get a better
view, discovering when I got there that our carriage was now also several
metres away from its neighbour. I was looking through a small window in its
end door at a man's face looking through the small window in the
neighbouring carriage's end door. The man looked rather like a vampire
with the way the filtered light was shattering over his gaunt face; a vampire
trapped in a spaceship that was moving away from me.

But the real action was going on next door, on the other track. One
carriage was way up in the air. The other one, the one next to ours, began
to move too, almost imperceptibly slowly. Through the window in the side

door of that carriage I saw the Australian/Norwegian couple. We waved at each other. And then their carriage went up. It was disconnected from its bogies. A pulley inside one of the two railway tracks beneath it began to move. And then suddenly, a long line of bogies began pouring under the first carriage and through to the second. About halfway through the line, the bogies became visibly different. These new ones stopped and were placed in the required positions under the carriages. The cables and bolts were connected and the lifts disconnected. The other half of the train now had Mongolian wheels. But what about our half? We were a little miffed that we'd been in the warehouse first but that the other half of the train had got their wheels changed first!

We were shunted backwards a little way, and then forwards again. We went forwards, out of the shed, and then back into it again. There was more bumping, but we weren't raised into the air. Then we went back into the dark again. For quite a way, forwards. Then we went quite a way backwards, still in the dark, eventually arriving back at the station platform. Up until that last sentence, we'd been convinced that we either didn't have wheels at all or that we still had Chinese wheels, when all along the changeover must have happened more than an hour before - somewhere in between the dodgem car moves and rollercoaster noises and the appearance of the other cars on the track beside us. If I see that Australian/Norwegian couple again I'll ask them if we were way up in the air when they came in. We didn't even notice.

We sat at the station for a while again. There were no soldiers running around on the platform anymore. The military-uniformed lady came to give our passports back (she'd kept them for three hours!!). She asked us to lift the bottom bunks/seats. This is how we discovered that there is a hidden compartment under there, which she wanted to check to make sure we didn't have any contraband. We didn't have any contraband, but we most certainly had reds under the bed.

The train moved away with the communist music playing again and the guards standing to attention. After a short distance, it stopped again and I wondered what country I was in, until a Mongolian passport officer came to our cabin, looked under our beds and took our passports. Then another officer took our arrival cards, signed them and gave them straight back to us. They kept our passports for a while, but nowhere near as long as the Chinese did. Got away at 1:45am, the border crossing having taken over five hours.

7th of May:

I had a rather restless night's sleep because every time I rolled over, I kept obsessively looking out the window to see what was out there. At 5:30am, I discovered that the sun was rising. I yelped, kicked off my covers and grabbed my camera, and that is how I came to see both the sunset and the sunrise over the Gobi Desert.

We sat in a station for a while and then moved off. I sat up for a while watching the desert as the sun rose higher. I finally convinced myself to go back to sleep because I didn't want to have to sleep through Mongolian towns in the day, and desert is exciting but it's just desert, right, it's all the same (yet mesmerising still). So I got another three hours' sleep, but I still kept waking up to peek out the window because I wanted to know how long the desert went on for. We left it at around 9/9:30am.

We've seen only a handful of villages all day, there are barely any animals and no shepherds, but I'm still looking out the bloody window. The different tones of yellow in the grasslands, with just brief bits of green or brown, are mesmerising. They look pretty much the same as the desert: flatness going on as far as the eye can see, but with grass and a few more bumps. And more habitation - but after China it doesn't look like much habitation.

They have a few new buildings too, but they're much smaller. And there are yurts, and some underground dwellings!

It's now 11:30 and we have snow! Wow! I think I'm up to date now so I'm gonna look out the mesmerising window and eat chilli tofu.

8:25pm:

It's snowing in Ulaanbaatar. Not settling, but snowing. The area we went through on the train was completely white. Apparently the temperature here can range between 40°C in summer and minus 40°C in winter, springtime is always cold and summer is really short. It's really warm in the buildings, though. My homestay is in an old (mid-20th century) apartment building which has hot pipes running along the walls – even the stairway is heated!

My tour guide and driver picked me up at the train station at 1:30pm and took me to my homestay. I keep reading about Soviet-style apartment buildings and I don't know what they look like yet, but I assume this is one. There are a few buildings arranged around a rather drab courtyard, and the buildings are also drab and colourless, but the courtyard has colourful play equipment and a painted amateur statue. The stairwells, including the stairs themselves, are brightly painted, and the doors to the apartments are coloured. "Mongolians love colour," said my tour guide, Tunga. This was the first thing I noticed when the train reached the outskirts of Ulaanbaatar: there were suddenly bright splashes of colour everywhere, beating loudly through the white snow, the roof of every fixed building and the door of every ger (yurt) covered in bright paint or Colorbond. It's quite a sight.

I had an hour and a half to acquaint myself with the apartment - very small, very creaky floors, hot pipes on the walls, analogue television, amazing cast metal kitchen sink - and my host mother and the neighbourhood, before Tunga picked me up again for a walking tour. I learned many interesting things, including:

- Mongolia was ruled by China for about 200 years, becoming independent in 1911. In 1921, there was a communist revolution led by a man called Sukhbaatar. In 1924, Russia took over. Mongolia was never part of the USSR, but the Soviets ran things anyway. Consequently, Ulaanbaatar has lots of incredible European architecture, stately grand buildings including an opera house and ballet theatre: apparently Mongolia's ballerinas rival Russia's.
- The Mongolian communist party still has a lot of power, but the President is independently elected, US-style.
- Just about every building in Ulaanbaatar is from the 20th century. (Or 21st – there are several office buildings and apartment blocks being built now.) Before that, it was all gers (yurts). It was known as the "felt city". There are lots of gers in the suburbs. They have suburban fences around them. It's odd to look at.
- Ulaanbaatar has a population of about 1.5 million, and Mongolia about 3 million (in a huge country!)

- The city's roads aren't designed to cope with this number of people and cars. When Tunga was growing up, the only cars were company cars, and only for the bosses. Not many people could afford their own, and those who did buy one were subjected to so many questions it wasn't worth it, because they would be accused of getting the funds by illegal means. Now, though, everyone has a car. They buy a lot second hand from Japan, which means that:
- Mongolia, a right-hand-driving country, has many right-hand drive cars! They have both! The government tried to make a ruling that you could only have left-hand drive cars, but there were already so many right-hand drive cars that they couldn't get it through, so legally you can have either – and people do!
- The traffic is terrible. People push in and honk a lot, and manoeuvre without warning. Tunga said it's because traditionally everyone rode horses across broad open steppes (grasslands), and they never had to stop or go around anybody. People still do this now, even city people when they're on holiday in the country, so when they come back to the city and get in their cars, they are the most impatient drivers in the world.

We saw TumenEkh, a traditional song and dance group, perform. It was incredible. They did maybe ten different pieces from different traditions – social dance, song, "long song": where the notes go on and on, several different notes in a fast melody, without the singer drawing breath. And string instruments, a traditional orchestra, contortionists, a shaman dance (with a very earthy costume and a heavy drumbeat), a mask dance with elaborate masks of gods and devils... And the famous Mongolian throat singing was mind blowing... the performer was whistling in his throat!

Then we went to a "Mongolian fast-food restaurant" to try a kind of dumpling called buuz, which is pronounced the way a Jamaican would say "boat". It really was fast food – I went to the loo right after we ordered and it was on the table before I came out again. I haven't seen any McDonald's: Tunga said Mongolians have their own fast food. These dumplings are designed to be fast because they're eaten at lunar new year, when every Mongolian has three days to visit every single member of their family who is older than them. All that visiting requires a lot of food. Tunga said people will make up to 1,000 buuz ahead of time and store them outside, where they freeze, because it's January or February. Then, when the rellies arrive, they only need to be steamed and they're ready in minutes.

They're so fatty. Lard was caked onto my fork. I've stopped being a vegetarian just for this trip because I heard it's pretty hard to get vegetarian food in Mongolia and Russia. Right now I'm looking forward to becoming a vegetarian again. The buuz were *so* fatty! But fortunately, they're served with salad (I would have died otherwise). Tunga said traditionally it would have been root vegetables or seasonal vegetables, but now they can grow anything in a greenhouse.

I should probably go to bed. I got through today on caffeine, guarana and excitement.

Follow the cows

8th of May, 4:55pm:

Well this is an interesting turn of events. We're bogged, somewhere on a Mongolian plain in the middle of nowhere. And it's snowing. This is one of those situations where I don't panic because I know it'll make a good story later. So I don't think I'll say anything more now because a story is much better if you don't start it in the middle.

We left Ulaanbaatar at 10ish this morning. On the way out I once again marvelled at the colours of the roofs, especially in the hillside suburbs, and the sheer number of gers sitting on fenced off suburban blocks.

Our group is composed of myself, Tunga, a driver called Bata and a cook called Dorj. Because of circumstances (primarily the fact that the tourist season hasn't started yet), I am the only tourist on this tour. I have a private tour of Mongolia!

Tunga told me that where there are only one or two gers on a fenced off block it's a family, but where there are more and the block is larger, the gers are accommodation for the workers who are going to build something there. For some reason they always seem to build the fence first!

She also said that all Mongolians can get about half an acre of land for free in a city or town, but that in the countryside all the land is owned by the state and the nomadic herders move their gers around seasonally. The reason land is privatised in the city is part of embracing capitalism, but they couldn't do it in the country because the nomadic system has been in place for centuries, and the herders need to be nomadic because the good pasture changes and they need to move around to access it.

By the side of the highway in the outskirts of Ulaanbaatar was a man in traditional (warm-looking) dress with two incredibly furry camels and an eagle. I paid 3000 tugriks (about AUD$1.40) to hold the eagle on my arm. It was heavy and its wingspan was enormous! The man said it weighed about 8kg. In western Mongolia, there's a tradition of eagle hunting. They keep a blindfold over the eagle's eyes until they find some prey – rabbits, foxes, sometimes even a wolf – and the eagle goes and grabs it and holds it down until the hunter gets there.

Next stop was the Chinggis Khan statue. I was confused by the two spellings of Chinggis Khan and Ghengis Khan, but it seems Ghengis was a misspelling done by someone who pronounced g's as j's. Pronunciation-wise, Jengis Khan will work, or Chinggis Khan. It means Ocean King – so vast were the lands he conquered.

The statue is the largest statue on a horse in the world. It's big and shiny, and he is holding a golden whip. You can climb up into the horse's mane and have Chinggis Khan towering above you.

In the building beneath it there is a Bronze Age museum. There are items from two different periods, the latter one being the time of Chinggis (late 12th-early 13th centuries). Did you know that they had steel, bombs and guns? And their arrowheads had holes in them which made a noise when they were flying through the air, so that when hundreds of arrows were fired at an enemy army, the noise would be very loud and the enemy would panic!

We drove through a few different weather systems today. The area around Ulaanbaatar was green. The area where the eagle was was windy and bloody cold. The area where Chinggis was had snow on the ground but was sunny and warm and Tunga exclaimed, "Yes! The weather is getting better!" Then we drove into rain, and then snow. I later explained to her what jinx means, but I don't think she fully grasped the concept.

When the rain became snow it was quite quick and suddenly all we could see was the car in front of us, which had its hazard lights on. If it weren't for that car's wheel marks, I wouldn't have been able to see the road at all. I realised that there were absolutely no road markers - even though this was a main highway! Fortunately we drove out of that heavy, settling snow area fairly quickly.

I had a Toilet Experience at a petrol station in the outskirts of a coal mining town. I knew we were stopping for lunch soon, but I really had to pee and we were stopping for petrol anyway, so Tunga said, "Well, OK, but it's only that wooden one." She was pointing in the direction of the shop, which had a wooden door I started walking towards until she said, "No, no - that one over there!"

My eyes refocussed and spotted, in a corner of the petrol station's yard, a tiny lean-to outbuilding. *Aha!* I thought. *This is sure to be a Toilet Experience...*

It was a small pit; not smelly, fortunately – I think not many people had used it. But you could certainly see the business of the people who had. Over the pit were about five thick wooden slats with spaces between them about 20cm across. You just stand on the planks and squat. It may have been the first time I have ever actually seen my stream of pee before it hit anything.

We had lunch in a roadside café. Kimchi soup was on the menu – apparently kimchi is popular because there are many Koreans here – but unfortunately they were out. Everything else was meat, meat, meat - but there was one dish that had mushrooms too, so I ordered that. Unfortunately, when it came out it was just a pile of boiled meat with enormous chunks of fat in it, and some side dishes (coleslaw and rice). They had neglected to tell us that they were out of mushrooms too! My face must have portrayed my horror, and just as Tunga was telling me I could order something else, Bata's plate of fried dumplings came out, which my face must have shown it liked the look of, so he offered to swap with me. I was very grateful, but ended up feeling a bit bad because Bata couldn't manage all the chunks of fat either – he left a pile of it on his plate.

Fried dumplings are so much better than steamed dumplings! Tunga said it's because the flavour is less strong and they aren't sitting in fat and juices. I really liked them. Unfortunately they were covered in lashings of mayo, and I'd also ordered a potato salad dish, so I came away with the same feeling of fat pooling in my belly that I'd had last night.

Bata and Dorj don't speak English, but sometimes Tunga tells me what she and they are talking about. At some point while we were driving, she said they were discussing what the dirt road we would later turn onto would be like after all the rain. "We think it will be very muddy," Tunga said. (Writing this after our Land Cruiser's nose has been submerged in said mud for two hours, I have to say, "No shit.")

Upon turning onto the "dirt road" I immediately realised that it was not a road at all. It was a track. There are scores – probably hundreds – of them winding all over the grasslands. In Australia I suppose we would call them four-wheel drive tracks, but Mongolians don't only use four-wheel drives on them – we saw a two-wheel drive truck abandoned with its nose in a puddle a few kilometres back. These tracks are just how people get around out here. And if the track's washed out or they realise they're on the wrong one and they need to go in a different direction, they just make a new one. The tracks are created by people just driving across the steppes (grasslands).

We stopped at an ovoo near the start of the track. An ovoo is a pile of rocks which are an offering to the gods. For good fortune, you have to throw rocks onto the pile while walking around it clockwise. There were some prayer wheels there as well that we spun, and a tall stick with coloured silk flags hanging off it stuck in the middle of the ovoo. The dominant colour of the silk was blue, and Tunga said that blue is the most important colour in Mongolian culture because it's the colour of the sky. People hang blue scarves at the entrances to their homes, and there is one wrapped around the rear-view mirror of our Land Cruiser. It's not giving us much luck at the moment. I see no blue sky.

As for the rocks, you can get better fortune if you bring them to a higher altitude, which is why ovoos are always made on hills. Tunga said Mongolians never throw a rock down; especially not into a river, because the river will wash the rock away, and with it all your money.

Also on this ovoo were two crutches and two steering wheel covers. Tunga said people leave crutches and the like there so that they won't need them again – they believe that if they hang onto them, they'll get another injury. The steering wheel covers were there to pray for a safe journey. Again, we're not having much luck with that, but we don't have a steering wheel cover so maybe we should have left our hubcaps there or something.

We've been here so long that the snow has started to settle. It's now 6:15pm. Maybe we'll be here so long I'll get to tell the story while it's happening!

Bata was driving along all these little tracks, and sometimes a fork in the track would appear and he'd confidently pick one side, and I wondered how on earth he knew where he was going when there were no signs or landmarks. I was just about to ask Tunga how when he finally wavered and stopped to ask somebody – some park rangers and researchers at the edge of the national park. Other than them, we've passed two families I think, one with one ger and one with three, and it took us a bit over an hour to get here.

We stopped to take photos of the group of three gers. There was an open wooden structure/yard next to them which Tunga said was the winter home for the animals. They wander around grazing in the day and sleep in there at night. There was also a fairly new-looking four-wheel drive, a solar panel, a satellite dish for the TV, a fairly new-looking tractor, and lots of dogs. Tunga said the dogs are to keep wolves away.

The track was good but we were going through the odd washed out section, sometimes slipping on mud - and a couple of times we drove right through what can be described as either a large pond or a small lake - but Bata always did it confidently and without issue. My guidebook says Mongolians are always very confident. Early on, I asked Tunga what would happen if we were to get bogged, and she shrugged and said, "I don't know – we get out and push!"

I couldn't help noticing that a: we don't have a winch and b: even if we did, there are no trees or boulders to latch one onto. I also couldn't help noticing that there were no gers for miles around and no phone reception.

When the track got really bad, and we were basically driving through a bog, with wheel ruts winding all over the place as people tried harder and harder to find a way around the wet bits, and Bata started swinging his wheel all over the place and sometimes getting out or reversing back to investigate all the options, I asked Tunga again. "Do boggings happen often?"

She looked rather uneasy with this question and reluctantly answered, "Yes... of course."

"What do people do?" I asked.

"They have to get out and walk to the nearest family to ask for help, but it can be some distance. They might be walking for quite some time. You can see there are no gers anywhere around here."

The premonition in her words was uncanny. It was less than five minutes, or maybe even two, after she said that that it happened.

All of a sudden, we spun out. I felt the car tip, and I thought we were going to roll. Bata hit the brakes, and we stopped. My relief was short lived, as we had stopped with our nose in a waterlogged wheel rut... He tried to reverse, but of course it wasn't going to happen. We all got out, and the other three tried to push while I took photos, but it wasn't going to happen.

"I'll help if I can put my raincoat on!" I announced. Tunga and I opened the back and I got my anorak out of my pack. When I came back around the vehicle, I realised that Bata and Dorj weren't there anymore. "Did they go to the nearest family?" I asked Tunga.

"No," she said, "They're getting some wood." She gestured to a nearby hill, where there are (yes, are: this is still present tense for me) some spindly small pine trees. I could just see Bata and Dorj's figures through the falling snow.

They came back with some long and spindly branches which we began to break into bits. Dorj stuffed some under the back tyres, where they would go on to achieve nothing at all, as they are sticking up in the air as, indeed, is most of the back end. Bata attempted to shove some around the front wheels, but there wasn't even anywhere for them to go. We pushed again, but she wouldn't budge.

Then Dorj began looking through all the very many things we have in the back. He pulled out a very small jack and kept looking. I wondered if he had a spade in there somewhere, but no such luck. Apparently Mongolians are so confident that they don't think to bring a spade when they're going off-roading through a bog in the snow without a winch or support vehicle.

What Dorj was actually looking for was a missing piece of the jack, something that turns the screw around to make the jack extend. He didn't find it. Bata, fag in his mouth, propped the jack up on a chunk of wood by the front wheel and began moving the screw with a small piece of stick. It did extend, but it was never going to achieve anything. How was such a tiny jack on a chunk of wood in the mud halfway up the wheel going to move the wheel? I thought Bata must know something I didn't, because he kept trying for quite a while, and has tried periodically since.

I didn't have a clue what was going on because they were talking in Mongolian the whole time. I just kept thinking they must have some kind of contingency plan, but then something very, very worrying happened. All three Mongolians suddenly got out their phones and began looking at them intently. They were looking for phone reception. *Oh my god*, I thought. *They're going to call for help? They don't have anything with them other than that little jack? Their contingency plan is to call for help?* Well, I guess Tunga had told me that that is what people do.

Tunga and Dorj put their phones away, but Bata kept staring at his. I thought this meant that his phone had reception. It didn't – he was just more stubborn than the other two.

Dorj started putting the back seats back up and clearing them off. Tunga came over to me. "OK," she said, "You get into the car and get warm. Dorj and I are going to the top of that hill to look for reception. And we know there is a family in that direction somewhere."

"And you know their phone number?" I asked.

"Just get in the car," she said.

So I got in the car, and that was where you came in. It was 4:55. Bata kept playing with the jack for a while, then he got in and tried reversing again - to no avail, of course. He really is very stubborn.

After about thirty to forty minutes I saw him look out the window, so I did the same. Tunga and Dorj were approaching along the track. Bata walked over to meet them. I saw Tunga point towards the farthest hill. They talked some more, and then Dorj pointed in the same direction. Then they walked back to the car. "We couldn't get reception on this hill, and we tried that way a little way, but we couldn't find any," said Tunga. "But there were some cows here earlier, weren't there?" There were. I had been taking photos of them through the snow. "It's getting late, so they will be going home," Tunga explained. "So Dorj and I will follow the cows and we will find their home."

They were going to find the nearest family.

Bata and I sat in the car for ages again, he occasionally trying fruitlessly to reverse - I've no idea why. Meantime we've been sinking! At some point he put waders on, but I'm not sure why because nothing came of it.

It's nice in the car, though, because Bata's had the heater on for about two hours now. This, of course, requires the engine to be on. At one point, I looked at the dash when Bata was out of the car (either smoking or trying the jack again) and I noticed that the fuel gauge was dangerously close to empty. I wondered whether Bata was so confident that he thought running out of fuel was not an issue. If it was me, I definitely would have been rationing the heater in case we were stuck here all night!

When he got back in I asked him, "Is the fuel OK?" and pointed at the gauge.

"No problem," he said (he likes to say that). "This broken."

I found out that he does speak a little bit of English, because he went on to tell me that we'd done 86km since we'd last filled up, and that the tank would do 600km. This was a great relief.

We kept looking out the window, but nobody was coming. At one point, I thought he said, "No problem," but he actually said, "Snow problem." It was. It started to settle, but now it's gone back to rain. All the more water for the growing river beneath our wheels.

Suddenly, Bata got out. I quickly wound down my window (I couldn't see a thing through the condensation) to see Dorj and another man. I eagerly looked behind him to see what vehicle he had. It was a motorbike...

The man had a good look at the car whilst talking to Bata and Dorj, and he did some pointing over the hills as well. Then he and Dorj got back on the motorbike and rode off.

"He will bring small tractor," said Bata. "Family is five or six kilometres that way."

Thank god, I thought – the motorbike wasn't going to help much. But did that mean that Tunga and Dorj had walked for five or six kilometres? Was Tunga waiting in the ger getting warm?

No. About twenty minutes later the lonely, wet figure of Tunga appeared over the cloudy pass up ahead. When she got back to the car, she told me that she and Dorj had found that man alone on the motorbike. He was the owner of the cows, and he was looking for a lost one. He got lumbered with us instead.

He knows where all the families in the area are. He said one family has a car, but they went to town this morning and are not likely to be back, given the weather. Another family has a tractor. That is where he has taken Dorj.

Good tour guide that she is, Tunga began telling me about how the man knew all the families. "Even though they are far apart, they are his neighbours," she said, "so he knows where they all are. In the Gobi, the families are much further apart – maybe 100km between gers. But the people will still say, 'They are just over there, not very far away'!"

She said that when a nomad points, you have to watch their finger. If it is fully outstretched, it means that what they are pointing to is far away - more than 100km - even if they are saying, "It's just over there." If the finger is curled, it means the place is not very far. I think all the people I saw pointing had their fingers curled. I think...

Well, that's it - you're all up to date, folks! It's now 8pm, and that is everything that's happened. I never imagined three hours ago that I would actually get to tell this story while it was still happening! Even when I started telling it, I didn't think I would get to finish what's happened so far. But I have. So that's it, folks: this story doesn't have an ending!

The nearest family

9th of May, 6:15pm:

I am sitting in a pine forest on a hill, overlooking the vast plains and snowy mountains in the distance. I can hear wind – lots of it – but where I am is perfectly still and quiet. I'm up above the tourist village we are staying in, which is basically just six log cabins and a pit toilet, but there are also some local people living nearby. I could see three gers from the top of the hill, and there are lots of animals around - including some very cute dogs who introduced themselves to me when I was squatting over the toilet this morning. It has no door, so they just poked their heads in! There's a gap between the door and the land around – I think they do that to stop local animals wandering in and falling into the loo pit – so the dogs didn't fully invade my personal space, fortunately!

Well, you want to hear the end of my bogging story, don't you? It was incredible. The story has the best end possible – I think it'll end up being the highlight of my time in Mongolia!

The man with the tractor arrived just on dark, at about 8:15pm. "I thought the tractor would be bigger," said Tunga. It was small and green, and hanging off the back was not a tow bar but an old tyre. The man and Bata tied this tyre to the back of our vehicle using rope and, somehow, a big stick. Don't ask me how this works. I was thinking, *Oh dear, I'm not sure a tyre can rescue us*, but Tunga said later that because of the rubber it's actually very good for tension and... something. An engineer could tell you more. Or a Mongolian nomad.

The tractor pulled, the car revved, and nothing happened. Bata and the tractor man conferred and tried to dig around the wheels a bit with the spade the tractor man had brought – smart man. Bata's waders got a good workout because the front wheels had sunk quite a bit by this stage, and the wheel rut they were trapped in had flooded.

They tried again. The engine revved, the rope went taut and the tyre went *BOING!*, detached itself from the car and went sailing towards the tractor.

I got back into the car. I had hoped to be able to photograph our triumphant emergence from the bog, but it was bloody freezing, quite dark and I'd already allowed far too much rain to fall on my camera. So I was in the car when, on the third try, it was finally pulled free.

The tractor man stayed with us, leading us back to his ger, where he'd left Dorj. Apparently when they'd arrived there on the motorbike Dorj had been shuddering with cold, so he was left there to warm up.

The ride to the ger, in the dark, following this Mongolian nomad tractor man who'd so valiantly rescued us, was nothing short of awesome. Bata let him go in front to guide us, as it was now pitch black and he certainly didn't want to get bogged again. After less than 100m, at the top of the first rise, we hit snow again. This proceeded to get thicker and thicker. I have imprinted on the back of my mind the image of this tractor man, illuminated by the headlights along with thick streaks of white snow falling alternately right towards us (and hence right into his face) and sometimes diagonally down. He was set at an angle on the tractor, both because of the angle of the terrain and because he had to hang on for dear life. He was hanging on with his left hand and steering with his right.

Let me tell you, the tractor is the original all-terrain vehicle. My god, it's good. It'll get through anything. I remember at one point he charged across a creek and up a hill on the other side and then looked back, a smile on his face, to check that we, in our massive snorkel-equipped Toyota Land Cruiser, had managed the same feat.

The back wheels of the tractor churned up a lot of stuff. Chunks of snow and mud were flying everywhere. The snow stopped after a while but the mud didn't, and tractors have no mud guards, so by the time he got back to his ger, the tractor man was absolutely covered in the stuff.

As Tunga had said, "Oh, it's just over there" can mean a fair distance. We found out later that the tractor actually hadn't come from the nearest ger; it had come from the motorbike man's own ger, because he had wanted to help and had already begun doing so, and he hadn't been sure if the other nearby tractor owner would want to, so he'd taken Dorj to his own ger instead. So, the motorbike man and the tractor man were the same person. I didn't get to see his face properly until afterwards, and even then it was covered in mud! His ger was some distance away, and it took us about half an hour to get there – but of course a tractor can't go very fast.

The whole time, the tyre was sliding along behind the tractor, churning up a track of its own.

Eventually, the small scope of the headlights illuminated a white ger up ahead with lots and lots of cows gathered around it. We got out and picked our way around the cows, with their big eyes and wet streaky fur, to the entrance of the ger.

One of the things that had attracted me to Mongolia was that it's quite easy to have homestays and stay in gers in the middle of nowhere with local people. However, the places in which you do that are usually designed for tourists – I'm sitting in a tourist cabin right now, all by myself. My homestay in Ulaanbaatar is a real home, but tourists stay there often and it's more a place to sleep than a place to experience real Mongolian culture.

This, on the other hand, was a real nomadic ger, the home of the family who owned the cows; a shelter from the pouring rain, homely and warm -

and I never would have gotten to go inside it if we hadn't needed their kindness.

I stepped across the threshold feeling great excitement, but wasn't able to see anything at all at first because I had to stoop so low to get through the door. Once inside, though, there was more than enough room to stand tall. It was a lot more spacious than I expected – about the size of a small cottage.

The first thing I noticed was that my feet landed on something hard – it was not a dirt floor. Actually, in many cases a proper base is made for the ger, and is used again the next year if the ger is put in the same spot. It usually is – in the winter spot it certainly is, because they have the animal shelter built there. I later realised that what I was standing on was lino.

I moved around the wet and mud-covered people in front of me, offering them some lollipops I'd bought in Ulaanbaatar. The people were standing in front of the stove, which is right in front of the door. Tunga told me this morning that you should always go to the left when you enter a ger, because there's a Buddhist/cultural thing of always going clockwise – it's something to do with energy circles. I hadn't known that last night but fortunately I went to the left anyway, making a full circle over to the woman, who was sitting on the bed on the right of the ger, rolling dough and making dumplings. I gave her a lollipop and Tunga gave one to her child. The child was only two so I'd thought she might have been too young for lollipops given the choking hazard, but Tunga said, "No, no - it's fine," and gave her one. The child went on to eat several lollipops throughout the evening, even finding her way into the lollipop packet at one point, and the adults didn't seem to mind at all. Tunga said, "Mongolian children are very independent." I noticed that they are given lots of freedom, and basically do as the adults do.

I was given a small stool to sit on next to a small table, and the woman poured us tea in small bowls. I was wary at first, but I've found I quite like Mongolian tea. Tunga told me they salt it because of the dryness of the climate, and different regions have different levels of dryness and so use different amounts of salt. Fortunately, we seem to be in a wetter region, so the tea I've tried so far hasn't been too salty. It's white, with milk and sometimes butter added, even though it is green tea. You can hardly taste the tea, actually. The flavour I was hit with when I first tried it, in the roadstop where we had lunch, was rice. I remarked this to Tunga and she said, "No, it's wheat. They fry some flour and then add tea and boil. It makes it more filling and warming for you in the cold climate." The tea I've had since then hasn't had flour, though.

So, there I was in a real life nomadic ger receiving tea from the tractor man's wife. Unfortunately I never found out her name. Tunga told me later that the tractor man's name was Yurey, but I didn't get anyone else's. There was he and his wife and another man in the ger, who was a kind of herding (I can't quite say "farming") employee who lived in another ger at the back; and the little girl. Apparently the couple have two older children but they are at school in the town where we had lunch, which is quite far away on those little tracks, so they stay with relatives in the town during the week. This is normal for nomadic children, and every school also has a dormitory for those children who don't have relatives in town.

The woman gave us some tea and then some amazing homemade bread which she'd baked right on top of the stove – it rivalled European bread, honestly, and that's saying something! Next to it she placed a small bowl of homemade cottage cheese and a large jar which had a commercial label that said "apple sauce". That sounded boring, so I went for the cottage cheese. It was nice – very mild.

Meantime, the tractor man was sitting in front of the stove talking animatedly and frying the dumplings as his wife handed them to him. They were deep fried in a large metal bowl which sat in the circular hole at the top of the stove (at other times there's a lid for it). I'll stop calling them dumplings now, though, because pasties would be a more appropriate word. When they came out, they looked a bit like battered fish or chicken fillets – long and flat, but it's dough, not batter - with a small amount of minced mutton inside (and I think a little spring onion or onion). They're called khooshoor. I really liked them then, but I had them again cold for lunch today and didn't so much.

In a break between rounds of khooshoor I watched Bata put some of the apple sauce on a piece of bread, followed by some sugar. I thought it seemed a bit excessive to have sugar as well, but decided I might as well give the apple sauce a try.

It definitely wasn't apple sauce. It was yellow and a little bit chunky, and it tasted a bit like butter - maybe butter that's been left to melt and has congealed a bit. Tunga said it was actually the same cottage cheese, which had been encased in some kind of animal guts and cooked and left somewhere... I added some sugar.

Now I will tell you a bit about the ger. The stove is always in the middle, closer to the door. To the left (if your back is to the door) is the "man's side". To the right was a cabinet containing kitchen things and then a bed, presumably the woman's. To the left was what appeared to be a chest freezer, but it was open and they appeared to be using it as a fridge. Then there was another bed and then an altar to the shaman gods. Shamanism and Buddhism coexist peacefully in Mongolia, rather like Shintoism and Buddhism do in Japan. Tunga said it's because it's easy to make new gods in Buddhism so you can easily worship nature, and Shamanism is a naturistic religion.

In the back of the ger there was a longish dressing table with a mirror, TV, some photographs and some beauty products. It opened up a bit like a sideways chest, and the family's clothes were stored inside.

Sitting next to any ger outside you will always see a solar panel and a satellite dish. The former is for power, the latter for signal. Gers have phones, which connect to the mobile network via an aerial on the roof. A cord comes down into the ger and they plug an ordinary landline handset in.

A phone was just what we needed to get us going. Because it was now dark and the "roads" muddier than ever, Bata wanted to phone someone he knew nearby to come and guide him, as the only thing worse than getting bogged in the snow in the daytime would be getting bogged in the snow in the dark.

However, this family was having a problem with their phone and it was currently sitting under the stove drying out. Earlier in the day, the mother had been outside doing something and the little girl had been alone in the ger. She had filled a dish with water and dishwashing detergent and first she'd washed her hair with it, and then she'd decided to be like her mother and clean the ger. She'd cleaned the table and then she'd cleaned the phone! With sloppy dishwashing water. So now the phone was drying under the stove. Once it had been there for a while, the men started trying to get it going. They took it all apart, wiped it, blew it, put it back together again, took it apart again... they were trying very hard to fix the phone.

Meantime, everybody was talking jovially, and I had no idea what they were saying but I was really enjoying just sitting there drinking it in. The woman gave me some yogurt which was really nice. She'd made it herself. Every nomad makes all their own dairy products – quite a variety of them too.

It was still pouring with rain outside. At one point, I went out to go to the loo (a ger's loo is the wide-open spaces). Bata gave me his torch, and this helped me to navigate around the cows, but it did not occur to me to attempt to navigate around the cow poo until I felt a particularly slippery, squelchy bit of earth beneath my foot and realised what it was. I tried to navigate around them after that, but given how wet and brown the rest of the ground was, I had real trouble figuring out where the cow pats were. I ran into Dorj on the way back and he tried to point them out to me, but I couldn't even tell what he was pointing at. I hope I didn't walk cow shit into the ger...

When I came back in I was cold, so I sat by the stove near the door. The woman started using an interesting method of cleaning up the piles of mud we'd walked into her house.

I don't like calling her "the woman", but I don't have anything else to call her – other than "Yurey's wife", which is equally sexist. I've realised that Mongolians don't put nearly as much emphasis on names, introductions or pleasantries as we do. The whole time I've been here, I have been introduced to no-one but Bata and Dorj. Yes I have the language barrier too, but I can point to myself and say my name, and so can they I'm sure. But they don't, and I've seen no-one introducing themselves to other Mongolians and no-one shaking hands. They don't seem to say "thank you" very much either. I know the word for "thank you" and I try to use it a lot (even though I mispronounce it horribly), but I don't hear others saying it very often. It's interesting. I think they're very reserved people but also very kind, and they also expect kindness from others - so I think they just go up to them and interact as if they already know them well.

But Tunga said that it isn't kindness, it's their way of life. You have to be kind to people in trouble; you have to take them into your ger and give them tea and food, and let them stay the night if they need it or give them whatever other assistance they require, because next time it could be you who needs a stranger's help. These people travel great distances without any protection from the weather, either on foot, on a horse or on a motorbike. They don't carry anything with them. They often have to do this in extreme conditions of cold or rain looking for a lost or injured animal. People do get stuck too far away from home and it's pretty easy to freeze to death out there, especially in winter, when temperatures are sub-zero almost all the time. So, people just help each other out. It's a way of life.

Another thing I've noticed about Mongolians is that they don't worry about getting mud on the floor. There is no rule about taking your shoes off before entering a ger, so we trekked mud everywhere, and the woman made an attempt to clean it but she did it in a very ineffective way: she wiped all the lino, which had been covered in up to a centimetre of mud and water, using the same cloth and bucket of water. She did a good job, but there must have been a thin film of dirt everywhere still. Also, she did it while we were still there, trekking our mud around, and she didn't mind - she let us continue to walk about. Her daughter told Dorj off for leaving new mud prints; it was very funny!

We couldn't help but walk mud into the place because there was no mat to speak of outside. Inside she laid her cloth down, but it was very small and when you tried to wipe your feet on it all it did was move about beneath you. The next place we stayed at had a cloth instead of a mat as well.

The strangest thing was, though, that actually most of the mud that she was cleaning off was not from our shoes; it was from her husband's jacket. When he'd come in, the farmhand had scraped the mud off his oilskin coat using a knife, right onto the ger floor. Fair enough that he was cold and wet enough already and didn't want to do that outside, but they could have put a mat underneath him, couldn't they? They didn't.

The next morning, Dorj was in our cabin grabbing his shoes, which had been drying out under the stove all night and were now covered in dry mud. He was standing literally one metre from the front door. He banged the mud off his shoes right there on the cabin floor.

Eventually the men got the phone working, at about 10pm. It was a black landline phone plugged into a cord that went straight up to the ceiling, just hanging there. It didn't appear to have a handset, so they were using speaker phone. They rang the number of Bata's friend but his phone was switched off or out of range, so Yurey rang his neighbour who has a car - the one who'd gone to the village. This confirmed that yes, he was still in the village and he wasn't coming back. It was looking like we'd have to spend the night right there in the ger - which I would have been fine with because it would've given me an even more raw local experience – but perhaps the others didn't want to because there wasn't enough room, or whatever. I don't think the family would have minded because culturally they just have to do it - anyone has to open up their home to anyone - but they came up with a new plan. Yurey would come with us and tell Bata where to drive to avoid the worst mud. Then Bata would drive him back home and spend the night with the family.

It was well over an hour's drive, even though it was only 10km. I didn't know what he was saying, but I could hear Yurey guiding Bata the whole way. They just know everything, these locals. At one point they struck a rough part where a bogged jeep had been abandoned, so they stopped at a nearby ger to ask the best way 'round. It was well after 11pm by this stage, but apparently it's still totally fine to knock on someone's door and ask for directions.

Eventually, we arrived at our accommodation, which was a collection of wood cabins in the middle of a windy steppe, with small mountains and trees around. I didn't see that until the next day - at this point it was just a wood cabin in the dark! But it was warm, because the people had been expecting us and they hadn't given up on us, and the stove was well stoked.

The cabin was very charming, made of split logs, with woven carpet mats around the walls; two of them with pictures of antelope on them. Gers have mats around the walls too – extra insulation I suppose. This cabin was the kind of place I'd expect to find in the American Rockies, but it is a traditional design because in that region, unlike much of the rest of Mongolia, there is plenty of timber. I say plenty – they're the spindliest pine trees I've even seen, but it's plenty compared to the rest of Mongolia. They are built by slotting the timber together (no nails!) and insulated with moss.

Goat guts

The next day, we went to Baldan Baraivan Monastery. Again, the track was very muddy because we had to pass a lake which had swelled, so a man from a nearby ger came along to help us navigate. It's like using a local pilot – he was number two of three such men who helped us. They know the land so well because they live on the land, and have done all their lives. So they could say to Bata, "You'll get through that muddy cesspool on the left but not the one on the right," and he would do what they asked - even if he had trouble believing it was true - and they would invariably be right. Bata was amazing too – I was very impressed with him. Four-wheel driving must be hard work – there are so many different things you have to watch out for.

Baraivan Monastery is a rather desolate place by a small lake with some small mountains and rocky outcrops around. It's desolate because there aren't any monks there. There used to be 3,000, plus 5,000 staff and students. It was the biggest monastery in eastern Mongolia and it had scores of buildings and temples. But in 1937 the Soviet Army came in, took the monks away and executed them. Around 30,000 Mongolians were killed that year in the Communist crack down on religion, power, money and free thought. Some were executed and some were taken to gulags in Siberia, which amounted to the same thing.

All the buildings of the monastery were destroyed and the carved stones on the mountain desecrated. And so it became a desolate place.

In 1998, only a few years after religion had been re-legalised, some Mongolians built a small wooden temple in log cabin style. Later they commenced rebuilding the monastery buildings in the way they would have been built originally, which is in Tibetan style of whitewashed stone buildings with thatched roofs and colourful rhombus-shaped window frames.

Mongolians are not very religious. Tunga said this is because religion was completely banned under communism for so long - to the extent that when she first started guiding at Baraivan Monastery she didn't know a thing about Buddhism, and she had to ask. The only reason Buddhism has been able to be revived successfully in Mongolia is that the period of the ban fell within some lifetimes, so people who were young when it began were able to, in their old age, educate the younger generations when the ban ended.

But it's one thing to teach people about religion and another to make them believe in it. Many cultural rituals are still practised, like the ovoos, and Shamanism is still there among the nomads because they never let it go in the first place, but Buddhism doesn't seem to be a big thing here. Well, maybe it's like Christianity in Australia: it's there, but it's not that big of a thing anymore. Most of us celebrate Christmas and Easter for cultural reasons, not religious ones. Tunga has said that several times: "We do this because it's our culture, not because of any belief."

Now there are no monks permanently stationed at Baraivan Monastery, but there are a few who visit. In Mongolian monasteries most monks don't live on site; they're allowed to live in houses with wives and families, and they just go to work every day! So the only people living on the monastery site now are the caretaker and his family in a ger. He showed us around the temple buildings in an Adidas tracksuit and a t-shirt that said, "Women are from Venus, men are from bars." It was all very zen.

That night I'd been told dinner would be at seven, and I'd been sitting in the cabin writing in my journal and waiting for it, but when it came it was only one serving, just for me. Tunga came in a couple of minutes later and said that the staff had killed a goat that day - of which I had just been given some - and that they were also preparing a "special Mongolian dish" which wouldn't be ready for a while, so she'd asked them to make something else for me. She said that she, Bata and Dorj would join the staff to eat the other dish later, and I could come along and try a bit. I thought, *OK, that's fine*, and I ate my goat, hot potato chips and rice.

My stomach had started playing up a bit. At that stage I thought it was only that I was still full from lunch. I got all my meal down just fine and quite enjoyed it - because it was not the sinewy minced mutton in cold khooshoor that I'd had for lunch. I've discovered I really don't like mutton - it's too strong-tasting. This, by contrast, was quite nice fresh and hot (if a little chewy) goat pieces.

A while after I had eaten, Tunga came back and took me to the ger where some of the staff were living, in the back corner of a yard with a high wooden fence. "Why are the fences so high?" I asked.

"Because of strong wind and storms," Tunga replied. "And in Gobi, sand!" So that's why they have such funny-looking high fences around gers. Not the nomadic gers, though.

Stepping inside the ger, the smell hit me like a smack in the face. It smelled putrid, even though it was the freshest of fresh goat. The trouble was, it was the freshest of fresh goat's innards. The first thing I saw was a large pot/steel bowl on the stove, which contained a very large bulbous thing simmering in soup the colour of puss.

I was led to the table behind the stove, where Dorj and Bata were sitting around something that was prepared earlier. There was a circular green plastic tub, the kind you'd use to wash your dishes in when you're camping. In the green plastic tub was... ooh, how can I describe it. I'll just have to make a list. Another huge bulbous sausage-like thing, this one with one end cut off so I could see the grey pock-marked meat inside. "Blood sausage," said Bata, cutting a large piece and putting it on a plate, which he placed in front of me. It was followed by a longer piece of a smaller "sausage" that had huge globules of smooth white fat on one side and, on the other, deep red chunks of pure cooked blood.

It didn't take much to figure out that this was the small intestine and the other was the bowel.

This was soon followed by a piece of flat, rubbery yellowy stuff which I was told was stomach, and a couple of pieces of meat I was told was heart. Followed onto my plate, I should say. This was all on my plate.

Dammit, I thought. *Being a vegetarian used to get me out of eating this kind of thing!*

As Dorj deposited another piece of the mucous-looking fat-filled small intestine onto my plate, I finally found my voice and told him to stop, begging the excuse that I'd already eaten.

I looked at the pile of innards on my plate, slowly gearing myself up for it. I am no longer a vegetarian, and I am a firm believer in the philosophy of "try anything once". I attempted the large intestine first. As with most Mongolian meat it was quite tough, and they'd only given me a fork. And I didn't want to put too large a piece in my mouth - hell no. With the assistance of Dorj and the communal sharp knife, I managed to separate a small enough piece to put in my mouth. It was disgusting. And chewy. I poked my fork at the piece of bowel that had now detached itself from the sausage on my plate. I decided not to even attempt that.

I sized up the small intestine next. I wasn't going to touch the fat, but the soft, squishy blood came away easily. It tasted like... soft squishy blood. It was gross too.

The heart was fine. It tasted like iron. Not good, but fine.

Finally, I got to the tripe. Not being able to separate it with my fork, I stabbed it and brought the whole thing to my mouth. I couldn't separate it with my teeth either. Twice I tried this, with incisors and with molars. No tripe was removed. I gave up and went back to the small intestine. It still tasted like squishy blood. Blood custard. The interesting thing was that Tunga swore that the large intestine one also contained only blood – maybe some onion, she said, but no gristle or meat. The chewiness was only because it had been cooked longer. If you cook blood for long enough it becomes chewy? *Bloody hell*, I thought, with no hint of irony.

I had another couple of bites of the heart because that was the only thing that didn't make me want to spew, but I didn't finish that either. My plate looked untouched. I'm a firm believer in "waste not, want not", so that was a strange thing for me, but that food was utterly horrible and I wouldn't touch it with a barge pole ever again.

The thing was, Tunga had called it a "special dish". They were all waiting around for it. They were really excited, and it was a real communal event. The table wasn't big enough for everyone, so they would all take turns to sit down, hack at it with the communal knife, then shove great chunks eagerly into their mouths - most of them not even using a plate. I remember one short man who was sitting directly across from me, the simple solar battery light globe lighting only his face, and the sheer look of glee in his eyes as he hacked into first the sternum and then big chunks of bowel sausage, holding it in his hand and biting right into it. The sheer pleasure on his face.

I did not get it, and I was rapidly feeling sicker and sicker. I tried to ameliorate things with the salad that was on offer, but it didn't fix the thoroughly off feeling in my stomach. There was also a plate of raw onion there, which Tunga said went very well with the "meat". It might take the taste away slightly, but go well? No. Nothing about this situation was going well at all. I wanted to stay longer to continue to observe this strange communal ritual, but the smell was getting to me and I could no longer look at the food without literally feeling my stomach turn. I felt physically sick. I had to get out.

That does not usually happen to me.

I didn't vomit, but I almost did, and every time I recalled the image of that fat bowel sausage sticking out of the bucket, my stomach turned again. Back in the cabin, I was writing about my dinner with the ger family that night. The cottage cheese was fine. I just barely managed to write about the khooshoor. I had to stop at the part about the stuff in the apple sauce jar...

Ger pilot number three

The next morning, we awoke to find that everything was white. This made my morning trek to the pit toilet with no door quite exciting, although why I decided to wear open-toed slippers there I can't fathom.

We left at about 9:15, and I was immediately captivated by the intense beauty of the grasslands in snow, which I had a box seat view of from my position at the front of the Land Cruiser. It was still snowing quite heavily and the tracks were only visible as two slight gaps in the grass that stuck out of the snow. The grass looked incredible: it has different colours but the snow brought out the burnt orange in it, so there was white speckled with burnt orange, the prevalence of which varied according to the angle of the hill I was looking at. It was mesmerising...

Suddenly, Bata turned off the track. Tunga told me we were heading for a lake that day and it was a little-travelled track that was likely to be flooded, so he was going to ask his friend with a car if he would come with us in case we needed a tow again.

When we arrived at Bata's friend's ger, all the animals were in their night time homes making quite a lot of noise – all except the bedraggled dogs that were wandering about. A couple of men were on the roof of the animal house, and I think they were putting hay on it to waterproof and insulate it. They got down to speak to Bata.

I didn't understand what they said, but Tunga said, "Ohh," in a disappointed way. Then Bata got out of the car and went into the ger.

Tunga told me that Bata's friend had gone to the village, and that without a second vehicle he thought it was too dangerous to go to the lake, because no-one would be around to help us if we got into trouble. Particularly with the snow, she said: because it wasn't a well-used track it might become completely invisible, and even if Bata could see the track he wouldn't be able to tell when there were big cracks and washed-out portions that we could get stuck in.

Bata came out of the ger briefly to say that he'd phoned their boss, who said it was too dangerous to go to the lake. Then he went back into the ger again and Tunga told me that Bata had a new plan. We were going to go to the village, because that was a much more populated track. A boy from this ger was going to come with us to guide us. We would take him to the village and he would come back by another means later (a pretty big favour he was doing us, and giving up his work on the animal house too). I later found out that Bata's friend with the car was the boy's father, so he would bring him back later. Tunga said there was one village, or small town, that was the province centre, and then a little bit further along there was a bigger town that was "on the asphalt road". Once we got back to the asphalt road there was another way of getting to the lake, maybe maybe, if the weather had improved by then.

I was sitting in the car looking out at the two gers that were there, with their satellite dish and their solar panel and a traditional cart behind, waiting for Bata. The snow was still falling. I have imprinted in my mind the image of this boy, who was about 17, coming out of the ger and suddenly extending to his full height, which was almost the height of the ger. The ger was white and everything around it was white, and he was wearing a grey traditional robe with a blue tie around it, and he had a resigned expression on his face. Out into the snow he came, and into our car. And that was how we got Ger Pilot Number Three.

We drove and drove and drove. Our pilot led us to a small mountain pass, but it didn't end up being much of a pass for us because we couldn't pass it – it was too slippery to get any traction up the hill. So, we had to go allll the way around the mountains. It took 6½ hours to get to the asphalt road, but it was the second highlight of my time in Mongolia - after being bogged and rescued by the nomadic tractor man. It's the things that are unplanned which really make a trip.

It was just so beautiful to see the steppes in the snow. To stop and ask at gers for directions. At one point we asked a shepherd with a horse for directions! To see spring lambs and baby goats in the snow. And when it stopped falling and started to melt, the incredible colours that came out, and the shapes of the hills that were visible to the finest detail because some bits would melt before other bits, making the most breathtaking patterns.

And the way people can navigate in all that snow! I think Bata was mainly stopping to ask people where the less boggy tracks were, not what direction to go – he knew that already. Mongolians can navigate anywhere. Tunga had told me a couple of days before that Mongolians always know where north, south, east and west are. That's how they always pick a track confidently when there's a fork, and why, if the track then verges in a different direction and turns out to be the wrong track, they can easily just veer off and drive over the grass for a bit until they find a better one. They can always see where the other tracks are, too – even if it's just the faintest shadow in the distance, they can tell it's a track. More than once that day Bata randomly veered off the track and I had no idea where he was going, but there'd always be another track hidden in the snow somewhere that he was heading to.

I asked Tunga if Bata still knew where north, south, east and west were - given the white-out situation. Her reply was very simple. "We're heading south."

It took nearly four hours to get to the village where we dropped our pilot off. The sun had come out by that stage but, as the village had no paved roads whatsoever, the streets were very muddy. This caused an impromptu lake in the middle of the road we entered the village on, and a matted mess of wheel ruts at the entrance to the petrol station we visited. Somehow even such a small town had three petrol stations. It wasn't a village really; it was a town. It's called Ümnüdelger, and it's the administrative centre of the sum, or district. It has a town square, with statues of a local revolutionary hero and a local composer in it. Tunga pointed out the buildings around the square to me: the post office, the cultural centre, the Communist Party office, the Democratic Party office and the administrative office. There was also a school, a shop and a pub.

We returned our ger pilot to his father, who was a ranger of the Protected Area where the lake is. He informed us that all the tracks in there were impassable and that the main track from Ümnüdelger to the asphalt road was also incredibly boggy - so we would again have to go the long way 'round. This meant taking a higher, drier route, but it didn't feel that high because it was still going through the middle of the wide-open steppes - the widest I had seen by far. The one that Ümnüdelger was at the edge of was utterly enormous. We stopped in the middle of it for a picnic. Bata pointed at the furthest mountain at the edge of that steppe and said it was 60km away. We were in the middle of the steppe at that stage. That means the steppe was at least 100km across!

After three days of seeing not a single other vehicle, all of a sudden we were on a main highway. We saw four other vehicles while crossing that steppe! The track widened into two or even three "lanes"! We got up to (gasp) 50, and even 60km/h!

But still people drove all over the place – there were still ruts and bogs.

At 3:45pm, we finally reached the asphalt road. We'd left our cabin at 9:15 that morning.

I almost immediately fell asleep, as I no longer had to hold my eyes open to see the amazing scenery. We were still driving through a beautiful place, but there's something about a paved road that adulterates it. One of the best things about Mongolia is that it has barely any.

After another 3¼ hours of driving, Bata dropped me and Tunga off at Guru tourist ger camp in Terelj National Park, and he and Dorj returned to Ulaanbaatar.

The tourist ger camp consists of a large ger for the restaurant and many small ones for "hotel rooms". I am in number 8. It's a bit touristy but it's OK.

Terelj is beautiful. One of the things you can do there is horse riding, which was booked for me after a bit of mucking about because the horses are all local nomads' horses who are left to graze anywhere they like during winter, so it can take a bit to find them come spring time. They're also incredibly skinny because they haven't been given any supplementary food over winter. Tunga thought they might be too weak to ride, but a herder was convinced and a horse booked for 1pm yesterday afternoon (the 11th of May). It had to be in the afternoon because the herder needed the morning to find the horses! So in the morning I went walking. I asked Tunga if there were any tracks. "No tracks," she said. "You can go anywhere."

Such is the Mongolian landscape, with so few plants - almost no undergrowth and barely any trees - that not only do they not need roads for cars, they also don't need tracks for hikers, because you really can go anywhere over the grassy hills – it's very easy. You don't have to bash through undergrowth, and you also don't have to worry about trespassing because there is no private land.

At first I thought, *How will I find the good places? I don't know where I'm going!* But all you have to do is climb a hill and look around you. You think, *I'll go to those rocks at the top of the next hill*, and then once you get there you think, *Hmm, now I want to see what's behind that hill on the left*, and then you just keep going. You know where the scenic parts are because you can see them from afar, and you can have the freedom to pick your own route. I thought it was great. I kept going for nearly three hours.

Then it was time for my horse ride. I saw the horseman coming over the hill, riding one horse with two others tied closely to it – two because after me a German couple, Alex and Sascha, were going to ride together.

First, the horseman tied three of one horse's legs together with a loose leather harness, so that it could move around and graze but not go too far. This was the horse he was going to leave here.

Tunga told me to get on at the horse's left, not to pat it because Mongolian horses aren't used to that, and not to make any sudden movements. I asked her to tell the horseman that I wanted to go very slowly. I'd tried horse-riding once before, as a teenager, and hadn't liked it at all. I'd completely botched the technique and completely botched my back in the process, and I remember hating the sensation of galloping and trotting, which is why I asked to go slow this time.

I was given no technique instruction whatsoever, just told to hold the saddle and the reins. I was a little uneasy when we moved off and I realised I wasn't wearing a helmet, but then it became apparent that the horseman was going to lead me the entire time so I didn't have to do anything, which was brilliant! I just got to sit back and enjoy the scenery for 45 minutes. And what scenery. We went through a flock of sheep and goats and horses too!

The horseman was whistling and humming the whole time. Maybe to calm the horses, I'm not sure, but it calmed me too. Then, when we were on our way back, his mobile phone rang! The tinny, bouncy ringtone was a strange juxtaposition...

In the afternoon, I climbed a hill next to the tourist ger camp to a rocky outcrop with an incredible view. It was only ten minutes' walk from the camp! I sat there writing in my journal for a while, until I got very cold and had to return to my ger. I attempted to light my stove, but didn't do very well owing to the fact that there wasn't any kindling and the camp seemed to plan for only their staff lighting the stoves, not guests. I judged, however, that I was still better at it than the staff member who comes into my ger every morning and turns the place into a sauna within five minutes. When Mongolians put a heater on, they go large. Gers are hot. Particularly this one, because it's smaller than a regular ger.

In these tourist camps we're staying in, there's always someone who comes in about an hour before your pre-determined breakfast time to light your stove for you, so you can get up in a warm room. I appreciated this in the previous cabin because we were living in there - eating there and everything - but in this camp the ger is basically just a bedroom: I have to go to the big main ger to eat. So I was thinking about it last night and thinking, *I don't need the lady to light my stove in the morning, because it's not snowing anymore and I'm only in the ger for ten minutes after I get out of bed anyway.* I decided I didn't want to be woken by the clunking of the stove at 5:30 in the morning when I really didn't need to be, so I locked my ger door last night, mistakenly thinking that this would get me out of the whole experience.

No. I was woken at 5:30 by an incessant soft knocking on my ger door. I mean incessant: the woman did not stop knocking for at least two minutes. And I couldn't tell her to go away, that I didn't want my stove lit, because she wouldn't understand me, so I just had to ignore it and go back to sleep – which I managed, amazingly, although I certainly wouldn't have if I'd got up to let her in. Then I was awoken again by more knocking. Again I ignored it and fortunately she only knocked once that time. Then I was awoken again at 8:14, and this time she'd gone and grabbed Tunga, who was calling out to me, saying, "Carrie, the lady wants to come in and light your stove!" I let her in this time because my alarm was set for 8:15 anyway, but I told her that I didn't see the point as I was, by that stage, already up, so the whole "so the room is warm when you get up" purpose was already defunct, and I was leaving in ten minutes anyway. Which the woman surely knew; she would have known my breakfast time. She actually made me late for it, because instead of being able to get dressed straight away I had to sit and watch her make the fire first. And she crammed that stove so full of wood. God it got hot quick! Last night, when I got it going myself, one time I put on seven small pieces of wood instead of four and that made me too hot, but this woman must've used about twelve...

The hot pipes in my homestay in Ulaanbaatar make the apartment very hot as well, and Tunga said there are no controls for them! You can't even turn them off, let alone regulate the temperature, and they're not maintained by the apartment building - the hot water is piped in from the power station! So everyone in every building (almost) in Ulaanbaatar has to have their rooms heated to 25°C or more, every hour of every day! But Tunga said it's only from the 15th of September to the 15th of May. Then they turn them off. Now that's weird.

I find it bizarre that I am from a relatively warm country and yet I regularly find myself too hot in very cold countries because they crank the heating up so high. In Australia, we just don't do that – either because we have no need to and we choose not to, or because that absence of need means our insulation and heating are inefficient in all but the newest buildings. Perhaps they physically can't get that hot! So when I visit cold countries, I always find myself complaining about the heat...

The metropolitan Land Cruiser

<u>13th of May, 2:21pm:</u>

All aboard, the train to Moscow is leaving in four minutes. Not that I'm going to Moscow yet; I'm going to Siberia. I have about a 17-hour journey in which to update you on my final 42 hours in Mongolia.

On our last night in Terelj, I had a very interesting conversation with Tunga about communism. She said that when her youngest son was a small boy (in the early 90s), they had ration cards and there was only very basic food available. "Maybe one month there would be some vegetables available and the next month there wouldn't," she said. One day, sugar was available and she got a box of sugar cubes. Her son saw them sitting on the kitchen table and he didn't know what they were because he'd never seen sugar before. He tried one very delicately and he liked it, and he asked her if he could have another one. She said she cried.

She also told me how she grew up living in an apartment in Ulaanbaatar. Because there was no ownership, apartments were allocated to people based on their jobs, but there weren't enough of them so you had to work hard at your job for a few years to get one. Her father got one three-roomed apartment. Her mother's sister and her family didn't have an apartment, so they came to live there too. They had four children. Her mother and father had two (they had had two more but they had died). So each family lived in one room and the third room was mostly used by the older children, and then later on when Tunga's cousin got married, she and her husband and children lived in the third room.

There just wasn't enough housing, and under communism the economy was stagnant and the money wasn't there to build more.

That was all Tunga said about her own personal experience, other than to say that her grandfather was one of the people who was shot in 1937 because he was a member of the ethnic group in the northeast who live in wooden houses. Because they weren't nomadic they were able to do more trade with the Russians, so he was "wealthy".

They targeted the wealthy for obvious reasons, but also monks because they had a lot of power - because people always went to them for advice. Also, the communists executed and/or imprisoned many of their own people, the Mongolian communist leaders, for disagreeing with the more extreme elements of the policy (like executing tens of thousands of people).

There was no property. The nomadic herders were allocated to collective farms. They were each given a set number of livestock to look after. Tunga said that the number of livestock in Mongolia became stagnant, because no matter if the herder worked hard to breed more or if he didn't look after them and let them die in winter, they all got paid the same. Everyone in the whole country got paid the same monthly salary no matter what, so there was no incentive for anybody to work hard. If a herder bred more goats or sheep, it would just be more work for him to care for them but he'd still get paid the same. So, they didn't bother. They kept the animal numbers stagnant.

Now, by contrast, the livestock numbers are ever growing – there are at least 15 times more animals than people in Mongolia!

So a lot of things didn't get done under communism because there was no financial incentive for people to do them, and no investment either. Many businesses, factories etc. went bankrupt.

In 1990, some young people held a hunger strike in Sukhbaatar Square. There was no bloodshed. The communist era ended. It was just time. The first democratic elections were in 1992, but the Communist Party still won because many people were too scared to vote for anyone else. There was a plethora of democratic parties. For the 1996 election they united to make a democratic coalition, and they won. So, communism properly ended then, but of course changing the entire economic system is a long process and it's still going on. The first thing they did was to privatise livestock. Every herding family was given the same number. Since then, the numbers have skyrocketed.

Then, they privatised property. Everyone who was living in an apartment at that time could have it for free. Everyone who didn't have an apartment was entitled to one block of land in a settled district – not in the countryside because of the nomadic herding practises, but in Ulaanbaatar or any of the towns and villages. That is why Ulaanbaatar is now sprawling with what they call "ger suburbs", and every block has a nice tall fence or wall around it because that is how people delineate their private land. They are given the land for free, and they can afford to build a fence but not necessarily a house, so they just live in a ger on that block. There are thousands of them.

Looking out the train window now, I can see random fenced blocks in the countryside too. There must be certain zones around towns that are allowed to be built on. A few kilometres back I saw a ger on a hill in the middle of nowhere with a tall, thick Besser block wall around it!

Mongolians can still get blocks of land; their own little piece of their homeland, for free. There's a deadline by which they are meant to get them but Tunga said it's been extended a few times. Because of this policy, though, Ulaanbaatar is now sprawling well into its surrounding hills. The government is now talking about building apartments in the ger suburbs and giving people the option of giving up their block of land in exchange for an apartment.

The awful thing is that many nomadic herders are now moving to cities and towns because climate change is having a greater impact on their high up, unsheltered landscape than it has yet had in other parts of the world.

Extremes of temperature and lack of rainfall is diminishing – and in some areas eliminating - the available food for livestock, and many families who have made their living from the land for centuries are now being forced into poverty in fenced-off gers in the city.

The next morning (yesterday), Bata came to pick us up and we drove back to Ulaanbaatar. It took a while, solely because of the traffic. For the first time I got a little worried about Bata's driving, because as soon as he got to the city, he started zipping around like a mad thing; never spending more than 200m in one lane because there was always another car he wanted to go around, and he was never head-checking or indicating.

Only then did I understand what Tunga had said days earlier about the traffic in Ulaanbaatar being crazy because people are used to charging over the steppes with no-one in their way. She'd said charging across the steppes on horses, but after three days of watching Bata charge across them in a Land Cruiser I realised it was exactly the same thing. There he was in the city weaving from lane to lane, going around this car and that car, and I thought, *Oh, he's going around the mud pools!* It was exactly the same movement: the same method of driving.

When we got closer to the city centre, we inevitably hit gridlock. There aren't any traffic lights on the side roads, so if you're coming from a side road to a main road, all you can do is push in. Traffic on the main road will be moving at about 1km an hour and the side road cars just inch forward, and then when a gap opens up they sail in as far as they can, which usually leads to this:

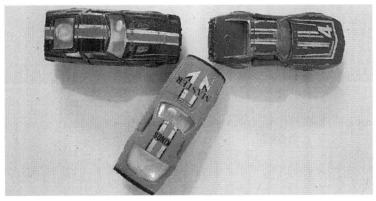

and then this:

or sometimes this, if they're crossing to another lane:

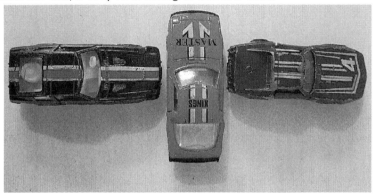

and then eventually, after three of four manoeuvres, they manage to successfully merge. Note that in my demonstration images the car behind is always incredibly close to the merging car. They're almost touching. They don't give way – the merging car just gives them no option but to stop. Somehow everyone drives in this very pushy way and yet still knows how to tell when they've been out-pushed; when to honk their horn and charge forward and when to stop and let somebody past. Collision is centimetres away in every case, but somehow they manage not to touch each other.

At one point, I thought we were going to be crushed. We were in the right lane and neither our lane nor the left lane was moving, but someone behind us was turning right, so they went around us. Other cars followed them but they weren't turning right, so initially they were creating three lanes where only two had existed before. Then the cars in front of us started to move, so the new third lane started to merge in front of us. We were stationary so we'd been out-manoeuvred by them, and we were stuck in the middle here:

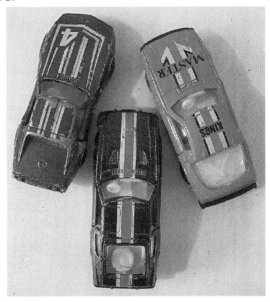

with more and more cars going around us, and that triangular gap was contracting and contracting and it looked like we were going to be crushed!

Bata got us out of it, though. He just had to do some aggressive manoeuvring of his own.

Last night, I had an interesting experience at the supermarket. If I'd thought about it properly I barely even needed to go, because I still have those snacks from Erlian and noodles from Beijing, so all I really needed was breakfast and water. But I got overexcited. There were packets of kimchi, which I don't come by often, for the equivalent of $1, and there were some premade deli foods that looked good, so I just bought too much. I bought four packets of kimchi, which I knew were 1,680 tugriks ($1AUD) each, but the other stuff didn't have a price on it, and I had no idea how expensive it would be - I ended up having to get more money out of my money belt at the cash register! But when I got back to my homestay apartment I realised that, minus the 25,000 tugriks I intended to give as tips to Tunga, Bata and Dorj, I only had 1,350 tugriks left to get through today, which wouldn't even buy me lunch!

At the same time, I realised that it said on the kimchi packets to keep them refrigerated, which I can't do, and that four packets was way too much anyway. I had one with my dinner last night and didn't enjoy it as much as I expected I would, so I thought, *Well, three packets of kimchi is worth, what, 5,040 tugriks, and that plus my 1,350 will get me lunch and maybe something more...* The supermarket was still open, so I thought I might as well try to return my three remaining packets.

I went in there, showed them my three packets and my receipt, and the first thing they did was count the packets, because obviously there were four packets listed on the receipt. I held one finger behind me, saying, "I keep one," and then I pushed three fingers toward them, saying, "I return three." They didn't speak any English and I didn't speak any Mongolian, but I figured actions speak louder than words, and shoving three packets of kimchi at them along with a receipt should have a pretty obvious meaning.

They called the manager, who took a while to arrive, so I was standing there for ten minutes watching the staff serve other customers and occasionally poke my kimchi packets, which they'd sat above one of the registers, and talk to each other about them. The only word I understood was "kimchi".

Eventually the manager arrived and she spoke to some of the staff, and I was thinking, *I hope she approves the refund; I'm gonna have to give them away otherwise...* Finally I saw her type her manager code into one of the machines and scan one of the packets and I was thinking, *Yes! Hooray!* and one of the staff came over to hand me some money and a new receipt. Then, the manager came over and handed the three kimchi packets back to me! I said, "Huh? What?" and then I looked at the money in my hand and realised that it wasn't the value of three packets of kimchi; it was the value of one packet of kimchi!

So apparently there was a whole other interpretation to my one behind my back, three in front of me sign language that hadn't even occurred to me. They thought that I had gone back in there because I had been overcharged; that I'd bought three packets of kimchi and been charged for four, so they had refunded me for one! When all along I'd bought four and paid for four, so I got to have one packet for free! I now had 3,030 tugriks for my final 24 hours in Mongolia, and I *still* had three packets of kimchi!!

Do you know what, Tunga found me lunch for 3,000 tugriks. Part of it was potato salad, which wasn't the best because it was freezing today, but part of it was also tea, so it was OK! And I kept one packet of kimchi, which I put into my noodles tonight, and gave the other two to her. I really don't know why I bought four...

Every woman and her tracksuit shop

After more than an hour - maybe even two - of happily chatting to Alex and Sascha (who are two compartments along from me), we stopped at a northern Mongolian town, and suddenly every man and his dog got on. Or, should I say, every woman and her tracksuit shop.

Previously I'd only had two nice Mongolian men in my compartment. They speak no English and I speak no Mongolian, but they're friendly. We exchanged a bit of food, they looked at some of my photos and at my Ulaanbaatar travel guide pages and it was nice, but then I went to Alex and Sascha's compartment so that I could have a conversation – and had a good one.

Then we stopped at this town, and I moved up and down the carriage a bit taking photos because I could see what looked like communist propaganda mosaics on some walls there. I tried to get off, as we had at the last station, but the large Russian conductor lady said, "No! Three minut," so I just moved around to different carriage windows to take photos. As I was moving I passed a Mongolian lady who was hustling several enormous black bags onto the train – like those big tartan tarpaulin bags but stronger, and massive.

I went back to the doorway of Alex and Sascha's compartment and Sascha said, "I think that lady's for you!" I looked and sure enough, she was taking those bags into my compartment, so I quickly came back here to stake my claim on my space.

A group of Mongolian performers, who boarded the train with all their drums and instruments back in Ulaanbaatar, were already using the top storage shelf in our compartment to store an enormous rectangular musical instrument case. If it weren't for that, the lady's bags would've fitted perfectly, but there's no room on that shelf so the lady is now scouring the carriage looking for space to store her stuff. I haven't seen her for several minutes, but her bags are still blocking the doorway of our compartment.

Tunga told me that Mongolians like to travel with an awful lot of stuff which they then sell. Sometimes they sell it on the train, but usually they take it to Russia to sell. Then they bring other things back to sell in Mongolia, things that aren't available there – that's the more profitable part of the operation, apparently.

The contents of these enormous black bags are scores and scores of flat packed Adidas tracksuits. I know this because when she saw that her bags wouldn't fit on the shelf, she started pulling the tracksuits out all over the floor of the corridor and storing them everywhere they could fit. The young guy in our compartment even put some in his suitcase for her! Previously I'd thought that my guys were with the performers because they let them put their instruments in here, but now I think they were just helping them out. People expect that people will travel with a lot of stuff, so they give them space. Only when they ask, though. I've been sitting in my corner ignoring the woman and I haven't been asked to share my space yet. I hope she comes back soon, though, because there's still 1½ bags sitting in our doorway!

9:20pm:

She came back right after that, after I'd tripped over all the bags to leave the compartment. She came back from another carriage! She hadn't been scouring the carriage for space; she'd been scouring the *train* for space! I hope she's going all the way to Moscow, because it'll take her hours to get it all back again...

We're going through border formalities now, but I'll tell you the whole story later.

This morning, we went to Gangnam Monastery. The first thing I saw was loads of pigeons. Apparently in Mongolian culture you have to be nice to (and feed) birds, dogs and children. This will give you good luck. And if you do bad things to them, you will get very bad luck. To get into the monastery you can drive right through the gate (we saw a tour bus coming out of it and it was quite a squeeze), and you are instantly surrounded by birds. There are old ladies there selling grain to feed them and if you do this you get good karma, but I only had 3,030 tugriks so I couldn't. The birds were everywhere, and when people threw the grain on the ground, they would climb on top of each other to get it. It was like watching iron shavings charge toward a magnet under a piece of paper.

We went in the morning because the monks do ceremonies in the morning. The main component of these ceremonies is chanting mantras or sutras (I forget which; maybe both) in Tibetan. The chanting is supposed to create positive energy. However, the monks I saw in the first temple we went into seemed hardly enthused by it. First I noticed one near me yawning; then I saw one walk around to another one and start smiling and talking to him; two at the back on the other side of the room were also talking animatedly; and two at the back on my side were hunched over, intently looking at something that was underneath their desk. I went closer to see what it was. One was playing a game on his smart phone, and the other was watching!

Then one who'd previously been one of the few who was actually chanting answered his phone, but discreetly, leaning right over and listening, but not saying much. Of the monks I saw in the monastery, I also saw the phones of at least 50% of them. If they weren't talking or playing games on them, they were checking the time or just glancing at the screen like we all do, and they were more sophisticated phones than the ones I saw ordinary Mongolians using. Monks in Mongolia today are paid a wage, and can earn more if they say sutras for individual worshippers.

The weirdest thing I saw at the monastery was the cashier station. I couldn't believe my eyes. Or my ears, because there was that old-fashioned cash register sound constantly ringing up, ringing up as more and more sutras were ordered.

It was a little room, one of the few that were heated, with a bunch of monks behind a counter and lots of people lining up to buy sutras. There was a list on the wall of all the sutras and which problem each would help you with - e.g. if you have a problem with your animals; if someone's taken something from you; to pray for safe delivery of a baby - followed by what it cost to have the monks say that sutra on your behalf. The price was 500 tugriks per sutra, or there was a deluxe service for 10,000 where the monks would say absolutely all of them for you. "This is recommended to do once a year," said Tunga. I asked her how long they would say the sutras for you, and she said not very long.

There was a price list on the wall and they were all numbered - it was like a Chinese restaurant! Tunga said the prices are only fixed at this monastery - elsewhere you just make a donation direct to the monks. She said you can also do that here if you want a specific monk to do it for you, or if you want advice first, and that's how the monks can make some extra cash.

"Once you've paid for your sutras," Tunga said, "You can just leave. The monks will say them for you." How strange.

In one of the temples we went into, there were boy monks having lessons. They were sitting around the room in groups of four or five with one older monk (but still very young) quizzing them on things. Tunga said that one can commence training to become a monk at any age - there is no limit - but usually the earliest is five years old. The decision can be made by either the child or the parents. According to Buddhist reincarnation theology, one's last incarnation before attaining enlightenment will be as a monk. Tunga said that such people usually know this when they are a small child of two or three – I think they say that memories of the former life hang around until that age. So the child can make the decision themselves.

They continue to live with their families, and they attend religious schools which teach them the three Rs as well. If when they grow up they decide they don't want to be a monk after all, they can stop. Anyone can quit at any time. What's particularly modern in Mongolia is that the monks don't live on site; they live at home with their families and they can have wives. I asked Tunga how long this has been the case and she said only since the 90s, and some of the older monks disapprove of it.

At the end of our monastery visit, Tunga told me some interesting things about Buddhist superstition and her family, including that she believes her brother-in-law died before his time because he ran over a dog! For someone who repeatedly says she doesn't believe, she actually does believe quite a lot, but more for superstitious reasons. For example, she has ceremonies done by monks after each lunar new year. She told me about the zodiac animals and how different years have different meanings and risks for different people, and that particularly when the same animal year as you comes around, you can have a bad year. Men are prone to have one at 36 and women at 48 if they are a tiger, for example. They can even die. She said she knows about tigers because her ex-husband and elder son are both tigers, and when two people in the same household are the same animal the risk doubles, unless you get a monk to perform a "separating ceremony". They didn't do this in the year that her ex-husband was 36, and he had an accident falling from a train and he nearly died, and broke his leg below the knee. The same year, their son fell over playing basketball and broke his leg in the same place. They asked a monk and the monk said, "It's because you didn't do the ceremony!" So now Tunga believes in that part of it, but it sounds more like superstition than religious belief.

It was time to go to the station. We met Alex and Sascha, whom I'd discovered were going to be on the same train as me when we were at Terelj, but now I discovered that we were also in the same carriage!

The train was starting from Ulaanbaatar; it hadn't come up from Beijing. I'd thought it might've had Mongolian staff because the Beijing one had had Chinese staff, but no. Mongolia is only the "trans" point of the Trans-Mongolian Railway - it's actually all about getting between China and Russia. This is a Russian train with Russian staff. On Russian long-distance trains there are staff members looking after each and every carriage. The men are called provodniks and the women are called provodnitsas.

The first provodnitsa I saw waiting at the steps going up to our carriage – and preventing me from getting on yet because it wasn't ready – was a large brown-haired Russian lady with a deep voice. She's a matron if ever I saw one. She does things like prevent us from going to the next carriage. However, she's a matron with a heart of gold. She's quick to smile, and when we stopped at a Mongolian station where we could get out for fifteen minutes, she picked some flowers and let us all smell them, and then she asked Sascha, who speaks Russian because he was born in Ukraine, to ask me if I had any Australian coins, because she collects coins from around the world.

I had had 5c which I'd given to a beggar in Beijing to get rid of it! I don't like carrying useless coins around with me. She was disappointed, so I said, "I'll show you what I do have," and started getting my wallet out of my bag. The train engine started up again at that point and we had to get back on board, so we were standing in the area where the door and the hot water urn is when I took out my "lucky dollar". It is one fifth of a $5 note that I found about five years back and have kept in my wallet ever since. It's been handy when I've been overseas and people have asked me about Australian money, as it was now – I showed her how it wouldn't rip, and she was very impressed. She asked Sascha to ask me if she could keep it. She was quite excited about it. I said, "Sure, OK," because I have a new lucky dollar now, or a lucky 60-odd cents – 1,000 tugriks. At Baraivan Monastery there was a hole in a rock where you're supposed to wave some money around so the gods will grow your money for you, but this will only work if you don't spend it. (So technically I had 4,000 tugriks I could've spent on lunch, but Tunga said, "No no no, you can't spend that!") So my lucky 1,000 tugriks now sits in the same window of my wallet that my lucky dollar used to sit in. The two shared the space for exactly four days.

Just after I'd given the provodnitsa my lucky dollar her boss stepped onto the train, and Sascha told me he said something like, "I'm the boss! You should give me something! Don't give it to her - she is nothing!"

And then when she told him it was Australian dollars he said, "Oh, I don't want that - that's useless." I think the Russians have a good sense of humour. I like them.

Sascha said that when that man asked him how he spoke such good Russian and he told him, he said, "Ah, so it is your mother tongue!"

And Sascha said, "Yes, but unlike when I'm speaking German, I have to think when I'm speaking Russian."

The train boss man said, "Yes, we also try to think before we speak..."

There's another provodnitsa in our carriage who's short and blonde; the exact opposite of the other one. She's also quick to smile.

We spent about an hour and a half at the Mongolian border control point (Sukhbaatar). This is all timetabled, by the way. We knew it'd be an hour and a half. The customs officer came through first. She took my customs exit card and customs entry card which had been signed and handed back to me when I'd entered the country. The Mongolians in my compartment had different cards. She signed them and gave them back to them. Then the immigration officer came through, checked our passports and took them. We weren't allowed to get off. Soldiers in camouflage uniforms were encircling the train, and when I poked my head out the carriage door one of them told me to go back.

According to the timetable in the carriage, we were to leave Sukhbaatar at 10:05pm. This happened. But as soon as the train crosses the Russian border, it switches to Moscow time. This doesn't mean Moscow imposes its time zone on all of Russia – it doesn't. But it just makes sense to have the whole timetable in the same time zone, so everyone knows how long it takes between stations and how long before they need to get off, even if they don't know the local time zone (which is hard to keep up with when you're travelling east to west).

So, even though it was now firmly night time, we were scheduled to stop at the next station at 7:14pm. I therefore assumed that Moscow time was three hours behind Mongolian time and that we'd be at that station in ten minutes.

No. Moscow time is four hours behind Mongolian time. It took an hour and ten minutes to get to the Russian border control point! I have no idea when we crossed the border.

Our arrival at the Russian town of Naushki was at 11:15pm Ulaanbaatar (and Beijing) time. Absolutely nothing happened for a very long time. I fell asleep leaning against the wall of the compartment. The blonde provodnitsa woke me, and one of the Mongolian men, at 12:10am saying, "Passport!"

I got out my passport, but nobody asked for it for another twenty minutes. Sascha said the provodnitsa had to wake me, though, because if I wasn't ready when the passport officers arrived, she'd get in trouble. They were probably already on the train at that stage - I was aware of them being in our carriage for a good ten to fifteen minutes before they got to my compartment, which is in the middle.

The reason this took so long is that, unlike the Mongolians and the Chinese, they did not take our passports – they did it all right there on the train. They were each carrying either a laptop or a scanner, which had access to a database containing everybody's visa information. My passport was taken by a fair-haired man with a laptop who turned around, balanced the laptop between the rail and window in the corridor and started typing in my details. Then a female passport officer appeared and took the documents of the Adidas lady, who was travelling with an ID card, not a passport. She took it away and brought it back later. A third officer came and took the older Mongolian man's passport, while the one who'd done mine now did the younger Mongolian man's. There were just so many of them, and I guess they were trying to make it go quicker by going into any compartment to find people who hadn't had their passports done yet. I counted about ten of them in our carriage.

They were quite thorough with their checks. I was watching the man with the laptop and he had all sorts of information on there, including our photographs. The woman who took the older Mongolian man's passport was looking at it for ages because she deemed that the photo didn't look enough like him. She asked him to produce an ID card as well. Then she scanned his passport in two ways with one machine – at the front was a laser and at the back was a slot. I wonder what they did before they had this technology.

Then, the customs officers appeared. Their uniforms were less formal and their attitude seemed to be slightly more relaxed, but this was only because they had to talk more, stay longer and look harder. The first one who came seemed to be asking the Mongolians if they were carrying x, y or z. They said no, and he sort of rolled his eyes and said something like, "Are you sure?"

Then he searched all their bags. Not thoroughly; he more glanced in them and asked the Mongolians to rifle through them a bit. He moved right over mine.

Evidently it is not entirely legal to bring things from Mongolia to sell in Russia, but the customs officers will let it slide. Sascha said that the ladies in their compartment are bringing t-shirts, and that the customs officer put some food on top of them so he couldn't see them.

Adidas Lady, though, had to pay a fine. She was a special case the whole time. She must've declared something or they must've known about her for another reason, because well before any of these checks happened, one passport officer came in looking specifically for her, and asked her to sign a two-page document about something. Then, during the customs checks, I saw her pull out her wallet a couple of times, and one of those times a customs officer – who wasn't even the one who had searched our compartment – took her down to the end of the carriage. He kept smiling, and it really looked like they were flirting. Maybe that's what you have do when you pay a bribe!

I'm not sure if it was a bribe or a fine, but Sascha said he heard them saying she had to pay €30. They definitely didn't confiscate any of her Adidas products, though - she spent ages repacking them while I was trying to go to sleep. They're still cluttering up our compartment...

The passport and customs checks were done by about 12:50am, and we were allowed to get out and wander around. The train wasn't due to leave for more than an hour and a half - we were timetabled to stay there for 3¼ hours!

The first place I headed to was the station toilet because, of course, the train toilets had been locked for an hour and a half by this stage. Upon entering the toilet corridor, I found myself faced with a lady with an expressionless round face sitting behind a counter with a cash register. There was a sign saying "10 pysomething something". I don't have any roubles yet, so I wandered back outside. The lady hadn't reacted to my presence at all.

I wandered back outside, where I ran into Sascha. I asked him, "Does the word for roubles start with something that looks like a p and a y?"

He replied in the affirmative.

"Right," I said, "It's 10 roubles to go to the toilet." I was just telling him that I would hold it when he said he had a spare 10 roubles he could give me. He told me it was worth about 30 US cents. "OK, I owe you 30 US cents," I said. I went back inside and gave the 10 roubles to the expressionless lady. She took it, said nothing and began punching some buttons on her cash register. Thinking I didn't need a receipt for going to the toilet I moved away, but I heard a flurry of movement behind me and looked round to see a flap of toilet paper had appeared and was hanging out the window of the lady's booth! It was a pretty serious booth; it was all glassed off, and there was another lady in there too. I don't know what she was doing. Near the entrance to the toilet there was a display case containing soap, toilet paper, paper towel, tooth picks, toothbrushes and sanitary items, all with prices on them. I guess that gives the two ladies something to do.

The toilet was a squat. I guess I'm not in Europe yet.

Alex, Sascha and I wandered around the station for a bit. Inside the main building we found some information panels with detailed instructions of what to do if you find a bomb, see a terrorist, find out about a terrorist attack, or if there's a chemical or biological attack or a natural disaster. They were very detailed. Sascha thinks they're trying to scare people.

An announcement came over the loudspeaker which not even Sascha understood, but everyone started going back to the train so we figured we'd all been called back. This was odd since the train wasn't due to leave for another hour, but we just went to bed. It was 9:15pm in Moscow and 1:15am in Ulaanbaatar.

Exaltation

When I woke up, to see bright sunshine and charming wooden Siberian houses, I looked at my phone and it told me that it was 6am. *Crap!* I thought. *I've been in bed for nine hours! I've only got four hours left on the train!* (which always goes really fast).

So I quickly got up, at precisely the time that the toilet was being closed for our impending arrival in a city where we would stay for half an hour. So I started writing in here and didn't realise for some time that the time on my phone was Ulaanbaatar time, not Moscow time, and it was in fact only a little after 2am in Moscow, I had eight hours left on the train, and had only been in bed for five!

But I was wide awake by that stage and loving looking out the window. It's now 3½ hours later and I'm still doing it. We are now riding along the southern shores of Lake Baikal, about 40m from the water. It's lake all the way to the horizon! Lake Baikal appears on a world map - it's that huge.

There's ice floating at the edge of it! And tiny bits of snow on the ground.

What I love most about being on this train is watching how the scenery changes and the architecture changes. Siberian houses are wooden and usually not painted, just varnished or stained. But often they have really colourful shutters, and if they are painted it'll be done in really bright colours.

That's what I've seen so far.

Now we're passing an ice sheet! It looks just like Antarctic pack ice when it's breaking up. It extends about 20m from the shore, and sometimes there are teeny tiny icebergs! And it's been going and going for several kilometres now. There was one bit in front of a breakwater that was still solid!

I have heard that to get to Olkhon Island (where I'm going tomorrow) in winter, you have to take a bus. Not a ferry, a bus. An ice bus.

14th of May, 8:17pm Irkutsk time, which is actually one hour ahead of Mongolian time, even though I've just spent 25 hours travelling west!

I grossly underestimated the amount of time I had to spend on that train, because a: my itinerary was wrong and b: we gained four hours at the border. Thank god I had enough food. I didn't have enough water, so I now have a massive headache.

I spent fifteen hours on Moscow time, even though I could tell from the state of the sunlight that that wasn't real time - but I could never check what the real time was because all the station clocks are on Moscow time too! So when the t-shirt selling ladies in Sascha and Alex's compartment started handing out Mongolian vodka at 9am, Sascha couldn't believe they were doing that at such a time - but being old hands at the trip, they must've known that the real time was in the afternoon!

Fifteen hours on Moscow time is just long enough to get used to it, but then I arrived in Irkutsk at 10:39am to be told by the man who picked me up, Damian, that the local time was nearly four o'clock and I'd just lost most of the day! I was taken to my homestay but didn't stay long because I wanted to see Irkutsk. There aren't many big sights there, but it is a very pleasant city to stroll around. It's not at all like what I've been told about boring block-style Soviet cities. It does have plenty of Soviet-built buildings, but they're all grand pastel-coloured administrative buildings - similar to the Russian buildings in Ulaanbaatar, but more of them, and these ones still have their Soviet propaganda porticoes attached.

The most exciting thing I found out upon my arrival in Irkutsk was that you can drink the tap water. Unfortunately my excitement was short-lived as, after imbibing said tap water heavily, I found that you have to pay to use the toilet every single god damn time – even if it's a crappy public toilet there'll be a woman in a booth. I'd rather pay for water, honestly.

I found two gorgeous churches. One was old and one was new. Brand new, possibly – there were some small bits that looked like they were still being finished. It took me a while to notice that, though, because the whole thing looked incredible and there were too many things to distract the eyes. It had a couple of golden onion-shaped domes as you'd expect from a Russian Orthodox church, and also a couple of towers with incredible colours and murals on them. I couldn't believe what I was seeing on the outside, but it was nothing compared to what was on the inside. There was not a single piece of wall, ceiling or vaulted window arch that wasn't covered in frescoes. The style was one I'd never seen before: the lines and slender grace of it reminded me a bit of the art deco style.

The best part was that there was a service going on at the time, which seemed to be made up entirely of singing – not of the whole congregation (which numbered about eight, as it was only a Wednesday evening), but of three soprano women standing at the back who were occasionally replied by the priest. They were singing the words from a holy book, just like the Buddhist monks I saw yesterday. These Christian women were singing and the monks had been chanting, but the rhythm was incredibly similar. It's fascinating that I can be in an Asian Buddhist monastery one day and a European Christian church the next and see similarities in their worship styles.

And yes, Russia is in Europe. Everything I've seen today has been European. Every person has been European. There is no way I'm still in Asia...

The singing was incredibly beautiful, and the location was awe-inspiring (which is the idea). The priest was quite young. He had long hair, a big beard and a red robe and hat, and when I entered he was swinging the incense orb all around the room. Then he disappeared behind the altar screen and didn't come back, but he was occasionally heard singing from back there.

There were absolutely no chairs or pews - everyone was standing. All the women were wearing scarves on their heads. I quickly reaffixed my sunhat upon seeing this, and didn't realise until I was leaving that there was a pile of scarves on a table by the door.

The worshippers were in a chapel to the side, not at the main altar. This meant I got to walk right up to the main altar in my lap of the church. It was through a couple of archways at the back in a sort of separate room, and I realised as soon as I stepped into it that the ceiling of this room extended into the entire main dome. It was tall, spectacular and, as with everywhere else in the church, no surface was unpainted, other than those that were gilded.

The perfect soprano singing continued the entire time I was in the church. I couldn't take photos out of respect for the worshippers, but photos wouldn't have done the place justice anyway. No lens could be big enough.

The music of ice

15th of May, 10pm:

Olkhon Island is incredible! Wow! I only got here at about 2:30 this afternoon and already I've seen so many amazing things! I don't know where to start...

Well, I have to start with the journey. I had no idea how long it was from Irkutsk – six hours! About 4½ just to the ferry! But Irkutsk is the closest stop on the train line, and this place is awesome so it's totally worth the journey.

I had a transfer to the bus station this morning from Damian. I'd known when I was wandering around Irkutsk yesterday that I'd been near the bus station, but didn't realise I had walked right past it because I didn't notice it. That's because all it is is a car park full of people movers. They were 13 seaters.

The first thing I noticed, when the driver started talking in a slightly agitated way to Damian whilst looking at the pack on my back, was that there was no room for luggage. He wasn't agitated really, though – that's just the way Russians speak. They always seem more serious than they really are – the provodnitsas were definitely like that. This driver was well used to cramming lots of stuff into tiny spaces. Damian just told me to leave my pack at the side of the van and that the driver would deal with it.

He then told me that I could claim a seat by putting my hand luggage on it. He pointed out that the front and back seats were already taken as they already had random stuff on them – plastic bags, a lunch box etc. Later, a boy claimed the seat next to mine by putting a bottle of soft drink on it.

I didn't understand why people were doing this. My instinct was to get onto the bus along with my luggage, so I kind of missed Clue No. 1.

It was about twenty past eight in the morning. I asked Damian what time we would arrive in the main town of Olkhon Island. Damian translated my question to the driver. The driver laughed. That was Clue No. 2. "No later than three o'clock," was the response.

Then Damian left and I had to connect all the clues together. Clue No. 3 was that there were no passengers on the bus but there were several hanging around: they weren't ducking off anywhere. The answer was obvious. A Russian minibus doesn't leave until it's full.

This took at least half an hour, but when it happened it happened so quickly that by the time I realised it I was the last one on. I hadn't realised how many people were waiting around for this thing – I'd seen about five. I saw another lady approach and start talking to the driver and when she agreed to go, suddenly four more people appeared out of nowhere. By the time I noticed them, they were already seated on the bus.

The bus wasn't full - it had two seats spare - but I guess eleven must be the minimum number (either that or the driver was sick of waiting), so everybody piled in. I mean piled, literally. Two foldable seats had to be put down too, so there was not a bit of spare space in the tiny bus.

Just as we were about to leave, two more people appeared: a young couple, each with packs larger than mine. "Yes, come in, we have plenty of room!" said the driver. First, he took a large box from the empty seats and put it on top of a pack that was in between his seat and the passenger seat, thus blocking most of his rear view. Then he opened the boot, which was not a boot, just a door with about 30cm of space between it and the back seat. (He had put my pack and another beneath the back seat earlier – he had to lift the seat up to do this.)

Two smallish things that may have been sleeping bags or small tents were removed from the "boot" and flung forward to the people sitting in the back seats. The driver did some cramming that was invisible to me as I was trapped in my seat by the window. It took about three attempts to get the boot closed again. The people sitting in the back were left holding the camping things. They shoved the smaller one vertically into the very middle space behind the back seat, thus eliminating whatever had remained of the driver's rear view. The other one they shoved behind their heads.

The long drive was quite boring, but I enjoyed looking out the window anyway.

The vehicle ferry goes to the south of the island, which actually looks quite dull – I was thinking, *Oh no, it's only brown grass hills...* But as the bus drove north, every glimpse we got of the coast was beautiful. The water was so so blue, and the hills on the mainland on the other side of the strait were made of some kind of white rock, which was reflected into a mirror surface on the lake.

Then I saw some white bits and realised that what I was actually looking at was ice! I'm not sure if the mirror surface was – I thought it was at the time: it looked like the ice went all the way to the mainland – but where I am now there's only a very small amount at the water's edge. However, I spoke to some people who arrived yesterday and they said that yesterday there was lots more ice; they were told they couldn't do a boat tour today because it hadn't broken up yet, but it definitely has now. It changes every day, they said.

Now, a little information on Lake Baikal. It is 636km long, 1,642m deep and contains one fifth of the world's non-frozen fresh water (less in winter, I suppose, when the top is frozen). In winter, you get to Olkhon by driving, even if there are cracks in the ice and a danger of sinking. In summer, there's a vehicle ferry. In between times, there's a hovercraft. A major industry on the island is fishing. In winter they still fish, they just do it by car!

<u>16th of May, 7:30pm:</u>

I arrived at Nikita's Homestead at about 3pm yesterday. It's a brilliant place to stay – a large complex of buildings all done in timber with elaborate carvings and murals. Friendly people, a folk concert every night, and three square meals a day included in the tariff!

And a wonderful location. I walked through the back gate at about 25 past 3 yesterday and my jaw dropped, and I've been slack-jawed ever since.

There are lots of high up coastal paths from which to see incredible views. I first marvelled at the blue water in the bay in front of me and the remaining ice at the bottom of its cliffs, and then I turned left.

Not far along, I saw something that reminded me of Mongolia. It wasn't an ovoo, but there were many coloured scarves very similar to the ones I'd seen tied to an ovoo centrepiece, and they were tied to some trees at the cliff edge, blowing in the wind.

Maybe I'm still in Asia after all, I thought.

The native people of Olkhon are called Buryats, and their religion is shamanism. I've seen pictures of them dressed in bright blue fabric with patterns very similar to ones I saw in Mongolia. I also saw some Buryat people today, and they look Asian. So, I was wrong. I'm not in Europe at all. I just got confused when I arrived in Irkutsk and everyone was so white and the streets were so clean and the buildings so European. Here, that is not the case. There's not a single paved road - not even the main streets in the villages. There are dilapidated buildings and a cess pool of a "lake" in the middle of Khuzir township that's full of rubbish.

So anyway, I'm walking along the tops of the cliffs toward Khuzir's beach, and it's awesome. I pass a church, and then I arrive at the fishing port. There are some derelict buildings, a dilapidated jetty that looks like it's suffered a fire, and some old boats up on the sand that obviously haven't been used in a while. I later read that far less boats went out after fishing became de-collectivised. However, the port is still in use: there were some men doing repairs to some boats, and they had what I'd like to call a "tank van" (a stout and cheap all-terrain vehicle that's very common here) right out on the sand in the shallow water helping them.

A couple of boats next to the one they were working on still had ice around their bows.

I reached the beach, where a French tourist was posing for photos in bathers! She was not, I hasten to add, swimming – it was too cold. There seems to be old metal things on many Olkhon beaches – on this one I found a car door in the shallow water. Another good reason not to swim, I think.

I walked into the township, via an abandoned factory with a big red star on its rather large, pulley-operated gate.

The town has plenty of those gorgeous wooden houses with the coloured shutters. I took photos of them, some goats and the "lake". Then I looped back through Nikita's and out the back gate again, and I turned right.

I'd already been impressed, but I became more impressed - as has happened many times since. Even better views; more shaman scarves on wooden pillars; and a large rock I later found out was called Shaman Rock (they do ceremonies there) which forms its own tiny peninsula jutting out between a small rocky cove and a bigger sandy one.

There was some ice at the edges of the small cove, so I went down to have a closer look.

From a distance, even a small distance, it looks like snow. Up close you can see that it's actually ice and that, as it's melting, it has formed thousands of long crystals, like chips, each one about the size of two fingers. In the ice I looked at first, which was in the sunlight on the eastern side of the cove, the crystals had already separated and were just lying there in big piles. It looked solid from a distance, but it was just piles of loose ice chips – you could pick up handfuls of them. They made a sound a bit like the sound you hear when you pick up handfuls of Lego. I later decided it was safe to eat one. It had a hole down the middle, so I was able to make an ice flute! That was nothing, though, compared to the incredible music that was made by the ice chips that had fallen into the water and were gently banging into each other with the water's movement. They sounded exactly like wind chimes.

Occasionally (sometimes assisted by me), a large section of the ice pile would collapse, making a larger sound, and once - just once - a group of crystals in the water were pushed by a wave into a rock in quick succession, in such a way that they made the sound of a scale on a xylophone...

I was captivated. I knew that ice looked beautiful, but I hadn't known that it sounded so beautiful too.

In the middle of the cove, there were some very small remains of pack ice, which sounded like a slushy...

On the other side was some ice that was in the shade, so it still had its basic clump shape. The long crystals were there but they were still stuck together, making the clump look much more like snow. It was easy to get them unstuck, though. I walked over an ice clump like that today (very carefully – I only did it because there was grass beneath) and though it looked just like snow from above, it didn't feel like it to walk on. I could feel it cracking beneath my feet, and I looked behind myself to see that it had held its shape, but hairline gaps had appeared. Then my foot slipped off the edge of one section and ice crystals cascaded after it! If you're directly on top of them, the crystals are strong, but as soon as you apply pressure to the side they split apart - hundreds of them at once.

I'd been on Olkhon for less than four hours and I already felt like I'd seen so much. When I woke up this morning I had trouble figuring out how many nights I'd been here. One night? Really? Surely not!

Having seen so much of this area yesterday, today I wanted to get out a bit further. I went north and crossed a beach with sand dunes, which was very hard to walk over and took a long time. On the other side was a tall headland where I ate lunch, and then I walked to the next headland. I saw a small amount of ice there, and then I climbed a big grassy hill. Another thing Olkhon has in common with Mongolia is grassland. From the top of the hill I had an incredible view, right out to the distant snow-capped mountains on the mainland and the northern entrance of the strait with all its lines of ice sheets. I could also see, in the distance behind the next headland, a little bay which seemed to still be full of ice!

I walked excitedly towards it. I was so excited I rolled down a hill for an auto shutter release photo and then spent the next hour pulling grass seeds out of my shirt and pants! It took me easily an hour to get to the headland because I was going slowly and taking plenty of photos. Then I sat on the highest point of the headland for some time having a snack and feeling like the queen of the world because I had the most majestic view. It was more of a promontory than a headland, because the land veered to the east at that point, over to the icy cove.

Eventually, I made my way down there. From every angle, the ice looked different. I first came at it from above. From above, you can see the circles. White circles, with lower blue ice around them. They looked like lily pads.

There was a long white streak further back, and in the middle a thin winding crack that looked like a stream.

Down on the shore, I could see it all up close. It was whiter bits above, bluer bits below, and amazing patterns.

I tried to pick some up and it disintegrated. It really is melting – I fancied I could see it melting right before my eyes. I sat on the shore for a long time and I swear when I left there were bigger gaps between the lily pads than there had been when I'd arrived.

I had to throw a rock in. The ice didn't break. I tried a bigger rock. The ice still didn't break, and not only that, the stone slid. It skipped. I had suddenly acquired the ability to skip stones! I skipped more and more, and they all just sat there on the ice! Then eventually I got a big enough rock to break through – it was about half fist sized – but it wasn't very dramatic; it more slid off than broke through.

I sat there for the longest time just staring at the ice.

Near the cove there was a small village, which I'd been told was the next village along from Khuzir, about 4km by road. I decided to go back that way, but I cut back to the coast near the end, past the beach. The sun was just starting to fall, and I was impressed yet again.

All up I'd been away for eight hours, walking for probably seven, the first five with only one break!

The sinking van

<u>19th of May, 9:45am Irkutsk time; 4:45am Moscow time:</u>
After a sunny 23°C yesterday afternoon in Irkutsk, when people were sunbathing by the river and I was starting to worry that I hadn't brought enough summery clothes, I'm now looking at snow again. I'm not sure where I am, but it's only three hours from Irkutsk. It's pretty heavy snow – I can only clearly see 40 metres out the window.

I'm on board Train No. 1, which also terminates in Moscow but I am getting out in Yekaterinburg, which is fifty hours from Irkutsk. Fifty! Oh my god! And yes, that's definite, I checked the timetable and it's all written in one time zone, so it must be true.

I have not written anything for the past thirty-six hours so that I'd have something to do on the train! Thirty-six hours is a lot shorter than fifty, though…

I can tell you about the train. It's a lot quieter than the Mongolian train - only one Russian lady in my compartment. It's also a lot classier. The compartment has a telly and a plug for earphones, which are now playing me some kind of dance music. There are two toilets per carriage instead of one, and you can't see the hole in the bottom of the train where your pee goes. And even though this train started in Vladivostok three days ago, there is still toilet paper and the toilet floors and seats are relatively clean (i.e. someone has been cleaning them, unlike on my previous two trains). They're out of toilet seat covers, but you don't really need them when you have such white, comfortable toilet seats (the others were black and clunky).

Just passed a station called Tyret. It's snowing there. I wonder if it's higher altitude than Irkutsk. The forecast for Irkutsk today is 15°C. I was discussing it with Damian at the station, and he said that Irkutsk also gets ups and downs in temperature. Sometimes people get caught if they only stay one night and it's much colder the next morning and they don't have the right clothes. Then he started talking about university students who keep winter clothes with them only in winter and go home and swap them for summer clothes in spring, and vice versa. He said he sees out of town uni students wearing clothes that are too thin in autumn and too thick in spring. He made this point, and followed it by saying, "Because, you know, in March sometimes it can be quite warm; more than zero degrees..."!!!

On my last day on Olkhon I took a tour, because it's a big island and that seemed to be the only way to see more of it. The tour vehicle was one of those tank vans. I think they're actually called UAZs, but I prefer to call them tank vans because they're a van built like a tank. Almost everybody on Olkhon drives them because they're the only way to handle the incredibly bumpy tracks they have there. Some parts are really rough, even in the towns. Rougher than the Mongolian ones. Mind you, when I traversed the Mongolian ones they were wet, and many of the Olkhon rough bits looked like they'd been created in the wet, but when it gets dry a former muddy cess pool becomes a mountain range of wheel ruts. The tank van was going even slower than the Mongolian Land Cruiser, and any time we were going down a hill, the brakes squeaked.

The first stop was just past the pack iced cove I'd visited the day before. I had been able to see from there that the ice got even better past the next headland. On the tour I got to see it from above, and there were ice sheets maybe 50m across, and triangular; white, with the blue lower ice around them. It was an amazing view.

We stopped there for a little while, and when I asked a Russian couple I'd been seeing everywhere on Olkhon (including on the bus from Irkutsk) to take my picture, I discovered that they spoke English.

I'm really not sure about Russians and English. Most of them, it is clear, speak none. But more than you'd think speak some. But, more often than not, they won't let you know they speak some until you've spent rather a lot of time with them. At that point, I'd spent 6½ hours on a bus with that couple and run into them at least twice around Khuzir, and had no idea that I could communicate with them. I didn't find out until the tour that the woman spoke quite a bit of English and the man some. She then became my translator because the driver spoke no English (he was by no stretch of the imagination a tour guide - just a driver).

There was also a Russian family in our group, and I didn't find out until the last stop on the tour (stop 6, about seven hours in) that they spoke some English too. I only found that out because my by then self-appointed translator, Ralia, had trouble translating the driver's last explanation and the family stepped in to help out. It was only words then, not sentences, but later I ran into them at sunset and the man said at least four sentences to me!

So, I think Russians are shy with their English. The trouble is that I'm shy too, and when I don't speak the local language I basically become a mute, because I don't want to be so presumptuous as to talk a foreign language at people. So I think I'm not giving them the opportunity to use their English...

Well, it's breakfast time in Moscow and lunch time in Irkutsk, so I think I'll have lunch.

10:40am Moscow time, 3:40pm Irkutsk time, who knows where the hell I am or what time it is – I don't even know how big Siberia is so I don't know if I'm still in it or not. I have heard it's heavily forested, which this area certainly is, and most of what I've seen all day.

While forests are pretty, they're not as varied as hills, grasslands or villages – mainly because you can never see very much of them at once. The snow was nice, but that was only for a couple of hours. So, regrettably, the scenery is not as captivating to me as it was on the previous journeys. Doubly unfortunately, on this journey I have no-one to talk to. As soon as I got to Russia it became much more difficult to tell foreigners by sight, and I've walked around the train a bit and I haven't heard anyone speaking anything other than Russian.

That's a bit disappointing. It was the people who really made my last two journeys.

I wonder how long this journey would take if they used fast trains. These ones only go fifty or sixty kilometres an hour.

So there I was looking out at the crazy ice sheets with this young Russian couple when another tour tank van pulled up and someone started waving out the window. I couldn't see much from where I was standing but the hair looked exactly like... Alex's! It was Alex and Sascha! Ha! How funny. I ended up getting a bit annoyed, though – not with them; I was very happy to see them - but they seemed to be on some kind of English language tour, and I got annoyed at Nikita's for not booking me on that tour. They had a guide *and* a driver – their tour looked way better than mine.

Well, they borrowed Tunga a few times when we were in Mongolia, so I figured I'd borrow their Olkhon tour guide as much as possible. At that stop, he was saying something about how huge Lake Baikal is and how there are very few settlements. Of those that do exist, some are only accessible by four-wheel drive tracks - so it's easier to go by boat. I didn't catch all of it but it gave me an idea of how enormous Russia is. I guess the government can't build roads everywhere. Well, the Chinese government can build flyovers everywhere, but that's not a good thing. Even Australia is like that, though.

The next stop on the tour was an abandoned settlement right next to a beach with the remains of a pier and plenty of ice in the water. Alex and Sascha's tour guide said that the settlement was a gulag and the prisoners worked in a fish processing factory, mostly canning fish. The pier was to bring the fish in and take the cans out. I wonder who ate it.

I asked the tour guide about the sinking of cars that fail to make the ice crossing successfully in winter. It sounds like it is a pretty hairy trip. He said drivers will cross gaps a metre wide simply by speeding up, so you have to have some confidence and, yes, sometimes they fail. He told me a brilliant story of a tank van that sunk during a trip with a driver and two tourists heading to Khuzir. Its nose became trapped in a crack between the ice, so the people climbed through to the back and climbed onto the ice back there. There was nothing to be done for the vehicle – it sank. I asked him if people often die, and he said sometimes they do but if the vehicle is only sinking slowly, they can get out onto the ice. I was trying to anticipate what he'd say next, like whether there'd be a helicopter rescue of these poor people clinging to the ice or what, but I was forgetting that the majority of the lake is frozen solid; there are just some cracks and holes in it. So, the people simply walked to Khuzir over the ice. It was 25km!

He then told the amazing story of how the man who owned the tank van went on to retrieve it from the icy depths of Lake Baikal. He went around asking everyone in Khuzir to lend him whatever lengths of metal cable they had, and he borrowed an underwater video camera off somebody too. Putting the camera on the many lengths of tied together cable they were able to find the vehicle, and then they hooked it somehow and cut a hole in the ice to put a big log in, and they made a manual winch around the log and five men were able to pull the vehicle back up. They towed it back to shore, and the man got it working again! It helps that it's a freshwater lake...

Babushka

On this train the beds are separate to the seats: they fold down over the top of them. The last train gave us weird floppy mattress things that we had to put down over the seats. Both Alex and I thought they were doonas and put the sheets down first, and then found out they were mattresses and had to remake the bed! On this train, however, the mattresses are already laid out behind the back rests of the seats, so you just have to put the back rest down and voila, you have a bed!

The Chinese train didn't have any mattresses. It needed them – the seats were fairly hard to sleep on. But the seats on both Russian trains I've been on have been soft and nice, so actually I don't think I need a mattress. I went to sleep not long after getting on this train this morning because it was bloody early: the train left at 6:45am. Since I'd already been up I didn't really think of it as going to bed, plus the seats are comfy so I was all ready to lay down on them, but a lady from another compartment insisted on putting my bed down for me. I didn't put the sheets down, though.

Do you know, I don't think I've seen a brick house the entire time I've been in Russia. They are all those stained wooden things. Or apartment blocks, but I haven't seen many of them yet either. In the many many country towns I've seen today I've seen only houses in the small towns and only a handful of smallish apartment blocks in the big towns. Nothing like those Chinese tower blocks.

3:10pm Moscow time; 8:10pm Irkutsk time; and I'm going to make a new time just for me: I'm going to try to guess what time it'll be in Yekaterinburg, because when travelling to a new time zone I hate hanging onto the old one – it mucks my body clock up. Yekaterinburg is 26 hours from Moscow, so let's say it's a two-hour difference. So, 5:10pm Yekaterinburg Maybe Time:

Aha! I'd read that ladies come to the stations selling food, and I finally saw some, in Ilansky! They all had little handmade trolleys with wheels and usually a handmade box on top that sometimes has floral patterns on it. They were selling things like bread, coleslaw, boiled potatoes, fried fish, various crepe-type things, pasties – all homemade (except the bread, I think). One of them was even selling home-dried sunflower seeds! Some of them also had chips, cigarettes, soft drinks and beer.

I bought a fish, because it was the only homemade thing that I knew what it was. I'll eat it later. Maybe when it gets to dinner time on Yekaterinburg Maybe Time. I already had dinner on Irkutsk Time. The packet of my dinner promised the world: I thought I'd finally found instant pasta, but it turned out to be just two-minute noodles with cheese. It wasn't so bad, though.

The lady in my compartment is called Lida. She's a diabetic too! That's what really got us talking, I think. She's about to have her insulin now. She has exactly the same Novopen as me, which is how she knew what mine was.

Other things I have learned about Lida, with only the assistance of a pen to write ages:

She's 67, she has two children and each of her kids has two kids.

She's going to Novosibirsk, and she tried to explain what she was doing there but I didn't quite get it – see a heart doctor maybe?

She asked me several times where I'm from, and she didn't understand my answer. I even showed her my passport and drew a map and she still didn't get it. She understood "New Zealand" but not "Australia". Then just now, as we were leaving Ilansky, we were talking to a man who knew about five words of English but he had been to Australia, so he understood my accent when I said, "Australia". He said, "Ah, Afstrahlia" or whatever the Russian word is, and the penny dropped in Lida's head and she went, "Oh, AFSTRAHLIA!" It turned out that it was only my pronunciation of the middle vowel that had been preventing her understanding.

I also learnt that she has an insulin injection once a day and tablets twice. Damn, I really thought I had more to say about her because it took about two hours to get that information! And to give her some information about me.

Also on the platform at Ilansky was a blue truck, a tanker of some kind. One man was driving it and another was connecting a hose from it to the carriages one after the other. He was connecting it to a kind of small tank that was underneath the middle of each carriage. At first I thought it was fuel, very briefly, until my brain caught up and thought, *No, carriages don't have fuel; only the engine has fuel!* Actually I'm pretty sure this one's electric, anyway. The Chinese and Mongolian ones weren't but the Russian ones are.

Then I thought, *Water?*, but surely that would go into a tank above the toilet. Then I thought *Waste?* but this tank wasn't underneath the toilet either. But the pipe was never connected for long, and from the direction of the movement and the absence of anything spewing out of the hose, I concluded that it was most definitely taking something out, not putting it in. Then I caught a glimpse of the liquid, and it was yellowy brown.

When I got back on the train I asked Lida, and she confirmed it. I pointed at it and said, "That truck... toilet?"

She laughed, nodded and said, "Da, da." She made some movement with her hands to indicate that previously the toilets had spewed onto the tracks but now they have a new machine. I heard "machina", anyway, and I had learned about two hours before then that "machina" means car, when we passed a freight train carrying lots of brand new Subarus. At first I didn't think they were new because they were dirty, but then I realised that the walls of their carriages were open mesh, and these trains get dirtier and dirtier the further they go, I can tell you. Window photographs get grimier and grimier. Then I realised that they were *all* Subarus - almost all Subaru Foresters - so there was no way they were second hand.

There are always so many rail workers. In all three countries. Even at stations the train doesn't stop at, in the middle of nowhere with nobody else around, there'll always be someone there. In China he'll be in a uniform and in Russia and Mongolia they'll be in a hi-vis vest; in China they might salute, in Mongolia they'll be waving a hi-vis flag – even if it's 5am, they will be there. Even if it's snowing or blowing a gale.

There are so many other workers too, in daylight hours. I saw some tightening the railway sleepers today and some cleaning sand out of the tracks in the Gobi Desert; but that's only two occasions I can call to mind where those workers were actually doing something – usually they're just standing there on the tracks, not doing anything. Maybe they were working on our track and they had to move aside for us to come through...

There are lots of staff on the train too. One to two provodnitsas per carriage; a man who walks around selling snacks; at least two, maybe three, in the café car; the drivers; the boss man... It's very good to see governments investing so much in rail. They give a lot of people jobs and they transport a lot of people and goods around. And it's electric, so its ecological footprint must be very low... unless the electricity is generated by coal. It could be. Dammit.

I'm not sure about this fish. It's very chewy, and sweet for some reason. And Lida keeps looking scornfully at it, shaking her head and rubbing her tummy! Maybe buying something just because I know what it is is not a good idea when the something is fish.

Just passed another shipment of cars. Toyota Land Cruisers this time!

<u>20th of May, 7:02am Moscow:</u> and I realised a couple of hours ago that if I just turn my phone off battery-saving flight mode briefly it'll automatically pick up the local time (that wasn't working before). It's 10:02! We're just leaving Novosibirsk Station, which is where Lida got off ☹ Two middle-aged men got on at bedtime last night and slept in the top bunks; one of them

snoring heavily – boy am I glad I brought earplugs! So they're my cabin mates now.

I did it again this morning. I got up on Irkutsk time thinking it was Moscow time. Thought it was 8am, but it was 3. Oops. Had breakfast with Lida, then realised the time and went back to bed!

When I got back from Olkhon I had the afternoon to look around Irkutsk some more. I went to the Regional History Museum. The ground floor had some displays on the native people of Siberia, including the Buryats. The artefacts, native dress etc. looked similar to Mongolian ones, apart from the ones that looked Native American! Tunga had told me about a people in northern Mongolia who live in tee-pees. There are some in Siberia too. The thing is that it's not that far away from Alaska.

The museum said that by and large these native people still exist in approximately the same territories and numbers as they did before colonisation (50,000 was one of the numbers), but now there are lots of Russians around too. So that's what it was – colonisation! I'd wondered how Russia got to be so big, and how Europeans had got to be so far east. They colonised the whole area starting from the 17th century – they had governors and everything. And *they* founded Irkutsk, which is presumably why it looks so European and its people look so white.

Upstairs in the museum was a display on the 20th century. Standing out at either end of the first gallery were big red images – I have to call them propaganda images because there's no other term – one of them a stained-glass window that was actually part of the building! The other one had a picture of a woman proudly holding a red flag, which said "1917!" in big letters.

There was a bit on WWI, then the revolution and communism, but unfortunately the English explanations stopped as soon as I ascended the stairs. This was a pity, because I really wanted to hear about it from their point of view. These kinds of places are always quite confronting to me because I don't realise until I'm there, and seeing "the other side", exactly how much *I* have been propagandised by my own side, and how much my own thoughts on what I'm seeing tend to tumble out through an "us and them" filter that I cannot control. This frames my mind and my thought processes as a result of my own upbringing and education in the West. The feeling of realisation of suddenly finding myself "on the other side" is exhilarating, illuminating and just a little bit scary - but more than anything else, I find that it is levelling. I've felt it before, in Germany and in Japan. And Vietnam. So far I have not been able to learn enough to understand - certainly not from a museum display with no English! - what it was/is really like to be of that "other side", and what it felt like to be a part of that cause at that time. But, while my curiosity to know that is there, I don't mind if I don't satisfy it because the overwhelming thing I've learned from these experiences of "the other side" is that *it doesn't matter*. The people of "the other side", whoever they may be, are just the same as the people on their "other side". Screw the "us and them" mentality. We're all the same. All wars, hot or cold, are pointless and stupid, and no-one should be thought of as an "other".

The only place I haven't had this feeling is China. They project their own "other" mentality onto any foreigner who enters the place, so I can't help but throw it back at them. They are an "other" I have difficulty feeling any solidarity with. And they're a huge nation and they're ever growing in money and power, and that is frightening.

But that's what people used to say about the USSR.

Suitors in the restaurant car

9:45 Moscow; 12:45 probably local time; 11:45 Yekaterinburg Maybe Time: The toilets aren't still nice. It doesn't help that in their new non-spewing-onto-the-tracks technology, which involves serious suction through a small hole, the small hole is too small to accommodate a medium-sized poo.

But hey, the poo's not on the tracks!

<u>10:28MT; 12:28YMT; 13:28PLT; Barabinsk Station:</u>

At this station the ladies didn't have trolleys; they were just walking around carrying their wares and hawking them to whomever they approached. The real reason I'd bought fish at the last place was that I'd read about those ladies selling fish so I knew it was a thing, an essential experience, and the person who'd written the account had said that it was good. This fish wasn't good, but I realised at this station that I'd tried the wrong one. At this station there were lots of women selling smoked fish. There were small ones, which they had attached to a coat hanger-like device by putting holes through their heads or sometimes tails; and large ones, that had been split and stretched flat and were being carried around in stacks that looked like stacks of hardened elephant ears. These ladies were wandering all around the station with them. I wanted to try some, but they all looked too big... There were baked goods, crepes, salads, vegetables and bread as well, and one lady was selling fur hats and scarves. Real? I don't know.

I ended up buying some crepes from a sweet elderly lady. There were quite a few very young ladies doing this too, especially with the fish! I ate my crepes right there on the platform because I was hungry. They contained some kind of ricotta. It wasn't bad.

Back to my last day in Irkutsk. After coming out of the museum I discovered that there was a fair going on over the road, by the river. The entrance was beneath a large statue of Tsar Alexander III, which I thought was an interesting thing to have survived so long. The sign said it was erected in 1908 to commemorate the construction of the Trans-Siberian Railway, then dismantled in 1920. The pedestal sat empty until 1961, when a concrete obelisk was made. This was removed in 2003 and replaced by a statue similar to the original, in time for the 100th anniversary of the railway. I find it very interesting that they chose to go *back* to an imperial figure.

I wandered around the fair for a little while, avoiding the 14 roubles public toilet, but as I was leaving I realised I did need to go, so I'd have to suck it up and pay. I was no longer near the public toilet so I began looking for another, and I spotted a row of portaloos in a park. *Aha!* I thought. *Portaloos! They're free, right?*

There was a lady sitting at a very small table on the path by the portaloos with a roll of toilet paper. Bloody hell. I hope toilets were free under communism. I'm close to starting a revolution of my own, I can tell you.

At least it was cheaper. 10 roubles. But it was a squat portaloo! Which was scary because those things are made of plastic, so they bow under your weight! And I nearly hit my head on the ceiling.

2:24pm Moscow; 4:24 YMT; and my phone says the local time is... no reception. Don't know what the local time is!

Yesterday morning I got up at 4:55am to take the train at 6:45 (Irkutsk time). Got the train, most of which you know about, but you don't know about what happened last night. All afternoon I'd been toying with the idea of having a beer in the café car just for something different to do, and I'd decided to do it at sunset. Unfortunately, not knowing what time it was or when the sun would set, I got there far too early. I spent most of my beer shielding my eyes from the still very bright sun, but by the end of my beer the sun was finally setting. I was listening to music and taking photos of the sunset when a young man came over, with his beer, from another table and asked to sit with me. I didn't hear what he said because I was pulling my earphones out of my ears, but I nodded and he sat down. I did hear the next thing he said, but I didn't understand it. My response was, "I'm sorry, I don't speak Russian," and the look on the guy's face was priceless because he'd clearly sat down to try and chat me up, and the look on his face said, "Oh shit! I've picked a girl who doesn't speak Russian! What do I do?"

Well, he spoke more English than Lida. Twenty, maybe even fifty words. He told me he'd learned it playing video games. His name was Nikolai and he was an officer in the army. He was going to Moscow.

The funny thing about being chatted up by someone who is not fluent in your language is that all the usual euphemisms, lines and innuendo are completely removed. He had to be very direct, because he didn't know how to say it any other way. So he was saying things like, "You...me...interest?" and something about did I want a Russian man (that sentence was half in Russian so I wasn't sure); and once even in sign language, pointing to me with one hand, pointing to himself with his other hand, and then joining the two hands together! Very direct. I just kept shaking my head, and eventually he gave up and said, "OK, I go," and he did.

I put my earphones back in and prepared to finish my beer (which was by this time some of Nikolai's that he'd given me) whilst watching the darkening sky, when seconds later, another man came and sat down opposite me! His name was Valentin and he was saying similar things to Nikolai, but was much more drunk and less attractive. Just as he was asking me about Nikolai, Nikolai came back and sat on my side of the table, and the two of them started talking! Nikolai evidently told him what he did for a living because Valentin said something like, "He artillery… boom boom… muzzafucker!" This was fairly appropriate for that particular statement, but then he started saying it all the time. Nikolai told me that he was swearing a lot in Russian as well, to the extent that an older man from another table came over twice to tell him to stop it!

Somehow both Valentin and Nikolai were still coming on to me. I looked around the café car and realised that everybody else in there were men, some of them smoking even though there was a "no smoking" sign. The waiter didn't look happy about the situation, particularly about having this drunk man swearing everywhere, but he kept bringing us more beer anyway… When did the restaurant car become a sleazy bar?

I was trapped next to the window, so all I could do was sit and enjoy the antics of these men and endeavour not to consume too much beer. I did enjoy it. At one point I asked to take a photo of them, and Nikolai initially said no but later agreed provided there wasn't any beer visible in the photo. Maybe the army has some rules about that?

Not long after the merry Valentin boldly declared, "I am from Russia, muzzafucker!", he suddenly got up and left. This left Nikolai to attempt to seduce me again, so I ran off when he went out for a smoke! I hid in the toilet for a while, in case he came after me!

I was a bit worried about Valentin; he's in the same carriage as me so I can't get away from him, but as I was going to bed I saw him leaning against the window in the corridor, apparently asleep! He wasn't going to do anything…

I've seen him on the platforms a couple of times today and he still looks drunk and obnoxious. Not in a dangerous way, though. But he's no Valentine, I'll tell you that!

Funny thing is, just as I started writing this account, the train stopped at a station called Omsk and I got out to have a quick walk around. Nikolai was waiting for me on the platform! Blimey! He's actually trying to court me! So I took a turn with him at Omsk Station, not having much choice in the matter, and he introduced me to his comrade, Konstantin. They're all such lovely names.

So. I'm being courted by an officer on a Russian train. Whatever shall I do!

21st of May, 6pm Yekaterinburg Time, which I had guessed correctly – it's now 4pm in Moscow and 9pm in Irkutsk:

Well the officer turned out to be married, so that was a no go. But I did have a very nice evening with he and Konstantin in their compartment. We watched some movies, not that I could understand them, but one of them was a Buryat movie which was a comedy, so I could kind of get what was going on. It turns out there is a decent-sized Buryat film industry!

Konstantin also showed me some army videos he had filmed. There was one of the soldiers listening to a Mongolian throat singing performance. I'm not sure whether Konstantin and Nikolai are posted somewhere near Mongolia or in Mongolia - "Mongolia" was all I really understood in their explanations. They're either posted somewhere in southern Russia near the border, or they sometimes do exercises in Mongolia, or both.

They also introduced me to a couple of deep-fried bread products, which were simple-tasting but nice, and a kind of green salad vegetable which they said is found only in Siberia. You can eat it with salt as a snack – the station kiosks and seller ladies sell bags of it, which is where they'd got it from. It has a real bite to it. Good stuff.

They also introduced me to Russian beer in a 2L plastic bottle – they had a name for the bottle size that started with a "b". I've seen them everywhere - you can buy beer very readily in Russia. I'd been expecting to see vodka everywhere, but I've seen a lot more beer.

Last night I had my first Russian vodka experience. The beer ran out, so Konstantin and Nikolai got some cash together and Konstantin went out of the compartment for a couple of minutes and came back with a small bottle (500mL) of vodka wrapped in newspaper. There was a secret place to buy vodka somewhere on the train!

I'd been told that in Russia you have to drink the vodka straight down, and they told me this too. I was very wary at the start because the last time I'd shotted vodka I'd very nearly spewed - but the Mongolian vodka I'd had on the last train had been fine, though I had had a little sneaky water with it. That was not going to be an option here.

It was absolutely fine. It was smooth. Not sweet like the Mongolian one, but smooth. We did four rounds, each one big enough to be two mouthfuls, and I got it all down three out of the four.

Once we'd got it all down, Konstantin would usually be ready with some of the salad he'd made earlier out of tomatoes, cucumbers, the Siberian leaf vegetable and mayonnaise. He'd get his vodka down first and then he'd stab some bits of the salad with a fork and be holding it out towards you, his other hand underneath it to catch the drips, as soon as you'd finished your vodka. He was doing this to Nikolai as well as to me, so there must be nothing strange in it.

For three of the four rounds we just sat around, clinked glasses and said, "Nazdorovye," which means "To your good health" (or "Cheers"). But for the third round – they said they always do this on the third round – the two of them stood up and encouraged me to join them. They said it was a military tradition that on the third round you stand, and you do not clink glasses, and you drink to your fallen comrades. This they did very seriously.

It was a great night, and overall not a bad two days on a train. In the absence of foreigners, I made friends with the locals, and once again, the people made the trip.

The holy family

<u>22nd of May, 4:20pm:</u>

Oh boy, I am tired.

   Arrived in Yekaterinburg at 5:37am local time, yesterday. The provodnitsa most annoyingly woke me up forty-five minutes earlier, signing that she needed my sheets back. I complained loudly, waking the other man in my compartment. She came back again two minutes later. God dammit, I had my alarm set for twenty minutes before arrival – do not try to steal someone's bed sheets twenty-five minutes before they finish using them!!

I was met on the platform by Konstantin, my tour guide. He runs a tour company and owns an apartment which contains the company's small office and two bedrooms for tourists to sleep in. He told me that the apartment building was very advanced for its time. It was built in 1930, part of a large apartment complex which was bringing to fruition a Soviet experiment of having self-contained apartment communities with their own doctor's clinic, kindergarten etc. on site – I'd seen one in Beijing! This one also had a laundry and a communal canteen, and the apartments only had kitchenettes because they were trying to free women from housework by providing these services, so that women could be "more productive" members of society by working in factories like men.

This experiment did not last: later apartment complexes - of which there are so many and they're still being built today - had schools, social and cultural centres, sporting complexes etc., but not laundries and canteens. But still the women were expected to work in factories - of which Yekaterinburg had many.

This apartment complex was also very advanced in that it had services like running water and electricity, which were not common at that time. It also has those hot water pipes for heating, but they have now been turned off for the season. Today it's a balmy 25 degrees or higher, so fair enough.

The thing about this apartment complex, though, is that while it looks quite normal from the outside, on the inside it looks exactly like a prison cell block. Long run-down corridors with metal gates at either end, and big thick metal doors all the way along. All the residential doors I've seen so far in Ulaanbaatar, Irkutsk and Yekaterinburg were the same. In my Ulaanbaatar homestay the internal doors were thick too, and the toilet in particular looked like a cell. In Russia, so many apartments have enormous metal front doors with multiple locks on them, and each lock has multiple bolts – you have to turn the front door key four times, and feel the four bolts slide clear one by one, before it is unlocked.

Konstantin told me that this is because in the 90s there was a lot of crime, and companies that made these locks and doors became very popular.

So, the corridor leading to my Yekaterinburg accommodation looks exactly like a prison, but inside the apartment is awesome – it's all been newly fitted out.

On the drive there, Konstantin pointed out a red line on the pavement and said, "You see the red line? We knew you were coming, so we painted it for you to help you explore the city!"

He went on to tell me that he was not joking: that his company had been the ones to make the line, which is a 6.5km self-guided walking tour, and that the city had been trying to encourage tourism because it had been closed to tourists until 1991. This was because in the Soviet era Yekaterinburg had many military factories, including ones making nuclear bombs, and a large KGB office (metres from our apartment complex) and military office. There were just too many important secrets in Yekaterinburg, so foreigners were not allowed to come here.

The military headquarters is still in operation – I've seen a few officers walking about.

First, I went to the Regional History Museum. The region is called the Urals; the Urals mountain range runs north to south, several thousand kilometres from above the Arctic Circle to Kazakhstan. It is still in Siberia – Siberia is that big; it covers all of eastern Russia. It covers the Asian part of Russia.

Yekaterinburg was founded in 1723 and named after Ekaterina II, or Catherine the Second, the empress at the time, who had some municipal control over it. I've been writing it as Yekaterinburg because I've noticed that's how the Russians say it, but it's sometimes spelt Ekaterinburg. During the Soviet era it was called Sverdlovsk, but they changed it back in 1998.

The Regional Museum had quite good English explanations. This made the contrast all the more stark and noticeable when I went upstairs to the Soviet room and the English completely disappeared again! In Irkutsk the museum was pretty basic, as was its English, so I'd wondered whether maybe they simply hadn't got around to translating the upper floor yet. But this museum had good English on both the bottom two levels and on the fourth level above the Soviet one... I asked Konstantin today and he said he thinks it's a new display they haven't got around to translating yet, but I'm not so sure...

So, I couldn't learn anything from that room.

The final gallery upstairs was all about the execution of the last Tsar of Russia, Nicholas II, and his family, in 1918. The English reappeared for this.

What I hadn't known was that Yekaterinburg was the location of their execution. Therefore, there's a lot of information on them here and sites dedicated to them, but in much of the literature they are referred to simply as "the Romanoffs", because that was their dynasty name.

The "tour" I am on, my whole Trans-Mongolian/Trans-Siberian experience, is called the Romanoff Tour. I decided I wanted to do this rail journey, but I heard that it was very difficult to get a Russian visa independently and that it was best to book a tour, so I did some internet research and I picked the longest tour I could find. It is billed as still being "independent travel" - which I like, obviously - so I am not in a tour group or with a constant guide, but the travel agency arranged my itinerary and hooked me up with local guides in some places. I was given a choice of tour and activity options in Mongolia and Irkutsk. Moscow and St Petersburg are definite stops on all the agency's offerings, but the so-called "Romanoff Tour" is the only one that has a stop in Yekaterinburg. I picked it simply because I wanted to stop in as many places as possible – I had no idea what was in Yekaterinburg or who "Romanoff" was. I thought that if they thought it interesting enough to make it a stop on one of their itineraries, then I would go with their recommendation.

Until I went to that museum I thought Romanoff was a person. On entering that upper gallery I was able to suss out pretty quickly that actually it was a family, so I thought, *OK, they were a noble family in this area and maybe they were killed during the revolution, maybe along with the Tsar...* I was a good quarter of the way through the gallery before I realised that the Romanoffs *were* the Tsar's family!

The revolution began in February 1917, and on the 2nd of March the Tsar was forced to abdicate. He and his family were sent to exile in Siberia and were imprisoned in the house of a merchant in central Yekaterinburg. On the 17th of July 1918, in the early hours of the morning, they were executed in the cellar there.

The overwhelming representation of this presented by the museum was one of great tragedy and regret. There wasn't much explanation of events and concepts – artefacts and photographs were clearly labelled, but other than that I was left to connect the dots. I was confused as to why the bodies had been hidden and why there had been two separate searches and investigations made during the Soviet era. Konstantin filled in some of the gaps for me today, but I still don't fully understand it and I've realised there were actually several different groups and periods within the Soviet era which were distinctly different and complicated, and I would like to learn more about them if I ever find a museum that has English translations of its Soviet section!

Anyway, basically the museum told me that the Tsar, his wife, five children and four of their servants had been killed in Yekaterinburg and their bodies hidden underneath a muddy road in the forest nearby. It also showed photographs of foreign delegations visiting the room where they were killed in the 1960s or 70s. There were many bullet holes in the wall. But the museum said that the house had been demolished in 1977.

After lunch, I went to walk the Red Line. It's a great walk, going past most of the city's beautiful buildings, of which there are many - and they are buildings of such culture. Russia is a place of such culture. Yekaterinburg has 1.5 million people and is relatively compact, but in the area covered by the Red Line alone there are nine museums and four theatres, and I can see several others on the map that aren't on the Red Line route. There's an opera and ballet theatre (gorgeous classical building), a philharmonic theatre (communist building) and a musical comedy theatre (new building). I am currently sitting outside the latter listening to a brass band that is playing on the footpath. This is the fourth afternoon I have spent wandering around a Russian city, and on three of the four I have come across a brass band! This one started up at about 5:30 on a Thursday evening. Quite a crowd of people have gathered to listen, including myself.

I also saw artists painting on the street in Irkutsk, which has several museums too - even though it's a much smaller city.

Also, of course, there's the odd beautiful church with eye-catching golden domes. I spotted a particularly large and beautiful-looking one and decided to go inside. The map said it was "The Cathedral in the Name of All Saints." Next to it was a small wooden chapel (with a wooden "onion" on top) which was just one small room packed with icons, but there was one icon in the middle of the room that I instantly recognised from photographs I'd seen in the museum. It was Nicholas II himself, in icon style - gold everywhere, holding a cross and with a halo around his head! At the side of the room, on the wall with a candle in front of it, I saw another icon with the entire royal family in it: mother, father and all the children, all with halos and looking very holy. And then I saw another!

Well, I thought. *They have a chapel dedicated to the memory of the royal family. That's nice.*

I continued around to the cathedral. Large photographs on the fence showed the royal family, in particular the children, in happier times. I realised that the enormous crucifix in front of the cathedral, which I'd previously seen but had only noticed two figures beneath it and thus assumed them to be Jesus and Mary, actually had seven figures. The one at the front was a man carrying a boy and the man was, recognisably, the Tsar. It was a big statue, beneath the crucifix, right at the entrance to the cathedral.

I went inside, finding a scarf by the door to put on. It was quite beautiful inside with lots of gold and looking quite new. I found some pictures of a tumbling down cathedral and wondered whether they were still restoring it after the Soviet times.

Outside, on a small English sign, I found the truth:

Church-on-the-Blood in the name of All Saints Shone
Forth in the Land of Russia
The memorial church was consecrated in 2003 on the
site of execution of the last Russian emperor Nicholas II
and his family.

The site! This is where that merchant's house used to stand, and the cathedral was built very recently. *Gee*, I thought. *These people really do feel bad about the death of the royal family!*

Every time I write these words I have to stop myself from writing "holy family". That's the term that springs to my mind every single time, because there is such a religious cult around them. But more on that later.

The next day, Konstantin made a Russian breakfast for me and Isabella, the Swiss traveller who'd arrived the previous night. It was a very nice savoury (but not salty) creamy porridge, bread and cheese and crepes like the ones I'd bought off the old lady at one of the train stations. Konstantin said the cheese was sweet cottage cheese.

Then we headed out on tour. We were heading west, and Konstantin said we were heading to Europe. Apparently I still wasn't in Europe yet, despite having seen all those gorgeous European buildings the previous day. I asked him how on earth someone had decided that Asia was here and Europe was there, and he said that the borderline was the Ural Mountains.

First, we stopped at the Gulag Memorial. It's right by the highway, at the site of a mass grave of 18,500 prisoners who were executed, mostly in 1937. It was 30,000 in Mongolia, but in total it was 750,000, and millions were imprisoned. This was done by Stalin. Konstantin explained that the Lenin statues are still up because he is still a popular figure – not with Konstantin himself because Lenin killed people too, but he thinks Lenin is worth remembering as an important historical figure. Stalin is much less popular because he was a cruel dictator, and after his death in 1959 all his statues were taken down and the gulags were closed. But still, Konstantin said, there are some people in Russia who think Stalin had some good ideas and that what he did was necessary. He said that even Putin said once that, "We can't do things Stalin's way anymore," but that the way he said it implied that he thought this was unfortunate.

The reason for the gulags was that Stalin knew that war was coming and he wanted to speed up Russia's industrialisation process. There were many rich mineral resources in Siberia that could be exploited, but there was a labour shortage – only 20% of Russia's population lived in Siberia, even though its land area is three quarters of the country. Stalin's solution was to send prisoners there to do the work. He took millions of people, the vast majority innocent of any crime. He also executed 750,000 people.

"If Stalin needed these people as a workforce," I asked, "why did he kill so many?"

"He killed thousands to scare millions," was Konstantin's response.

The memorial has all 18,500 names written, and their birth and death years. This information was obtained from KGB records, along with the location of the burial site. It's the second biggest gulag memorial. The biggest has 75,000 dead.

Next, we drove to the Asia-Europe Monument. I'd always been more than a little confused about the division between Asia and Europe (as you've probably noticed). Part of that is the contrasts visible in Russia as the two appear to coexist in many places, and part of it is that in primary school I was taught that the two were different continents, and so this was another example of my education funnelling my thought process and making it difficult to think outside the box. Consequently, I asked Konstantin for a lot of explanation of who says this is Europe and that's Asia and why is it so.

He said that the continent is the Eurasian continent – Europe and Asia are just two parts of it. It is not possible to have a continental divide thousands of kilometres from the ocean. However, Asia and Europe are on different continental plates, and about 300 million years ago the plates collided to form the Ural mountains. They were originally very tall mountains, about 5,000 metres, but because they are so old they've weathered a lot over time.

The one who decided where the border falls was cartographer Philip Johan von Strahlenberg in 1725. In charting the area he found that there were two completely distinct river basins on either side of the Urals – all rivers on one side flow east and all on the other flow west. He also noticed that the flora on each side was quite different. He therefore concluded that this was the intra-continental divide.

I was quite confused when we got to the monument because there were no mountains anywhere to be seen. Konstantin said that here the mountains had worn down to just hills and that that was why the Trans-Siberian was built through here. I didn't even feel like I was on a hill; I felt like I was on a mound by the side of the highway, and I didn't see any flora difference at all...

But, I had my photograph taken with one foot in Europe and one foot in Asia.

I have to say, though, that about an hour into this next train journey - by which time I was definitely in Europe - I noticed that the forest had changed markedly. I mean *completely*. Different species, and even a different kind of forest – the Siberian forest had no undergrowth, but this forest has lots. It is *completely* different - and I had 50 hours of looking at the other stuff, so I should know! So maybe that cartographer hit the nail on the head...

Next, it was time to learn about the Romanoff tragedy and its bizarre peculiarities. We drove back into Asia and to a beautiful wooden monastery in the forest. The monastery is very new: it was built in the noughties after the Romanoff family were canonised in 2000. That's why they get to appear in golden icons with halos around their heads! They are strongly linked to the Russian Orthodox Church for a few reasons: one is that the Tsar was head of the church; one is that many monarchists are religious (communists certainly aren't!); and another is that the Romanoffs were given the opportunity to leave Russia but the Tsar chose not to, because he wanted to stay with his people. The family also have a strong image as being a pure Christian family and they are viewed as having suffered and sacrificed their lives like Jesus did. It's pretty heavy stuff.

The Russian Orthodox Church and its followers love and worship the Romanoff family so much that they decided to build a monastery dedicated to them on the *wrong* site of their burial – which was mistakenly identified by the White Russians in 1918! After the revolution in February-March 1917 there was a civil war, primarily between the White Russians and the Bolsheviks, but actually there were several different groups fighting each other. The Bolsheviks had captured the Romanoffs and were holding them in Yekaterinburg, but the White Russians were coming. Only eight days after the execution, the Bolsheviks lost control of the city.

They feared that they would lose the civil war, so they wanted to kill all members of the Romanoff family so that the monarchy could never be re-established. But they did it in secret and they hid the bodies. I'm not sure why, since it was pretty obvious that they'd killed them when the White Russians got to Yekaterinburg and found bullet holes and blood in the house where they knew the family had been held. Maybe they just didn't want people to know where the bodies were in case a cult of worshipping them sprang up, as has now happened!

One of the Bolshevik ring leaders knew about an abandoned mine outside the city that had a lot of water in the bottom of it, so they planned to dump the bodies in there because they would be hidden under the water. Before doing so, they removed the Romanoffs' clothes and possessions and burnt them next to the mine, and poured sulphuric acid on the bodies to prevent identification. They threw them all into the mine, but found that the water at the bottom had frozen, so the bodies could not be fully hidden. So they came back the next night and removed them (that must've been gruesome) and buried them beneath a particularly muddy bit of road that had some logs over it to aid the passage of vehicles.

When the White Russians took Yekaterinburg a week later, they appointed an investigator to find the bodies. The investigator found the mine and the remains of a fire and some of the royal family's possessions that could not be burnt (jewels etc.). The investigator concluded, and wrote in his report, that the bodies of the royal family and their servants had been burnt at the mine site. This was accepted by the White Russians at the time and has been believed by the Russian Orthodox Church ever since.

Meantime the Bolsheviks won the civil war and there were various different periods of different Soviet groups and policy. In 1978 another investigation was launched, which found the real grave site. This was well before the monastery was built at the mine, but the Russian Orthodox Church is a bit strange. It reminds me of the Catholic Church - they even have a figure like the Pope. They still deny that the bodies were found under a muddy road and insist that they were burned at the mine site.

It's a beautiful monastery. It's in the forest, and all the buildings are made of whole logs, in traditional style. The sun was shining through the trees and picking out the bright green leaves and the shining gold of the onion domes. There are a few different churches, just like in a Buddhist monastery, but while in a Buddhist monastery the different temples are dedicated to different gods, in this one the different churches are dedicated to different saints. There's one to St Nicholas (that's Santa Claus, not Nicholas II); one to the royal family; one to a saint who was canonised by Nicholas II; and one to the Virgin Mary. We went inside the St Nicholas one and the royal family one. There were many monks moving statues about and ladies cleaning things, because apparently there's an event on this weekend!

Konstantin explained about the wall of icons. He said the main icon of the church is always to the right of the centre. He said people don't pray to the icons themselves, they pray to the saints, but that the icons provide a medium between the real world and the spiritual world. In the royal family church, I went over to look closely at a Jesus icon that was on the side wall. Unlike the others, which were painted on gold leaf, this one had gold coming out of the image, with gaps in it for Jesus's face to be painted on a canvas behind.

As I stepped away from it, I became aware that there was a Russian worshipper/church cleaner standing next to me who seemed to be telling me that I should cross myself. So I did. Then she came around to the icon and kissed it, explaining (which Konstantin translated) that she was not kissing the icon itself, she was kissing Jesus, and that if you had a photograph of your mum and you kissed it, you wouldn't be doing it to kiss a piece of paper; you'd be doing it to kiss your mum. She encouraged me to kiss the icon too, so I did. When in Rome... I didn't feel like I was kissing Jesus, though. I felt like I was kissing glass.

The mine site is behind the royal family church (the altar points to it). There's a wooden cloister running around it. Konstantin said that on the anniversary of the start of the Romanoff dynasty, 120,000 pilgrims went there.

There are only about twelve monks and about twenty students. They try out the life of a monk before actually becoming one. Then they can quit if they want. Monks can also quit, but it's much harder. The monks wear long black robes and caps, and women must wear something on their heads and a skirt that falls below their knees. They had wraparound skirts on the table at the entrance for those of us wearing trousers to borrow. Consequently, everyone there looked very traditional, even the little girl who was playing with some kittens at the entrance - she had a headscarf and skirt too.

It's interesting that communism has not had nearly as much impact on Russians' religious beliefs as it has on Mongolians'. This may be because religion wasn't actually banned here, just discouraged. Or maybe there's another reason.

Next, we went to the real grave site. It was discovered in 1978 during the second investigation, but the bones were not exhumed until 1991, when Boris Yeltsin initiated a third investigation. Then, they did extensive tests, including DNA tests, which proved who the bodies were. The trouble was, though, that there were only nine of them – eleven had been killed, including the four staff, but only nine bodies were found. Still, those nine were identified and they were laid to rest in St Peter and Paul Cathedral in St Petersburg, the traditional resting place of all Romanoff monarchs, in 1998.

Two of the children were still missing, Alexei and Maria. In 2007 yet another investigation was done and they were found in a separate grave only a stone's throw away from where the others had been. DNA tests were conducted using Nicholas II's own DNA from a bloody shirt that had been protected as a relic after he was attacked by a Japanese nationalist when he was a prince. The tests proved conclusively that the bodies were of his children. Despite this, their skeletons are still sitting in a box in an archives office – they haven't been interred with the others.

The reason is, superbly ironically, the Russian Orthodox Church! For sixty years, everybody thought that the bodies had been burned at that mine. When the first nine bodies were found the Church didn't believe it, which is fair enough because they were just nine, not eleven, unidentified skeletons in the woods at that stage - but even when they were dug up and DNA tested fifteen years later they still didn't believe it! And when ten years after that they decided to build a monastery dedicated to the memory of their much loved, now canonised and worshipped royal family, rather than building it at the grave site they decided to build it at the mine site, where the bodies spent less than twenty-four hours. And now the bodies of Alexi and Maria can't be buried because the church can't accept that it's them, even though there is incontrovertible proof that this is so. They are denying the burial of these innocent children that they adore. The boy in particular they have a fixation with: I saw so many icons of him... They're being kept from their family! I just can't get a handle on it.

Other interesting things I learned in Yekaterinburg:

- Konstantin said that Soviet apartment blocks have different eras and different styles, and they are named after the president of the time - just like we name historical architectural styles after British monarchs! He pointed out some Kruschevki and some Bresnevki. Kruschevki have five storeys (among the shortest). I think my Ulaanbaatar homestay apartment block may have been a Kruschevki.
- Isabella said she went to see Lenin's body in Moscow and people were bowing to it. She said she thought it was so ironic that communism bans religion and yet people were worshipping a communist leader!
- I don't think I've mentioned the many, many posters and enormous billboards of "9 May" I saw in Irkutsk. It's the day the Russians took Berlin – there was a photograph on the posters of a soldier raising the Soviet flag high above a burning city. It's the day Russians celebrate the end of WWII. I asked Konstantin if they'd had big posters in Yekaterinburg as well and he said yes, and a big celebration and parade. He said it's a big deal because 27 million Russians died in WWII, so every family lost someone, and they want to remember them and to celebrate victory over their invaders. Australians get pretty into Anzac Day, so it shouldn't have seemed strange to me when I first saw the billboards but it did. I think because it was the Soviet flag flying in the pictures. But I think again it's just a part of their history that was important and they don't deny it. That was their flag at the time so it's in the picture, but the day isn't about the Soviet Union, it's about Russia...

Isabella and I were talking last night about how we both do find it strange that there are still so many red stars, hammers and sickles and Lenin statues about. Konstantin said there are still many people who believe in Leninism and even Stalinism. But then there is also the historical thing. He said they leave it there because it's part of their history, and I thought about the statues we have in Hobart: we have a statue of an English king from 100 years ago; I can't even remember which one – he's certainly not relevant anymore. And we have a statue of William Crowther, an arsehole who stole Aboriginal remains, on proud display in Franklin Square. Nobody's taken him down – but I think most people don't even know who he is; our statues just aren't important to us now. But we still leave them there.

And you can't take the decorations off the Yekaterinburg Town Hall because it's a beautiful building. They can't even demolish the Kruschevki because people are living in them. The Soviet era really was so huge, so ground-breaking, so important, that they left stuff absolutely everywhere. It would take so much effort to get rid of it all. That statue we have of the king probably weighs a tonne – why would you bother? In England they don't get rid of the GRs and VRs you see about the place. They haven't had a regime change since those monarchs, but if they did - even if they became a republic - I don't think they'd get rid of them. It's an important part of their history, and it's basically just a way of telling which era the building was built in. But the Soviets built *so much* - their calling cards are everywhere. The Mongolians have mostly removed them, but for them it was a foreign occupier. For the Russians, it was themselves. It's part of who they are.

Dental emergency

<u>25th of May, 5:12pm:</u>

Well I am flat on my back because of a bleeding tooth infection. What? Really? A tooth can affect the whole body this badly? The extra annoying thing is that yesterday, apart from the sore tooth, I was absolutely fine *and* I got medicine! It's very very annoying because I'm in Moscow! Grr.

My journey to Moscow wasn't very eventful because I was trying to rest – ha! But I briefly made friends with the Russian in my compartment, a young woman called Karina, who spoke English. As usual, I didn't realise she did until several hours into the journey, when she suddenly said, "Do you mind if I open the window?" Then the window wouldn't open and she declared, "It's impossible!"

It still took another couple of hours for us to talk. It had to come from me. I wonder why that is. Are Russians shy, or do they just not talk to strangers? Well, Karina ended up enjoying talking to me so much that she left me a note when she got off the train because I was asleep!

I asked her how she learned English and she said, "I don't know!"!! Pop culture? She was fairly good at it.

The train terminated in Moscow at 9:23 yesterday morning (real time! The train time was the same as real time!). I was taken to my homestay apartment, in a lovely area with beautiful pastel-coloured buildings all along the main street, many many apartment buildings and lots of greenery along the little laneways between them. My tour guide came, a young lady called Kristen. The first thing I said, as she was the first fluent English-speaking person I'd seen so far, was, "I need to see a doctor – can you see my swollen cheek?" It's like I've got a golf ball in my mouth - it's very visible. I was stupid enough to think that all I needed was a doctor to give me some antibiotics, but fortunately Kristen thought it was the same word and began looking for a "tooth doctor".

Apparently you don't need appointments here. We found a dentist in this area at about 12:30pm and were told we couldn't be seen until 1, and Kristen said, "What? When you have pain, you shouldn't have to wait! Usually you don't have to." So we went into the city instead. She didn't even know where they were - she just said, "There will be one," and sure enough, there it was: a massive building with lots of medical clinics in it, right on the road we were walking on! There, we were told we couldn't be seen until 1:30. Kristen said, "Do you want to wait or we try somewhere else?"

I said, "That's fine," - we could go for a walk for half an hour and come back; I couldn't believe I only had to wait half an hour to see a dentist *on a Saturday afternoon* without an appointment!

We were walking along Arbat St, which is a downtown shopping and restaurant district with many shops and cafes and street stalls. Kristen said it was the centre for merchants in the 16th century, but you can't see buildings that old because of fires: Moscow almost burned to the ground in 1812 after Napoleon's invasion. They call that the First Great Patriotic War. The second is WWII, when Hitler invaded.

We went back to the dentist, and it was quite a chore to get into the place. I had been given a swipe card to get through the security gate, but it only let one person through - because apparently people never go to the dentist with their friends or relatives or interpreters. Kristen, who'd gone through first, said, "Oh, I'm sorry, I should've let you go first! Here, give me your bag - you climb over."

Nobody cared. Fortunately it wasn't a big gate.

The lift took us to one floor, and then we had to go through corridors and up stairs – Kristen said this was a typical old Moscow building! Total rabbit warren.

The dentist was late. That is universal. She had a look in my mouth, which would barely open, and said something to Kristen. Kristen said something back, and the dentist said something more, and they both looked very serious and I was getting very worried. I heard the word "abscess" and I thought, *Ooh no no, that must mean something else in Russian...*

Possibly the longest minute of my life waiting for the translation, which was a lot shorter than whatever the dentist had said. It was, "You should have the tooth deleted because it could become dangerous." I was told that the tooth is growing into the cheek, which could cause an abscess. My interpretation of this was, *Oh phew, it's not one yet.* But after a day laid out on my back and spewing last night with a fever, I think I've been convinced that the tooth does need to be removed.

The dentist gave me a prescription for lots of different medicines and made another appointment for 1:30 Monday. The dentist's fee was only 460 roubles! That's about AUD$15! Why can't our dentists be that cheap? The medicine cost much more, though. I hope I can claim it all back.[1]

After getting the medicines from a nearby pharmacy, we sat in a park and Kristen translated my medicine for me! She was great.

Then we could finally do the walking tour. We walked first to the Cathedral of Christ the Saviour, which is quite enormous and adorned with gorgeous metal statues. It was demolished by Stalin so he could build an enormous Soviet palace, which proved to be too enormous and couldn't be built, so the foundations were turned into a swimming pool for a few decades. It was the world's biggest, apparently, and Kristen said some people died in it! Then after the end of the Soviet era they decided to rebuild the cathedral.

Behind the cathedral is a bridge over a river from which you can see the Kremlin, but that's not what I was looking at. I was looking in the other direction at a statue the size of an office building. "What is THAT?" I asked.

"Oh yeah, that's the Peter the Great statue," said Kristen (clearly she'd been wanting to tell me about the Kremlin instead).

There's a massive sailing ship raised high on tall waves, and the statue is on top of it – it just goes up and up; it's enormous! Kristen said it wasn't even meant to be Peter the Great - it was meant to be a Christopher Columbus statue that somebody called Tsereteli made to be put somewhere in Spain. When the Spanish saw it they said, "Eugh, it's too bloody huge - we don't want it," so the Russians said, "Meh, we'll have it. We can call it Peter the Great."

---

[1] I couldn't. When I returned home, I read the conditions of my travel insurance policy to find that it had a $100 excess. Incredibly, my Moscow tooth crisis did not cost me more than AUD$100 – it was about $80, I think, for about four kinds of medicine, two dental appointments and Kristen's interpretation services!

On the other side of the bridge, we looked out at the Kremlin. It's pretty big too. The bits visible from that angle were a large palace and some strong red fortification walls with about eleven different towers, some bigger than others. The bigger ones had green spire roofs with a big red star on top. The Kremlin was built as a castle, initially wooden. The palace was the Moscow residence of the Tsars. It's now the president's official residence, but Kristen said she doesn't think he lives there. She said she's heard that when he is there, a flag will be flying. "Wow," I said, "That's exactly what the Queen does at Buckingham Palace – is he trying to be a king?"

Kristen looked very worried and said, "I hope not!"

I think many Russians are worried about Putin. Konstantin certainly was...

We walked along a main road that goes along the northwest side of the Kremlin. It was a big road: six lanes one way! We passed a gorgeous old library and its newer extension, which is dedicated to Lenin. "It's not called Lenin's Library now, it's called State Library or something like that," said Kristen. But it still says "Lenin" on the portico.

This is the Cyrillic that I can read now, just from seeing it around the place:

Restaurant

Café

Toilet

Metro

Moscow

and Lenin.

Then we passed Parliament House, which looks tall and serious with lots of security guards. I asked Kristen if members of the public could go in there, and she laughed awkwardly and said, "I don't think so..."

We were still walking past the Kremlin and Red Square and it was looking more and more impressive at different angles - but we went to the Bolshoi Theatre first. It's massive. As we were walking around I kept saying, "Whoah, that's huge - whoah, wow, this is massive; that's enormous..."

and Kristen said, "It's Moscow. Everything is big."

But they don't have skyscrapers. There are five that were built by Stalin which are called "skyscrapers", but I don't really think they are because they're not that tall. They're shaped a bit like a castle! Interesting architecture. Apparently Stalin meant to build seven, and the weird thing is, later in the evening I saw a new building being built that looked exactly like them. Hmm...

The current version of the Bolshoi was built after 1812, when the previous one burnt. I'd love to go and see a ballet production at the Bolshoi because that's where Anna Pavlova used to dance, but I wish I'd organised it before I left home because shows tend to sell out. I would like to see something somewhere, but I feel a bit overwhelmed because there are so many theatres and so many performances. I did find one ticket office, and they had a poster on the wall that was about three times A3 size. It had a table with all the dates of this week only, and all the theatres and what was on in them. The text was tiny. There is just so much on, and I don't think it was even all the theatres in Moscow - I think it was just the ones that ticket company sells for...

Finally, it was time to go to Red Square, via a bit of original city wall and past the Museum of 1812 (huge) and the State History Museum (huger).

Red Square is also massive and full of amazing buildings! St Basil's Cathedral is the one with all the many coloured domes. At first I thought it looked like Disneyland, but then Kristen said, "Some tourists say it looks like ice-cream," and I realised that was a more apt description. Or cream – some kind of really intricate baked good with elaborate decorations on the top, done by a pastry chef who wants to show off. The image it gives you is definitely food, anyway. Confectionery. It definitely looks like you could eat it...

It's actually ten different churches, which explains the different colour schemes, I suppose. One is for Basil the Blessed, who was a holy fool who predicted the downfall of Ivan the Terrible, so Ivan added Basil's chapel to the cathedral he had already built, and put it over Basil's grave. This was not successful in preventing his downfall.

I just can't take it seriously – I mean, I know no-one who has seen Fawlty Towers can ever take anybody with the name "Basil" seriously, but just the look of the place... If there was a religion for worshipping confectionery it would be appropriate, but otherwise...

I asked Kristen what "Soviet" means. She said it's a Russian word meaning unity or togetherness. I said, "Oh, that's nice,"

and she said, "Yeah, but..."

"But it didn't work out that way."

"No."

She said she thinks the Soviet statues and things should stay, though, "Because they are a part of our history too."

But the Soviets tried to overwrite previous history, which should also be respected. I guess they've restored a fair bit since the end of the Soviet period, though.

Kristen doesn't agree with Lenin's waxy corpse being in Red Square. She said it's against the Russian religion and dead bodies should be buried...

Soviet theme park

<u>26th of May, 8:25pm:</u>

Ow! I walked ALL DAY! Ow! That's the problem with big cities: there's too much to see, and you can't get a seat on the metro.

The Moscow Metro is famous. On Saturday evening, I did a DIY metro tour. I got on I think it was the green line at Teatralnaya: the theatre station. There are about four theatres there, and the station has stucco gold-trimmed musicians on the walls. I went to Mayakovskaya, which was the grand prize winner at the 1939 World Fair. I wasn't quite sure why, because it was mostly just a white hall with many small mosaics on the ceiling – everything from peaches to fighter planes to people playing sport. I cricked my neck looking at them all. But I've realised today that often if you go to the platforms of a different train line, you'll find a completely different hall with completely different things. I've since learned that Mayakovskaya was the first "deep column station" in the world. A deep column station is one that has only columns between the platforms and the central hall, opening up the whole space. I noticed quite a few of these in Moscow, including some which had mezzanine levels too, and it was impressive. Perhaps that's why Mayakovskaya got the prize.

I have to rewind for a minute because actually my first experience of the metro was with Kristen on my local line where my homestay is. The station is Baumanskaya, and it was built in 1944. The first thing that struck me was the entrance: black columns, with white (dirty) stucco behind. In the entrance hall where the ticket gates are, there is a red and gold mosaic on one side with a communist star in the middle and some war motifs. In most of these old stations, this hall is circular.

Kristen told me that they commenced building the metro in the 30s and continued through the war, and that the stations were intended to be used as bomb shelters as well as for transport. They made them beautiful, most with pictures and statues of ordinary Russians so that people could feel that they were theirs. Baumanskaya Station has some red granite statues downstairs of military people – ordinary people nonetheless, in that time – and a mosaic done in stone of Lenin's face on a red flag and the dates "1905" and "1917": the two revolutions. Apparently Stalin's face used to be there too, but it was removed.

In the evening I went to Mayakovskaya (1938) and Novokuznetskaya (1943). Novokuznetskaya also has mosaics, but bigger, set in a white stuccoed ceiling with repetitive patterns of hammers and sickles underlain with wheat sheaves (there is *always* wheat!!)

Underneath this, along the wall is a continuing stucco frieze of the city's and the country's defenders; and a black and white image at the end of the hall with some proud defenders, proud industrial workers, the Kremlin and Lenin's head. There's always Lenin's head. But even more often, there is wheat. The airflow grates of all these metro stations are moulded into the shape of a sheaf of wheat. Wheat was very very important to the Soviets, for some reason.

I shouldn't go on about things like that, though. Yes a lot of it was propaganda, but the stations are works of art and the fact that they celebrate ordinary people doing ordinary things (including harvesting wheat) makes them even more beautiful.

To get back to Baumanskaya I had to change trains at Ploschad Revolyutsii, which was built in 1938. It's the station for Red Square. It has life-size bronze statues on four corners of every column, all of ordinary people. At one end, they are military statues: an old man with a rifle; a young airman; and a seriously scary-looking soldier with a revolver in his hand, a star on his arm and a long belt of bullets wrapped right around him – but you're not meant to be scared of him because he is defending Moscow. Another soldier has a dog, and it's considered good luck to touch the dog's nose as you pass, so the dog's nose is now a completely different colour to all the other statues! I saw several people touch it while I was there.

Down the other end of the hall, there are statues of people engaged in more normal pursuits. In the middle are farmers (very important), and at the end are people engaged in study, playing sport and rearing children.

I spent the longest time there – I discovered it by accident, and it ended up being the best one!

Today my follow-up dentist appointment only took two minutes because the dentist said the tooth can't be taken while the infection is there, so bang goes my chance to have a cheap and easy wisdom tooth removal. I no longer have a golf ball in my mouth, though, so it's all good.

Then I went to VDNKh, the All Russia Exhibition Centre. Oh my. What a place. It's out of the city centre – has to be, because it covers a very large area, and umm... it's a Soviet theme park! The first thing I saw was a reeeally tall shooting obelisk with a rocket on the end of it, and some communist pavilions in the middle distance behind it. The rocket obelisk was in a park which also contained a statue diorama of the solar system and busts of several astronauts. At the bottom of the obelisk there was a frieze with images of dedicated workers in a style I am now well used to seeing - except that these ones were working on launching a rocket ship.

Ah, the space race, I sighed.

I realised that I was standing on top of the Cosmonautics Museum, which I knew was in the area but not in VDNKh itself. My guidebook tells me that the rocket-shooting obelisk was built in 1964 to celebrate the launch of Sputnik.

VDNKh was just over the road. There was a broad circular space in front of it, like a large turning circle or car park except that there weren't many cars there, and then an enormous grand entrance gate with stucco of wheat and workers all over it. At the top was a huge golden mosaicked statue of a proud man and woman standing tall, the man holding a simply enormous golden sheaf of wheat over his head.

I could already see a large ferris wheel off to the side and was getting a very confusing feeling. The thought, *It's a... theme park?* had already entered my head, but it was only when I got through the gate that this was confirmed by the boppy b-grade pop music that was playing over loudspeakers throughout the park. This was not just any b-grade pop music: it was American b-grade pop music. This was quite a contrast to the wheat-infested Soviet gate I'd just walked under and the grand, columned, trumpeting, star-topped pavilion that was facing me behind the Lenin statue. In between the two, however, was a broad promenade which felt exactly like the entrance to Disneyland or Movie World!

My day got weirder from there on. The American pop music did not stop. I passed the Russia Pavilion (the first one) to find an enormous golden fountain behind it that seemed to be dedicated to wheat, productivity, wheat, sunflowers and, of course, wheat. There were children swimming in it and young people climbing on it. All around the park there were people on bicycles and rollerblades. Everybody was having a great time: doing exactly what Soviet propaganda always implied the people were doing – being happy and having an enjoyable time.

There are two fountains and scores of pavilions. Originally they were built to represent each of the Soviet Socialist Republics, but now most of them are named evocative things like "Pavilion No. 42". I did see one that seemed to say "Armenia" (that's if I figured the Cyrillic out correctly).

Some pavilions are museums, but most are in a bad state of repair and are now being restored. It looks like they've done the Russia Pavilion first. I surmised that the reasoning behind the unremittent American music was that, upon deciding to restore the park for historical values, they needed something to counteract any negative influence all the Soviet propaganda may otherwise bestow!

There's a big rocket ship at the back of the park too. You gotta have the Space Race in there.

I had a wonderful time in the Soviet theme park, though it was without doubt one of the weirdest places I have ever been to.

That may have been matched this morning by Lenin's Mausoleum, but not in a good way. That was definitely one of the creepiest places I've ever been to. And I only say "one of the" because I've also been to the Capuchin Catacombs in Sicily.

It's a big granite thing at the edge of Red Square. It's open for three hours, four days a week. There are no windows, of course, so the doorway kind of looks like it's swallowing you up. You pass a guard and turn to the left and it gets colder and darker, and a stone stairway appears, going down. In the dark. With no handrail, and the temperature dropping with every step...

I was already creeped out. I clasped my hands together at the top of the steps and didn't let go until I left the building.

At the bottom of the steps, you pass another guard and turn right, into the tomb chamber. It's large and tall and there's a raised path going around the outside of it, right around Lenin, who's enclosed in a large glass case with regal red trimmings. It looks a little bit like a carriage without wheels.

He's well-lit and creepy-looking. Well, it's a dead body, what can I say. I've seen the pope who's preserved in St Peter's Basilica, but he didn't look real - he looked like a wax figure. Lenin looks real. Every time I pictured him as I walked back across Red Square, I shuddered!

The grace of St Petersburg

Next I went to the Kremlin, which is one of those must-do sights, but unfortunately that means every man and his dog does it - or every tour group and their flag-wielding guide. The churches were nice to see, though. There are four of them: one tiny, one small, one medium-sized and one big. The big one used to be used for royal coronations. Frescoes everywhere, of course, but they're *old* frescoes – the church was built in the early 16th century and it felt quite magical inside.

I sat in the so-called "Secret Garden" for a while having lunch, and then decided to walk along the Kremlin Wall - whilst looking out at the view - to the exit. And who did I walk past? Alex and Sascha! Ha! It's like there are magnets connecting us or something. We left the Kremlin together having a good old chat. They were flying to St Petersburg that afternoon though, so they had to rush off. We are now all in St Petersburg and attempting to arrange an actual planned meeting!

I took the train that night to St Petersburg. Only seven hours: my last leg. Over in no time; 7,900km done.

I arrived to my best accommodation in Russia! The travel agency I booked through uses mostly homestays, I guess as a way of doing it cheaper, but unfortunately in most places it was quite obvious that the hosts were only doing it for the money. Even though they were all nice people, I always felt like more of a cash cow than a guest. It was also quite isolating because they would just do their own thing and leave me to my thing and I'd have no-one to talk to.

Not so here. A lovely couple called Igir and Tatiana are pretty much running their apartment as a B&B! They're very friendly and giving, and they genuinely want to sit around and talk to guests in the evenings and make them feel welcome. It's a nice apartment too - much more spacious than the Soviet ones. It's on Vasilyevsky Island, one of the older parts of St Petersburg. The first thing Igir said when he was showing me where we were on the map was, "Bridges go up at 1am; then you can't get back!" This is so that ships can go through in the night.

I had a walking tour first, from a young woman called Sasha. The first thing I noticed is that the city is very European, and very not Soviet. I asked Sasha about that and she said that Soviet buildings are there, but not in the city centre. That day I saw only two, which was quite a contrast to Moscow.

There are also no skyscrapers, because there is a rule that no buildings can be taller than the Hermitage, which is only three storeys. The Soviets wanted to break that rule but the locals didn't.

There are very many rivers and canals, because the city is built on a swamp. It feels like Venice or Amsterdam.

There are many pastel-coloured buildings with statues of mythical figures holding up their upper floors.

Put simply, I have very definitely arrived in Europe. St Petersburg is a lovely place. Not the best weather at the moment - it gets a lot of rain (probably something to do with being in a swamp). But I'm quite used to changes in weather by now. It was less than two weeks ago that I last saw snow, then I had four days of 30°C plus in Moscow, and now rain and about 10-13°C.

St Petersburg was founded in 1703, so people keep saying that it is "new" - just like when they say the temperature is, for example, 8°C, they proudly say "plus 8", because apparently you need to specify whether it's plus or minus. And last winter was "warm": zero to minus 10. That is a "warm winter". My Australian sensibilities get very confused whenever I hear things like that. Inevitably the temperature is only identified towards the end of the conversation, so I'm understanding what they're saying and nodding along and then they say "plus" or "zero" or "St Petersburg is new" or "Do you live in a house? Wow!" and a firecracker of surprise goes off in my head. The blinkers through which we view our world...

St Petersburg was founded because Peter the Great wanted a naval base, but he also disliked Moscow so he made it the capital. There are three very large palaces around the place but none were built for him; they were all built later. The Winter Palace is huge but now makes up only one third or so of the enormous Hermitage Museum. The Hermitage was originally a small building next to the palace which was, as the name implies, a hermitage – not in the religious sense, just a private residence for Catherine the Great (Ekaterina II). Somewhere for her to be alone. The art collection began when she acquired some artworks from Europe in 1764, which she showed by invite only. But in 1852 a public "Imperial Museum" was opened in a purpose-built building next to the hermitage. After the downfall of the monarchy, the museum expanded into the palace.

The Hermitage Museum is open late on Wednesdays, so I got there at about four and stayed until about eight. Still didn't see everything. Apparently there are three million artworks, so it would take years to see them all.

The ground floor houses antiquarian items like mummies and Greek and Roman statues, but I decided I wanted to see European paintings so I went straight to the first floor - up a gorgeous grand staircase framed with gold and mirrors.

The royal family's living quarters were on the first floor and are now exhibition space. You can see some glorious frescoes and stucco, a golden ballroom, a pastel blue theatre room and Pavilion Hall, a white and gold light-filled room by a courtyard garden and the river. And then there's the art – oh so much of it. I saw Da Vinci, Raffaelo, Michelangelo, Rembrandt... after nearly three hours I realised I was still on the same bloody floor, so I thought I'd better go somewhere else. I saw a little bit of the ground floor stuff, including a Roman gravestone and some stone Egyptian sarcophagi, and then I went up to the second floor to the 20th century art.

The real reason I'd left the first floor was that my eyes had started to glaze over when I was looking at the Dutch Masters. I thought I should glance at the other floors before leaving, but I ended up being re-invigorated by the 20th century and late 19th century art and going around looking at all of it! There was Cezanne, Monet, Van Gogh, Picasso... I particularly liked the French Impressionists, but there was also some French realist work I liked by someone called Francois Goreng – he seemed to be one of Napoleon's court painters. But I went to the Impressionist rooms twice because I loved them.

The next day, I went to Peterhof, which is one of the summer palaces that used to be outside the city but is now in the suburbs. Its main attraction is the so-called "Grand Cascade", a fairly spectacular series of fountains, cascades and golden statues. It is known as "Russia's Versailles", and I can see why. Unfortunately, just to get into the gardens costs more than going to the dentist!! I had planned to visit the palace as well, but I got very mucked around by their ticket windows, which is a very Russian thing I haven't mentioned yet but it has been the bane of my existence at almost every tourist attraction I have visited in Russia. The ticket window is always separate to the entrance gate, often some distance away. I've heard that in Soviet times shops were like this as well – you had to pay somewhere separate from the place where you got your goods. I've heard some shops are still like this but I haven't encountered it, fortunately, but I have had a lot of problems with entrance tickets to attractions. Moreover, anywhere big like Peterhof has multiple parts to it which require different tickets, and you have to buy the different tickets at all the different places – there is no all-inclusive ticket. When I bought the gardens ticket I asked if I could get a ticket for the palace too. I was told that this ticket office was only for the gardens and that the palace ticket office was inside. Inside, I trooped around three different ticket offices! The first sent me to the second, which was only across the way but the doors were locked. This is another common thing in Russia: if there are three doors, only one or, if you're lucky, two will be open. And on the Moscow subway more often than not, one of the three escalators will be closed, even during peak hour. Sascha said he asked why this was and was told, "You cannot know the answer to everything!"

I had to go underneath a barrier to get to the second ticket office. There were two windows there, and at one there was already a customer whom I waited behind for a couple of minutes before checking the second window, to see the top of a woman's head. She was bent over, texting. I made a tsking noise, which was the only reason she looked up and saw me. I asked her for a ticket to the palace and she told me that that ticket office was somewhere else.

By the time I got to that somewhere else, I'd had time to reconsider spending more than the cost of a dentist's visit again. I saw a sign saying "No photographs inside" and I thought, *Screw this - I went to a palace where I wasn't allowed to take photographs yesterday and it's not worth paying that much to go to another today unless I can take photographs.* (Another Russian thing is that there are very many places where you can't take photographs.) So their loss: if they'd had an all-inclusive ticket or an all-inclusive ticket office they would've got my money, but they didn't, so I had time to reconsider! So I didn't go into the palace, I just checked out the fountains and a little bit of the gardens. The fountains were golden and terraced and very cool.

I headed back to the city, which was a challenge because it was on a minibus. I had nowhere near as much luggage as my Irkutsk-Olkhon experience and it was a bigger vehicle, a 20-seater (basically a transit van), but there were four people standing up and I was one of them! Because it was cold and raining all the windows had fogged up, so I couldn't see out – I started to feel sick...

The driver collected people's money and gave them their change while driving. As I was standing nearest to him, I was in charge of passing money back and forth. It was interesting.

In the evening, I went to the ballet! Me, watching ballet in a historic Russian theatre: the "Mariinsky"! I felt so sophisticated and cultured. It meant something to me because I did ballet as a kid, and when I was nine or ten I read a book about Anna Pavlova - who I think was from St Petersburg. I hadn't watched ballet since I was a kid. It was quite impressive. I couldn't believe they could move like that.

The next day I planned to meet Alex and Sascha at the Peter and Paul Fortress. Unfortunately, they're rather difficult to communicate with because they don't have a functioning phone or wifi device. I'd suggested via a Facebook message that we meet at 11, but hadn't received a reply. I showed up at 11 anyway, but they didn't. So I went around the fortress by myself, through a defensive tunnel and then the prison. The fortress has been there since 1703 – it's older than the city – but the prison was only operating for about fifty years, from about 1870-1924. This was the period when there was a lot of social protest, revolutionary actions, attempted assassinations of monarchs etc., and it was a political prison primarily. Did you know that Lenin's brother was executed in the 1880s for an attempted assassination of Alexander III? I saw his cell. Saw Trotsky's too. But the really ironic thing was that all these socialists were imprisoned and/or executed for years and years, and then the revolution happened, the Bolsheviks took control, and then *they* started imprisoning and executing people there. They had more prisoners and more executions, yet in the prison yard there's a stone with an inscription from Lenin saying something like, "In honour of those who were imprisoned and died here." How ironic.

Then I went to the church, which is the official burial place of Romanoff monarchs from Peter the Great onwards. Nicholas II, Tsarina Alexandra and Princesses Tatiana, Olga and Anastasia are buried there in a little chapel. There's an inscription on each of their gravestones saying they were buried there in 1998. There are also tombstones for Maria and Alexei, but they have no such inscriptions because those tombs are empty. I read somewhere that they were never found - I forget where that was, but maybe it's still the official line...

In the courtyard outside the church there were some benches, so I decided to sit down and have some lunch; and seeing as I hadn't run into Sascha and Alex yet I decided to check if there was wifi. There was! And there was a message from Alex! It said, "Sorry we didn't get a chance to check our messages last night, and it's now too late for us to meet you at 11, but maybe if you get this message we can meet at 2:30 outside the tower in the fortress."

I looked at the church tower above me. I looked at my watch. It was 1:55. I scratched my head. *Huh. If I stay right here for 35 minutes, Alex and Sascha will be here!* Magnets, I tell you.

Sure enough they came, and I went around the same sights with them! I think it's not just magnets; I think we're very similar people. Doing the same route would inevitably lead to some coincidences, but I think we were also interested in doing similar things while we were on that route. They'd tried to go to the ballet the previous night, but it was sold out! They had to get tickets for the next night instead - they showed them to me, and they were sitting three seats away from where I had been! Same row and everything! Magnets.

On my way back to my homestay apartment, I passed a group of middle-aged women dancing on the footpath outside the Hermitage, and on the other side of the river, underneath a statue, there was a group of people doing swing dancing! Russia is such a cultured place.

It's now 11:12am on Saturday the 31st of May, I'm on a bus, not a train, and I think we've just arrived at the Estonian border...

They were welcomed as liberators

1st of June, 5:10pm:

Tallinn is a beautiful town, mainly because of its intact Old Town, which was built between the 13th and 15th centuries and hasn't changed much since. Actually many renovations and reconstructions have been done to the buildings, but the point is it still *looks* original. It's a captivating labyrinth of narrow cobbled streets and pastel-coloured buildings. The best part is the walls and towers at the edge of it. The towers have conical red roofs and hanging beam walkways. The town wall was built in the early 14th century and was 3km long with 45 towers. Nearly 2km of wall survives, and 26 towers. You feel like you've walked into a medieval movie set – or, more accurately, that you've stepped back in time 700 years.

There's a festival on at the moment called Old Town Days. When I was walking through some laneways I heard beautiful singing coming from a church, so I went inside. It was part of the festival programme, a Danish choir. The church was quite a contrast to the Russian ones – very bare, and with straight line architecture. I later found out it was Lutheran. It was also very tall, and the acoustics were awe-inspiring.

In the early evening I found myself in a parade of medieval knights and townsfolk! Not by accident - I had been looking for it because it was on the festival programme - but by the time I got there the parade had already moved off, so I just followed it through the streets! There were some rousing drums playing and everybody was following the paraders to a grassy area by a fortification wall to begin a Medieval Knights' Tournament!

It was so cool. There were two jesters who were the MCs, and I had no idea what they were saying but they were hilarious anyway. There were horseback competitions, including charging at a cabbage and lopping it in half, and jousting with an inanimate object. There were archery competitions and swordfights; there were many cries of "Viva!"; there was fire twirling; horseback tricks; two people fell off; and one horse ran into the crowd!

2nd of June, 8:45am:

Last night I got up to go to the toilet, and it was still light outside. I thought I mustn't have been in bed very long. Then I checked the time. It was 3:40am!! Out the window I could see colours of what I thought was the sunset, but later I awoke again at 5:15 (creaky old floorboards kept waking me) and it was still bright as bright outside. I realised that it must've been the sunrise I saw at 3:40am, because I doubt the sun could've set and then risen again between 3:40 and 5:15. Still, there mustn't have been more than three hours of darkness, because it can't have set before midnight and then it was up again at 3:40!

I haven't seen darkness the whole time I've been in Estonia or St Petersburg. But in winter there are only three hours of daylight! How depressing! And it's cold! My hostel receptionist said that the snow provides more light because it reflects the moon! But he said that the coldest days are the sunny days, because there is no cloud cover. It's not as cold as Siberia or Mongolia, but it does get well into the minuses: -25° at least twice a year. He said that on the coldest days, which are sunny, it looks like people are afraid of the sunlight – the streets are bare because everyone stays in cars and buildings, but any time they do have to go onto the streets they run from building to building! Darting about like vampires.

Yesterday morning I walked around Toompea hill - where Town Wall meets cliff face, with buildings above it right on the edge, and amazing views of the Lower Old Town below. Then I fancied a coffee, so I set about finding a café with sunny al fresco tables and a nice view of cobbled streets and charming buildings. Found one in the town square, and it made my morning perfect because there was an orchestra on the main stage practising for a concert later in the day. They were fantastic. I sat there with my coffee, looking out at the 600-year-old town hall across the charming cobble-stoned square, soaking up the sun and listening to *Swan Lake*, "Dance of the Sugar Plum Fairies", "The Blue Danube" … it was heaven.

Then I went to see the Chimney Sweeps Parade! Apparently chimney sweeps are a thing in Tallinn. Like, they actually exist and sweep chimneys, and it's considered an honourable job for men, not boys. At the head of the parade was a sleek black motorcycle ridden by a man in a black outfit with two lines of brass buttons on his chest, a top hat and sunglasses. In the side car was a much older man with a very 19th century-looking grey beard, the same outfit and a much older-looking top hat. Behind them walked all the rest of the chimney sweeps, in the same outfit - looking exactly like a 19th century biker gang. Some had chimney brushes, which were on flexible cables or ropes, wrapped around their shoulders. It was a very interesting sight.

Next I did a walking tour. It was a free tour, something which is offered in many cities in this region. The expectation is that participants give a donation at the end of the tour. The tour guide was a university student called Mairi. Here are some of the things I learnt:

Tallinn was founded by the Danes in 1219. Estonia was ruled by the Danes, Germans, Swedes, Poles and Russians at different times. They declared their independence from Russia in 1918, and then fought a war of independence which they won in 1920 and remained independent until WWII. The Nazis came, and the Soviets drove them out in 1944. The Iron Curtain fell. Estonia was incorporated into the USSR. Mairi is too young to remember life in the USSR, but she told us a bit about some of the major events and regular goings on, including a record market that happened every week in a park just outside the Old Town. Western music was strictly banned, so all the record sellers had to pretend they were selling stamps and coins. Somehow they got away with it, though sometimes there were arrests. A record would set you back half a month's pay because of the danger money, but people would buy them.

This is a recurring theme – I saw Beatles monuments in Ulaanbaatar and Yekaterinburg, and I know rock music was revolutionary in the West as well, but behind the Iron Curtain it was a very important way in which people could reach out to the outside world.

Music and popular culture played a significant role in bringing down the Iron Curtain: Estonia had a so-called Singing Revolution. Every five years they have an enormous song festival which has 30,000 performers and more than 150,000 audience members. The audience members love to sing along, so we're talking earth-shattering numbers of people singing. In the Soviet era, the songs which could be sung were strictly restricted, but in the time of Gorbachev things relaxed just a bit. There was still the official list of Moscow-approved songs, but at the end of the festival people decided to sing something else. Unapproved songs, patriotic songs, revolutionary songs. 150,000 people did this, and the Soviets could do nothing about it – they couldn't arrest that many people, and they couldn't shoot them because Gorbachev was trying to make things politically nicer and freer than they had been before. The singers, to their surprise, got away with it. So they just kept singing. They had more events, more songs, more people.

Of the 15 countries that broke away from the USSR after the collapse of communism, Estonia was the only one to do so without bloodshed. They say that the Estonians sang their way to freedom! Which is probably not true, I'm sure it was a variety of factors - including a lot of luck - but the singing helped. It certainly helped the people.

In the afternoon I went to Patarei, which is an old Soviet prison. Everything is as it was left, bar a few contributions of vandals and artists. Beds, desks, fridges, posters on the walls... but everything's crumbling – all the paint peeling, the posters fading...

The ticket office is a caravan and the toilets are the worst portaloos I have ever seen or smelled. There is a café looking out over the bay and a beach, complete with deck chairs, on which people were relaxing and sleeping. But between the beach and the water there's a rusty, prohibitive barbed wire fence! The place is certainly weird, and the fact that it was a KGB prison is utterly scary. But the weirdest thing about it is how run down it looks given how recently it was abandoned. The prison closed in 2005. It wasn't a KGB facility then obviously, just a regular Estonian criminal prison, but the state it's in now clearly indicates that it was creepy even before it was closed. It was closed as a requirement for Estonia's entry to the EU, because the place was just that damn horrible. Several layers of paint are coming off the walls.

In the middle of the main prison yard is a high wall with razor-wire on top of it and a rusty-looking guard tower above. I wandered along this until I found an opening with a sign saying, "Walking yards". *Interesting that they'd close that off from the rest of the prison yard*, I thought, and I stepped inside.

Yards. Plural. Scores and scores of them. A long corridor stretching in either direction, open to the sky but with heavy rust-coloured mesh over it, and leading off it scores and scores and scores of individual exercise yards no bigger than your average bathroom. Walled on all sides, big doors off the corridor, and the same thick mesh for the roof. They were cells: they exercised the prisoners in cells. One of them even had a bed in it.

There are two rows of these cells, one on either side of the walled compound. Between them, up above, is a long guard's walkway. No matter what you did, a guard would be watching you through the mesh above your head.

126

Inside the prison building, it's cold. It's so cold the ticket vendor lends people blankets! And it's dank, and it's dark, and it's musty... and you can smell the moisture in the air.

Somewhere, there is an "execution room", but this is currently closed to the public. From the photograph it looks bare and dark and terrifying. It was opposite the showers, and they sometimes did executions without warning - whilst all the other prisoners were going to the showers. They never knew if they'd make it to the shower alive.

Horrible, horrible place.

Other things I learned while in Tallinn:

- The population is about 70% Estonian, 25% Russian and 5% other.
- Estonia is one of the flattest countries in Europe. The tallest thing in Estonia is a 370m hill! The second tallest is Tallinn's TV tower! As in all the world's most charming cities, there's a law preventing any bigger buildings from being built.
- Apparently Estonia is on the radar of Amnesty International for institutional discrimination against the country's sizeable Russian minority. Estonian Russians, even though they were born there and in many cases have lived there for generations, can only get a passport if they pass strict citizenship and language tests. And there are plenty of people, particularly in the border areas, who don't speak Estonian. These people can only get a kind of identity document which will get them into Latvia, Lithuania, Russia and Belarus, but nowhere else. They can apply for a Russian passport, but that would lose them the right to live in Estonia...

I left Tallinn at 9 o'clock this morning, by bus, heading to Kuressaare, a town on the island of Saaremaa.

3rd of June, 5:15pm:

OWWW I AM IN PAIN! ARGH! OW! Because I've been on a bicycle all day! Ow ow ow! What was I doing on a bicycle? Well, Saaremaa is a very good place to ride a bicycle because it's flat and has many smooth bicycle tracks. I considered hiring a car, but I thought I'd experience the place more on a bike. You can't hear the birds from a car.

I am now attempting to remedy my sore arse by sitting on the soft grass (haha, that rhymed) in the grounds of Kuressaare Castle. The castle is from the 15th century and it looks incredible from the outside, but inside it contains the best museum I've seen in a very long time. Much better than all those Russian museums which have barely any explanation, even in

Russian, with the Soviet stuff so censored – I had no idea how much until I saw this incredible Estonian museum. They're not shy about laying out all the facts and making accusations. Just now I went to a memorial in the castle grounds and they've written in big letters, "We remember!" and "They are responsible!" I realise they simply may have used a particularly aggressive translator, but nevertheless, Estonians, and Saaremaa islanders in particular, are very proud of who they are - and they do not like the Soviets one bit.

The islanders have always been a proud people, and one not afraid to defend themselves. Control of Estonia was shifted back and forth between different European powers for centuries, but they seem to have put up a bigger fight here than on the mainland. For me the most fascinating stuff is the 20th century history, which this museum does particularly well. I knew about the War of Independence in 1918-1920, but when I mentioned that before the reason I simply said Estonian independence "lasted until WWII," rather than giving a specific date, was that I didn't understand what had happened when. This museum filled me in. Estonia was actually invaded three times during WWII. The first time was marginally before the beginning of the war in 1939, which was actually two years before the USSR entered the war - they only entered in 1941 when the Nazis invaded them. In 1939, the Soviets invaded Estonia and immediately began a campaign of Red Terror. Among other things, they killed ninety people right here in the castle grounds (the memorial I visited was for that). The documentary video in the memorial says that the reasoning and the story behind it remains unknown, as all the records have either been destroyed or locked in secret archives. This and other poor treatment of the Estonians by the occupying Soviets meant that when the German forces arrived in July-August 1941, *they were welcomed as liberators*!! They occupied the country for three years, and the Kuressaare Castle Museum has pictures of them with their arms around local Saaremaans, all smiling. Some Estonians even fought with the Germans against the Soviets in 1941.

Now that's interesting. The Soviets were so bad that the Nazis were welcomed. It begs the question, though, that if Nazi Germany had won the war, what would conditions in Estonia have been after? Did people consider this and decide that they'd be better off under the Nazis than the communists?

Which begs the further question: were the US, Australia, Britain, France or any of the other Western countries to be put in the same situation and given the same two options; if they knew that they'd definitely be invaded by one of them and were they to be given the opportunity to choose the lesser of two evils, who do you think those Western countries and their people would pick? Nazi Germany. You bet they would. Especially in that time, when no-one yet knew how bad Hitler really was.

In 1944, the Soviets came back. They took only four days to get control of the Estonian mainland, but it took one and a half months to get full control of Saaremaa. The Sorve Peninsula, in the south, saw some of the fiercest fighting in the whole war as the Germans tried desperately to hold onto it.

It was at this point that many hundreds of refugees left Saaremaa, most in small boats bound for Sweden. The Germans co-ordinated an evacuation from the Sorve Peninsula. These refugees didn't leave in 1941 when the Germans were coming; they left in 1944 when the Soviets were coming, and most of them stayed away. The museum had a documentary about the Saarremaan diaspora in Canada.

Now bear in mind that these battles in 1944 were the Soviets taking back what the Germans had taken from them. This is what millions of Russians still celebrate on the 9th of May every year. Estonia did not become part of the USSR in 1945 as part of some Churchill-Stalin agreement for splitting up administration of territories liberated from the Nazis – no, Estonia became part of the USSR in 1939, and the Russians thought they had a perfect right to take it back in 1944. It had, after all, been part of Tsarist Russia for 200 years before the Estonian War of Independence. They viewed it as theirs, and they viewed the German occupation of Estonia as part of the German invasion of Russia.

The museum had some good displays on the Soviet times in Estonia. There was a particularly good documentary, which was voiced over the top of a propaganda video, about collective farming. It said the land each farmer was allocated to farm as part of a collective was very small, and that this was aimed at breaking the self-sufficiency of farmers and making them dependent on the State. Collective farm workers were paid in produce – very small amounts of it. To further restrict their ability to support themselves, even the size of their home vegie patches was restricted!

So, understandably, not many farmers wanted to be a part of the process - and it was voluntary initially. To encourage farmers to join, the State greatly increased the taxes paid by non-collective farms. The tax went up to 25 times its original amount, but still not many Saaremaa farmers joined the collective farms. Then, the Soviets started sending people to Siberia. Hundreds and hundreds of them, to prison and then exile. Of course, many died there.

The documentary also talked about how inefficient the collective farming system was, because it was so standardised. Farming practises were not suited to the Saaremaa climate. In fact, they were bad for the environment. Farm managers were chosen for their loyalty to the Communist Party rather than for their competence, and many didn't know what they were doing. The farms also weren't allowed to have their own machinery and had to rent it for a high price.

The way the documentary voiceover was worded, it was actually making fun of the Soviets for making such a balls up of one of the core elements of the communist utopia. How were they going to get all that wheat if they ran their farms so inefficiently?

In the late 1950s they changed the system so the farms had more autonomy and things got better, but there were still shortages of supply throughout the Soviet era.

There was a bit on the people sent to Siberia. 1,050 people were taken from Saaremaa, 30,000-odd from Estonia. It said that the overall population of Saaremaa just about halved: between Siberian exile, refugees fleeing, war victims and execution victims. But then, in the late 80s, there was perestroika and the Singing Revolution. I was impressed with the brazenness of the people of Saaremaa – they raised the Estonian flag on top of Kuressaare Castle in 1988, which was a while before the Soviet Union actually collapsed. It was only one year before the fall of the Berlin Wall, but they were within the Soviet Union – the Berliners weren't. The Saaremaans were very active in their independence movement.

Finally I climbed the castle tower, up a wooden staircase which had written on the steps, in Estonian and English, anti-communist jokes like:

"Capitalism: exploitation of man by man. Under socialism it is the other way around."

"Socialism – the most longest path to capitalism."

"What should you do if the Soviet Union opens its borders? Climb a tree, otherwise you'll be trampled to death!"

Below the tower I walked around the "defence gallery", which is completely in the open - just me, the turrets and the charming red roof tiles. It was awesome.

Best museum I've been to in a long while.

And the castle has a moat too!

A fairytale land

The next morning began my cycling extravaganza. I went south past the castle, found the bike track, and it was awesome. From the bike track you can look into the trees and see the forest. And you can hear it. And smell it. I was cycling along with my head permanently turned to the side. Unfortunately you can't do this when you're cycling on the road, because you have to concentrate. I did not like cycling on the road. There were trucks. It was scary. But for most of the day I was on bike tracks.

After not very long, I arrived at Loode Oak Wood. There was a walking track through it and a sign saying a bit about the species there. The sign said it was an "oak meadow", and I had no conception of what that could be, because surely a meadow is grassland and a wood is a forest, right? (Again I had my Australian blinkers on.) I went into the "oak meadow" and discovered that it was an open forest with meadow in between the trees! Grasses, leafy things and flowers – snowdrops, buttercups, purple flowers and oak trees all around! It was magical! And there were so many birds

131

singing! The track just went right through the grass; it had been created by people's feet, which meant the vast majority of what I could see was green.

After experiencing the "oak meadow" I got back on the bike, and the forest around me became pine forest, which stayed around me for the rest of the ride. I love pine forests. I stopped the bike and wandered into it a couple of times. The forest floor was what amazed me most – it had a carpet of moss all over it which was so thick that you could sleep on it comfortably without needing any mattress. It sank under my feet and then sprang right back up again.

Eventually I found Tehumardi, which was the site of the biggest battle of the Sorve Peninsula in 1944. It happened at night and most of it was hand to hand combat, over a fairly large area of pine forest and fields next to the beach. Mostly in the forest, I'd imagine – if I was in a battle I'd want some trees to hide behind. Pine trees aren't very fat, though. How terrifying would it be - you wouldn't even be able to see properly...

400 men died, 200 on each side. On the German side that number was more than one in two.

There's a Soviet war cemetery there, and a tall concrete memorial – they carved an image into the concrete! Those Soviets really took concrete to new levels. It said the memorial was put there in 1967, so that's why it's Soviet-focussed, but there is now a smaller Estonian memorial on the other side of the road.

4th of June:
Well here we go again. I realised a couple of minutes ago that I don't know what country I'm in. I'm one hour and 25 minutes into a two hour and 35 minute journey, and according to the map up to 70% of that journey is supposed to be in Latvia... I saw no border, but then I wasn't paying attention. Given the time, surely we must have crossed it already.

I'm well and truly in the Schengen Zone now, then! No border formalities at all. I guess I'd better start learning the Latvian words for "hello" and "thankyou".

I think I'll eat my sandwiches now, in a different country to where I made them.

12:25pm:
I discovered Estonian rye bread. It's great. It's really dark, but also moist and a bit sweet. It makes sandwiches much more interesting.

Now I'm on bus three of three, heading to Sigulda, Latvia.

I think Latvians look different to Estonians. I can't put my finger on exactly what it is that makes this so, but as soon as I got off bus number two

I thought, *Oh, people look different*! I'd read that Estonians have more in common with the Finns than with their Baltic neighbours. They're more Scandinavian, a different ethnic group: Finno-Ugric. Latvians look more Russian, I think. Again, I'm not sure exactly what makes this so, because they're all white northern Europeans. More brown-haired people in Latvia, maybe? But also the shape of the face is different, I'm sure... Am I imagining it? I should probably stop staring at the people on this bus and look out the window instead.

<u>8:40pm:</u>
I am sitting at the Emperor's View, a peaceful lookout with a 120° view over a tranquil, winding river valley. The river is brown, the trees are of every shade of green in the colour spectrum, and there's a red castle in the distance. And, over the past 4½ hours, I have walked over all of it. I did a big circuit, about 6km, passing through every part of what I can now see. I didn't quite make the castle, but I got to the ruins of another one. It was built in 1255.

And it's still the same day! This is the same day I took all those buses! It's light so late, I was able to complete a whole day walk afterwards! At the halfway point (the castle ruins) I stopped and had a meal, but it was dinner, not lunch!

I can't believe I'm in Latvia. My mum had a friend from Latvia. It always seemed like such a far-off, fairy-tale place to me. This view is pretty fairy-tale.

I didn't even know I was coming to this. I didn't know Latvia wasn't flat, let alone that I'd be staying next to a national park with walking and cycling tracks. I actually came to Sigulda to go on the aerodium, a wind tunnel that propels you into the air, like flying. But the people in the information centre told me that it had recently been sold to a rich man who'd taken it to Dubai, and that now they are building a new one. Sigulda actually manufactures them!

So I was left with the national park instead. Fine by me! The information centre people also told me that my hostel was 2.8km away. "Oh," I said disappointedly. "Is there a bus?"

"Yes," the lady replied, "But I think it doesn't go until 6pm."
It was 3pm.
"Well that's a dumb place to put a hostel," I said, "if there's no bus!"
"Oh, but the place is lovely!" she replied. "It's near the river, and you can walk all around!"
"Mmm, that does sound good," I said. It didn't solve the problem of how I could get there.

"If you like, I could drive you," said her colleague. "I can see how tired you are."

I was. Their information centre was very poorly signposted and I'd just wandered all around everywhere, with my bags, looking for it.

I couldn't believe what I was hearing. Was she joking?

"Really?" I asked.

"Yes, it's no problem!"

Was she going to ask for payment? I wouldn't have minded if she had, as it was either that or a taxi, but she didn't. She was just trying to help out. She told me that Sigulda was trying to become the most visited place in Latvia, and good service was how they were going to achieve it! Wow.

After briefly relaxing with a cup of tea at my hostel, I set out on my walk. I wasn't planning to go that far, just to have a little afternoon stroll so that I could have done something today other than sit on buses. But it didn't take me long to get to the first couple of spots on the map and the castles didn't look all that far away, and I knew it'd be light for ages, so I just kept going.

I think I'd better be getting back now, though, as it's gone 9:15pm. This'd be a great place to watch the sunset, but that won't happen for hours yet! The sun is low in the sky, and it has changed colour – not to red yet, but to yellow. It's sort of in that pre-sunset time of day, but the sun just takes ages to get around to actually setting.

5th of June, 9:35am:

On a bus again. It's funny how I did 7,900km on trains but since then I've taken nothing but buses!

So I walked through the green, green forest - totally different to what I'd seen the day before - for a bit over an hour and a half, and then suddenly a bunch of charming, slightly falling down farm buildings came into view. At first I thought I'd arrived in a village, and it sort of was - a couple of buildings were lived in and there was one café - but it was actually a country estate with a manor house. The buildings were from the late 19th century and very charming. For obvious reasons, it was no longer a manor estate – the last lord had fled in 1918. Then the manor house was used as a TB sanatorium, and it's still some kind of rehabilitation centre.

Just past it are the castle ruins: Krimulda Castle. They think it was built in 1255 or thereabouts. It was built by priests or monks. In 1601 the Swedish had it, and they burnt it down when Polish troops were approaching. Most of it doesn't survive, but what does is very picturesque, sitting there in the forest. I sat on the remains of one of the castle walls and had my dinner.

I did a kind of circuit loop, coming back another way. There were tracks everywhere, and they were all very easy to traverse because most followed the ridge or the riverbank. I only had to go down twice and up twice, to get between the two, and the ridge wasn't very high. But Latvia definitely isn't flat, I can tell you that!

Turn your school knowledge on its head

I'm enjoying a smooth, creamy latté in an alternative, arty, whitewashed wooden café in Cesis's Old Town. I've finished my sightseeing for the day, so it's good to sit down and have a rest. I'm off to Riga this afternoon – big city, blergh, but I'm hoping I can find some good museums to tell me about

Latvian history. So far I've found out that they had a War of Independence at exactly the same time as Estonia did, and that they fought alongside Estonians in some battles, including one in Cesis in 1919.

First today I saw the Medieval Castle, which was constructed in the 13th century and was another one of those religious castles. I find it very strange that there were knight-monks. They prayed every hour and were not allowed to have any entertainment for religious reasons. But they also wore armour, carried swords and killed people. There were holy wars, of course there were. This is how it was. The funny thing is, it just makes me think of *Doctor Who*. They did a couple of episodes set in the 51st century where there were priests and monks dressed in army uniforms, and they were soldiers. This was presented as being weird and futuristic, but actually it was just the past repeating itself.

I hope it doesn't.

The castle is not as ruined as the one I saw yesterday, but still pretty ruined. This is because in 1577, when Ivan the Terrible's army was at the gates, 300 townspeople who had sought refuge in the castle blew themselves up rather than be taken prisoner by the Russians.

You can go up one of the towers, and they give you a candle-lit lantern to do it with! "No electricity in a medieval castle!" said the young lady at the desk.

There are a couple of places on the narrow, steeply winding stone staircase where it is pitch black for a few metres. It was really interesting to have the experience of being guided by candlelight. It throws out quite a bit of light – a lot more than my phone. It also throws out quite a bit of heat, even though it's only one candle.

Going down was more of an issue, because a lantern doesn't throw light downwards, only sideways! And it's so flickery and mysterious... it would be really scary to be in a castle at night with only a candle. Of course, night doesn't happen at the moment, so it's all good.

There was a dungeon too, which did have electricity, thank goodness, 'cause there's no way you could hold a lantern whilst gripping the ladder to get in there! It's a small, cold, bell-shaped room, and the "door" is halfway up the wall.

There's a self-guided walking tour marked on the city map, which I followed. The Old Town is nowhere near as well looked after as Tallinn's, but that just makes it charming in another way. The buildings are a bit ramshackle, and the streets have dirt as well as cobblestones. I'm loving this café – it's one of the most charming I've ever been to. There are plenty of builders about doing restoration work, though. No hard hats or ear muffs in sight, and not even many shirts. At the castle I even saw boys doing it - they couldn't have been more than 15.

6th of July, 8:20pm:

So... many... things! I've had such a varied day! I misjudged Riga – I'd only seen the main road coming in and I thought it looked busy and boring, but actually it's awesome. So many varied architectural styles; completely different vibes and looks of different areas; a lot of music and a lot of life.

I arrived yesterday at about 6pm and made a friend at my hostel, a Londoner called Alex. He is cycling from the Arctic Ocean to the Adriatic Sea in 100 days – pretty much the entire length of the Iron Curtain, including Finland. So far he's been going for about 5 weeks. He said he's experienced temperatures from -7 to +35 and, of course, seen it never get dark. He and I actually saw darkness last night, at about midnight, when we were coming back to our hostel. I guess Riga is far enough south to have it. I hadn't seen darkness since the 27th of May; Alex hadn't seen it since the end of April.

We wandered around the Old Town a bit looking for somewhere to have dinner, found an Italian place that was affordable, and tried some Latvian beer too. Alex told me that Riga is a destination for English bucks' parties. The Old Town certainly is full of places to party, and there are lots of touristy trishaws that go around blasting loud music. There's also a weird cycle bus thing which has about nine seats, each with pedals, situated around a bar in the middle of the vehicle, which is shaped like a small old-style bus. I'm not really sure what the point of it is because I don't know how you can drink while cycling without spilling it everywhere. Particularly not cycling over cobblestones...

The next morning I walked into town rather than taking the tram, because I wanted to see a bit more of the neighbourhood where my hostel was. It's an interesting area. The main colour of the buildings is brown. There's the odd Soviet block of flats, but not many. It's mostly older apartment buildings, either wooden or rendered brick – the sort of classical buildings you see everywhere in Europe, but in that neighbourhood they are run down and the brown is from dirt, not paint. They're still indescribably charming.

Riga has one building like Stalin's skyscraper castles in Moscow, but smaller. Apparently they call it "Stalin's birthday cake." It's the only thing I've seen with a hammer and sickle on it (and some wheat) in the Baltics. Since this was part of the USSR, I'm sure it must have been just as blanketed in Soviet stuff as Russia was, but they've removed it. It is possible - the Russians just don't want to do it.

I went into Riga's Old Town, which is completely different to Tallinn's but just as remarkable. It's less well preserved, but that just means it has more variety, with buildings from many different time periods in many different styles. Riga is well known for its Art Nouveau buildings. There are 750 of them, more than in any other city in Europe. This is simply because Riga was growing and thriving when the style was popular. Some are more outlandish than others. There are beautiful patterns and colours galore, huge heads with various garish facial positions, and I saw one that had motifs that looked very similar to *Star Wars* characters! I clearly saw a Storm Trooper on the wall, and around the balconies something resembling either one of the droids the jawas were selling in *A New Hope*, or a dust buster.

70 years too early, of course.

Riga no longer has its old town walls, but that doesn't mean they're not there, it just means they're not visible. My walking tour guide explained that with the proliferation of gunpowder, walls became a less effective means of protection, so the city built earth ramparts instead. The walls were no longer needed. Seeking to cut building costs, local people began to build their homes backing onto the old wall - on both sides of it. That way, they only had to build three walls or, if they already had two neighbours, one. Consequently, the only places where you can now see the wall is in the backs of dwellings and cafes!

I went to the Museum of the Occupation of Latvia, which is right alongside the Vietnam War museum in Saigon as one of the most depressing and horrifying museums I've ever been to.

One thing I hadn't known is that prior to Nazi Germany's invasion of Russia, the two were allies. They signed a "Non-Aggression Pact" in August 1938. In it, there was a secret clause where they agreed on which countries each could have in their "sphere of influence" for invasion. They were going to split Poland between them, and the Soviet Union could have Latvia, Estonia, Finland and part of Romania to do whatever they liked with. They even agreed on exactly where Poland would be divided and to repatriate the other's nationals from the territories they would conquer.

If Hitler hadn't been stupid enough to go back on his word, repeat the mistakes of Napoleon and attempt to invade the largest country in the world... how would the war have ended? Not in the Allies' favour, that's for sure. All of Europe - not only the East - would have fallen into a pit of autocratic darkness. What a chilling thought.

Because Hitler went back on his word, his and Stalin's pact was not fully successful, but it *was* half successful. The two of them planned to invade and crush scores of sovereign countries and assimilate them into their own cults of power. Hitler failed. Stalin didn't. The Soviet Union terrorised upwards of 20 countries for 50 years. And yet the Western history books put Stalin right alongside Churchill and Roosevelt as one of the Allies who fought against history's most horrifying campaign of fascist terror, and won.

In school, I was taught about how these three Allies had split the countries of Europe between them purely for administrative reasons, just to get them back on their feet after liberating them from the Nazis. I was taught that Stalin had abused this arrangement and never let those countries go. But I was *not* taught that it had been his sick little plan all along - and that the only reason he aligned the Soviet Union with the Allies was that he hadn't got what he wanted from Hitler.

Stalin is a much-hated figure, yes, even in Russia. But the reason he is hated in the West is because of communism and the Cold War. The West is still so bloody terrified of communism that that's the thing they always focus on. But what his government's ideology was - what exact way of life they were trying to impose on millions of people - is irrelevant. The fact is that they were doing it by force: killing, maiming and imprisoning millions and controlling the lives of far more. That is wrong no matter what banner you do it under. The ideology behind it is irrelevant because the effect is the same. So even if you do hate communism or even socialism, that's not what you should think about when you think about what the Soviet Union did. You should think about the way they did it; what's wrong and what's right and how we, as humans, should and can be better than that.

Immediately after the Nazi-Soviet Non-Aggression Pact was signed, the Soviet Union set about invading Estonia, Latvia, Lithuania and Finland. Finland was able to resist more, but they lost a large chunk of their territory which they still haven't got back. I hadn't known that either.

The Soviets immediately began their campaign of Red Terror, which I'd learned about in Saaremaa, including deporting tens of thousands of people into forced labour in Siberia. This included 43,000 Latvians, among them 10,000 children. Whole families were taken away in the middle of the night. Who were they? People who were proud to be Latvian, and people who owned any more than a speck of land, basically. They were put into two categories, political dissidents and "kulaks". You were defined as a kulak if you had more than a certain amount of land and/or you had any employees, even one farm hand.

The women and children were put in resettlement districts and the men in gulags. In the gulags the prisoners had no mattresses or blankets and each day they were given a hunk of bread and a cup of broth and made to work 16 hours. It was exactly the same as Hitler was doing in the west. No gas chambers, sure, but that's only because the purpose was different –

Stalin needed his prisoners to work, but he killed plenty of them too. So many.

Just when I was thinking, *Jesus - Stalin was even worse than Hitler!* I got to the Nazi occupation section of the museum. Like in Estonia, the Nazis were welcomed at first. But their plan was just as evil as the Soviets'. They certainly weren't going to restore their independence, as some locals who fought with them thought. They had a plan to assimilate Latvia into a new German empire by moving 164,000 German settlers there and deporting 50% of the Latvians to Russia. Obviously they didn't complete this plan, but the Soviets moved 700,000 Russians there, and we know how many Latvians they deported. Between 1939 and 1991, Latvia lost more than a third of its population.

The thing about being incorporated into Hitler's German Empire, though, is that the Latvian population had to be subjected to all of Hitler's race purification nonsense. I didn't hear anything about this in Estonia, but there were less Jews living there. Latvia did have 70,000, but by the end of the war, there were only 1500 left. 25,000 WERE KILLED ON JUST TWO NIGHTS.

The Nazi occupation section of that museum made me want to cry. I couldn't believe people could be so brutal to their fellow humans. The 25,000 were from the Riga ghetto; the Nazi authorities decided to exterminate every single person. I think it said only six survived, by playing dead, but that four of those were killed later in concentration camps. And then the Soviets came back. There was one region in the west, Kurzeme, which managed to hold them off - the Latvians fighting alongside the Germans to keep their homeland out of Soviet hands. Then when the Allies defeated the Germans, they gave Kurzeme to Stalin, along with the rest of Latvia. I don't think the problem was that the Allies didn't get it - couldn't see Stalin's plans - but that they were afraid of him. The museum said they felt compelled to co-operate with the Soviet Union and not rock the boat - because if the Soviet Union had been fighting on the other side, the Allies would've lost the war.

I am so glad that Hitler was not so pragmatic...

The museum gave a bit of detail on life in the USSR – banned books, authors and artists forced to praise Lenin, children indoctrinated, food shortages because they completely changed farming practises etc. And then from 1988 people began protesting for freedom, just like in Estonia. There was some bloodshed – the Soviet army attacked Vilnius first, killing 14 unarmed civilians. Citizens in Riga erected barricades around key city buildings, and 80,000 volunteers poured in from the surrounding area to defend their capital. 5 were killed. This was in 1991. Then Boris Yeltsin came to power and gave the Baltic states independence.

There's a memorial to Boris Yeltsin in Tallinn. While I was there, someone splashed red paint on it. I asked my tour guide there why that would be, and she said it wouldn't have been an Estonian. It might have been a Russian, because while Yeltsin was quite popular overseas - including in the ex-SSRs he set free - he wasn't popular in Russia. She said that maybe the red paint was to do with the situation in Ukraine.

I haven't mentioned that yet, have I? The best explanation I got was from Konstantin in Yekaterinburg. He seemed to be a fairly liberal, free-thinking guy – critical of Putin, critical of Lenin, troubled by the extreme views of many Russians – but he was in favour of Crimea returning to Russia. Why? Because it is Russian. It was only in Ukraine because of an administrative decision in Soviet times: because Crimea is a small place it made sense to put it under the jurisdiction of a larger authority close by. This was the Ukrainian SSR. As they were all in the same country at the time, it didn't matter.

Konstantin mentioned Yeltsin then, saying he thought it was a mistake that when Ukraine was let go, he let Crimea go with it. He said that historically and culturally Crimea had nothing in common with Ukraine, and that the Ukraine government now is incompetent and it's not a good country to live in. So the people of Crimea decided to go back to Russia – their decision, Konstantin maintained, not Russia's.

The thing is, though, that there are plenty of small regions of ex-SSRs whose population is predominantly Russian. Narva on the Estonian border is 95%, and I'd say Karostas, where I am staying tonight, is too. Estonia and Latvia seem to be pretty good countries to live in: they've both made it into the EU and NATO and are on the Euro and are doing fine. I asked a Latvian tour guide if there were any problems with the large number of Russians living there and he said no, but that he worries what those Russians would do if a situation similar to the one that happened in Ukraine were to arise in Latvia. Who would they be loyal to?

Which begs the question: if Ukraine's government was better, would it have happened?

The Guardhouse

<u>7th of June, 9:42pm:</u>

I am sitting in my cell in Karostas Military Prison, Liepaja. I am not entirely sure how I feel about this.

My guidebook said that you can spend a night in a Soviet prison and "subject yourself to regular bed checks and verbal abuse by guards in period garb." I thought, *Well, I'll try anything once.* But today leading up to it I was actually quite scared. It turns out, though, that they've decided not to subject me to any reality show - maybe because I'm alone, I don't know. They've just given me a tour and a comfy bed in a cell and left all the doors unlocked. Phewf! And they've even given me a fake machine gun to reach the light switch with. The light switches are all really high up so the prisoners couldn't reach them.

What I hadn't considered was that I would be the only booking. I got a personalised tour of the prison, yes, but now I have to sleep alone in a prison. The tour guide is upstairs, though, thank goodness!

I am actually sleepy, so... maybe I'll just go to bed. The bed is very comfortable - not at all what you'd expect. Apparently what the prisoners had was a plank of boards on the floor...

I wonder if there's wifi.

No, no wifi. And only two bars of phone reception. There's nothing anywhere around here, just abandoned military buildings and forest. 100m along the next road the Kruschevki start, but there's nothing on this road.

I'll tell you about the Kruschevki later. Karostas is a very interesting place.

Umm. I think I might go to bed in my cell. I can even brush my teeth and go to the toilet in my own time. I am so lucky I'm not a real prisoner.

10:25pm:

I really hope I don't have to go to the toilet in the night. Walking along that cell-lined corridor is totally creepy.

Glad it's not dark yet. But you know what this cell could benefit from? A lamp. That I would totally leave on all night.

Also it could benefit from a light switch inside the cell that I don't need a gun to turn off.

I think I might sleep in my clothes. I'll feel less exposed that way. Also, it's cold.

My guidebook described Karostas as having "a particularly dour collection of Soviet tenements mingling with the gilded cupolas of St Nicholas Orthodox Maritime Cathedral." I thought I'd seen enough Soviet apartment blocks, but it turned out I hadn't. The dominant ones here were of a kind I hadn't seen before, made of large square light blue blocks with concrete in between them. The side of each building had maybe 20 of these blocks, the concrete between them was smeared over the edges of the blocks, and many were cracking and faded; some with graffiti tags on them. I later realised that the blue bit was actually made up of hundreds of tiny square tiles - like bathroom tiles!

So the architecture was already interesting from the bus, but I could not have been prepared for where the bus terminated. The woman at the tourist information centre had marked it for me on the map: it was a circle, like a roundabout or turning circle, and I had pictured a bustling suburban shopping area with some kind of centrepiece in the middle of the road, maybe with some flowers or a statue.

Ha! Nowhere near. The only part of that which was true was the bustling part. There were certainly plenty of people about – old ladies, teenagers on bicycles, mothers with prams – it was a very very lived-in place. And yet all it was was a bus turning circle in a wide-open piece of vacant land, with long grass and bits of gravel, a bus shelter and not much else. Around it were no less than 18 of those blue-tiled apartment buildings, and those were only the ones I could see from the middle of the vacant land - behind them were scores more. They were 5 storeys, which I think makes them Kruschevki, but long. I'd estimate there would be at least 40 apartments in each. 18x40 is 720, and there'd be more than one person per apartment (families were by far the dominant occupants of the area) so that's over 2,000 people living just around the bus turning circle, and thousands more in the area.

Further along the road I found some European classical style apartment buildings - much more charming and much smaller, but still full of people - and near the beach I found some stand-alone houses. They all looked very lived in, with washing hanging and children everywhere. But what did I not see? I did not see any sort of suburban shopping centre. I saw the odd grocery store: three, I think, in my three hours of wandering about the place. They were scattered about the residential areas, but there didn't seem to be any central shopping place.

What there was, though, mixed in with all these funny-looking apartment buildings, was quite a bit of beautiful forest, and scores and scores of derelict buildings. I later found out (from my prison guard/tour guide) that these were military buildings. The Karostas area was developed as a naval base in the late 19th century. For 50-odd years, of course, it was a Soviet military base... which I suppose would imply no shops. I mean, the Soviets didn't have many shops in general, but also I guess most people would've had army rations... It seemed weird that there were no shops though, given how many people were living there. The whole place was so full of contrasts. Soviet concrete buildings and European classical architecture; a thriving community and derelict buildings; cramped city living and forests; people and no shops; people and no workplaces; dirty residential buildings and the sparklingly shiny cathedral. What a fascinating place.

Oh yeah, and scores and scores of Russians in Latvia - that was the other contrast. I didn't hear anyone speaking anything other than Russian.

I also found an incredible fort down by the water. It was built during the reign of Alexander III (1880s-odd) and blown up during WWI. I asked my prison guard about it later, but I could clearly see when I was there that it had been blown up from the inside, and that they'd done a damn good job. The beach is covered in bigger-than-boulder-sized chunks of fort. In some places an entire section of building has been split in half and the severed half is now sitting on its side, or more commonly its corner, in the sea. My guard said the Tsarist Russians had blown it up as they retreated from the Kaiser Germans.

The prison I was in was a military discipline prison – it was known as "The Guardhouse". My guard told me that the prison and the rest of the base had been under the control of seven different armies at different times. The Tsarist Russians, then the Kaiser Germans, then the first Latvian Republic, then the first Soviet occupation, then the Nazi Germans, then the second Soviet occupation, then the current Latvian Republic.

The Guardhouse was for disciplining officers and soldiers who had either made a behavioural faux pas like getting drunk and fighting, or made more deliberate breaches of the rules like disobeying orders, desertion or, in one case, trying to start a rebellion against the Soviet government. Theoretically their imprisonment was meant to be for a short time, but it often ran longer. Even someone who had been sentenced for a simple misdemeanour could have his sentence repeatedly increased if he couldn't keep to the Guardhouse's strict rules - for example going to the toilet, washing and shaving inside two minutes, and keeping your uniform clean whilst cleaning your cell without any cloth.

The soldiers slept on boards on the floor with no mattress, pillow or bedding. The officers got a mattress, but no bedding. The temperature in the cells could be -10 to -5°C. I certainly noticed the cold, and that was in summer with a jacket and a blanket! And sometimes the prisoners' sleeping boards were used to clear snow from the yard, so they were wet too.

The conditions sound pretty damn horrible, although as it wasn't a civilian prison the prisoners never had to stay all that long. The longest was a year, apparently – nothing like the gulags or Patarei in that regard. But the thing is that if you have that bad a place to send your misbehaving soldiers, then your soldiers will not misbehave. They will do anything you tell them to...

146

Their food ration was the same as gulag prisoners. They were kept busy every second of every day. They were only allowed to go to the toilet twice a day, and then two toilets had to suffice for an entire floor to use and clean within half an hour. If the half hour expired and not everyone had been, not only would those remaining not be allowed to go, but everyone would be punished for not co-operating enough to get everyone to the toilet in half an hour.

My guard said all of the seven armies employed conditions like these and that it was bad even in recent times, under the current Latvian Republic. Now they don't do it because they are part of NATO, and he said now they have trouble with soldiers' discipline – they didn't before! Particularly the getting drunk and fighting thing - he mentioned that a few times. I wonder if that's why Nikolai and Konstantin didn't want photos to be taken of the alcohol we were drinking on the train. Maybe the Russian army still has a "Guardhouse".

Of course, the two armies that had the worst conditions were the Soviets and the Nazis. In Nazi times the prison was used mainly for deserters. One side of the upstairs corridor was entirely for the condemned. Those on the other side of the corridor had to dig the graves.

I had a private tour at around 9pm where the guard told me all that. He was no longer wearing his uniform, which relaxed me somewhat, but he did all this at night, including showing me the memorial for the guy who tried to start a rebellion against the Soviet government. There was a dummy of him that looked very lifelike in the dark and was right across from my cell... And then the guard just left me alone in the cell. He told me he'd be upstairs, but that seemed like miles away. I didn't sleep well because I was too scared! I was trying not to get up to go to the toilet, but I kept waking up because I needed to go, so I was having a very fitful sleep. Eventually I looked at my phone thinking, *Surely it'll be morning soon*, and it was 2:20am. So I had to go to the toilet.

I was so glad that it doesn't get properly dark here. I've been calling it "dark" since Riga because it does look like night (as opposed to how it was further north) but it's a very very moonlit night. Not twilight, but nowhere near pitch black, which was a damn good thing given my cell's lack of lamp situation. For the first couple of hours I didn't even want to open my eyes or roll over! My right side got sore because I spent too long on it!

I put as my Facebook status, "spent a night in a jail cell". Everyone's confused and concerned! I'm gonna wait a couple of days before commenting, "By the way, it was a voluntary tourist experience."!!

The next morning I took a bus to Klaipeda, Lithuania. I went there because it's near the Curonian Spit. The spit is a 100km long sand peninsula that's shared between Lithuania and Kaliningrad, Russia. It's World Heritage listed and it seemed nice enough, but it was similar to what I'd seen in Saaremaa and I'm not that into beaches. Though I think my favourite part, somewhat surprisingly, was walking along a crowded beach! It was culturally interesting: to see that many people there and that many stalls feeding them beer and ice creams – my Australian sensibilities were surprised. Alex said he went to some beaches in Australia where he was almost the only one there, and he thought that was really amazing! Well, I thought a beach crawling with people was really amazing. They had little platforms with a winding wall going around them for people to change in! People were queuing up to use them!

I tried to walk to Kaliningrad, but didn't succeed. On the map it looked really close, but it wasn't. If I zoomed my camera in as far as it would go it picked up what looked like fence posts on the beach. I couldn't believe that there could be civilians bathing and sunbaking so close to the Schengen border of a country that requires every single visitor to have a visa. If it was a fence I saw, it didn't look very long - it looked like you could swim around it! But I also definitely saw a big tower.

The section of beach I had wandered to was a clothing optional section. The Russian border guards, wherever they are hiding, would have some pretty powerful binoculars. They could totally spy on the naked people.

But then maybe they'd be sent to the Guardhouse for doing that.

The Hill of Crosses

In Šiauliai (pronounced "Shaolei"), I am couch surfing for the first time. It's something I've been meaning to try for years but was too scared. Then I had a housemate who does it all the time and she said it's brilliant. Šiauliai gave me the push to finally do it because there are no hostels there. I decided that if I liked it I might do it again when I get to Poland or Slovakia. So, maybe I will.

My host is called Gelmina, and she is a 22-year-old university student. She lives in a Kruschevki in central Šiauliai with a flatmate. For some reason, their flat doesn't have a bathroom sink. They use the bath instead. I'm not sure if the Soviets just didn't give them a bathroom sink, or if they didn't give them room for a washing machine and the sink was later removed to accommodate a washing machine. Either way, there's not much room in the bathroom, but I love the retro kitchen.

After I arrived in Šiauliai, Gelmina made me dinner and then gave me a short tour of the city. It has a chocolate museum, a bicycle museum, a very

149

nice lake and a Catholic cathedral with architecture I'd never seen before. White, rounded, and a little bit art nouveau-looking, even though it's from the 17th century. Gelmina said it was fairly typical of Lithuanian churches and that Catholicism is the main religion, in contrast to Latvia and Estonia, where it is Lutheranism.

Then we went to a bar where her flatmate works and she ran into two of her exchange student friends there, Costas from Greece and Sunjae from Korea. We had a lovely time talking to them and I tried two Lithuanian beers, both of which were completely unlike any beer I've ever tasted before! They had a richness of flavour and a sweetness that was almost like banana.

I came to Šiauliai to see the Hill of Crosses, which is 10km outside town. You take a bus and then walk along a country road to get to it. That was quite pleasant.

It is, as the name suggests, a hill covered in crosses! Actually two hills, and the crosses also spread out onto the paths leading to the first hill. There are thousands of them, from tiny ones to huge ones. Most of the medium-sized ones have tiny ones hanging off them too, and some rosary beads.

People have been putting them there since the 14th century. The Soviets tried to stop them, but they used to sneak in in the dead of night. Now, of course, anyone can do it anytime. Many are memorials for people who've died (some used to be for people who were deported to Siberia). Some are to mark group visits and pilgrimages, and I saw two that were marking military co-operation between Lithuania and the Czech Republic and France.

It's a pretty intriguing place to go, especially when you get around the back away from the tourists. I had lunch there. It was nice.

The big bonus of couch surfing is, of course, getting to know a local. Gelmina showed me some videos of Lithuanian folk dancing and folk singing. Like in the rest of the Baltics, singing is big. She told me she was going to show me some Lithuanian folk bands and I said, "Great!" but it turned out they were all choirs! A capella too, occasionally with a drum beat but nothing more. It was haunting. Even some of the folk dancers were accompanied by choirs rather than instruments!

There are some big folk festivals here, and many young people take part, which is wonderful. Gelmina showed me a video of one in Vilnius that had hundreds of dancers on a sports field!

That evening, I didn't take public transport, because Gelmina organised me a lift! She's a member of a Facebook group of students in Šiauliai who share rides to places. They post a message on the group page saying, "I'm going to Vilnius at this time and I have this many spaces in my car," and you message them saying you'd like to join and telling them where you live so they can pick you up. I got in on the second try – the first car had already filled up! The passengers get door to door service for much cheaper than the price of a bus or train, and the driver gets petrol money.

My driver was a young blonde man called Egedijus (the j is a y). He drove all over Šiauliai picking up three passengers, including me, and one package, and putting them into his VW Golf. He drove us to Vilnius, which was about 200km away, and drove all around Vilnius dropping us off. I learned the Lithuanian for "turn right" and "turn left" because the sat nav wouldn't shut up, but I've forgotten it now.

Egedijus spoke pretty good English, and we spent some time comparing Lithuania and Australia. We found that our speed limits are similar and that our laws on mobile phones and driving are the same. This surprised me greatly, because I'd seen so many drivers texting and calling – Egedijus did it several times in the 3½ hours I spent in his car. But he said the fines aren't very big and it's hard for police to prove you've done it, so nobody really cares.

I was pleased to discover that Lithuanians are safe overtakers and that they wear seatbelts.

The next morning I started my exploration of Vilnius at the so-called Gate of Dawn, which is a stone's throw away from my hostel. It's the only surviving gate into the Old Town, but what's most interesting about it is it has a chapel right above it. After I walked under it, the first thing I noticed was a woman standing with rosary beads in her hand praying to it. As I stopped to look at the gate and take a photo, which took me no more than a minute, I saw about six passers-by stop and cross themselves. Even people going in the opposite direction to the chapel would stop, turn, bow their heads, cross themselves, and then continue on their way.

And so I found myself in yet another charming Old Town. This one is too easy to get lost in. I use a city map all the time and check it frequently, but in Vilnius, even if you are checking the map frequently, and even if you're going back to somewhere you've been before and you know where it is, you'll still end up going in the complete opposite direction. The streets are like a three-year-old's squiggle painting!

Fortunately in the morning I just had to go straight for a few blocks, which was pleasant. It's mainly when you want to go across country that things get really hellish.

After about ten minutes I found myself in Cathedral Square, which is quite large and impressive - although not at all square-shaped! There's a tall white bell tower, which I've noticed in all the Vilnius churches I've seen is separate from the church. This church was the spectacular white columned, statue- and stucco-adorned Vilnius Cathedral. It looked so inviting from the outside that I decided to go inside. This is rare for me – I'm really not into churches... with the exception of baroque ones. Oh, baroque churches. Wow. Even the organ was baroque: curved lines, cherubs, gold, silver. It was gorgeous! The religious paintings were beautiful 18th century artworks. But the best part of the cathedral is Casimir's Chapel, in its furthest corner. A dome, some silver and so so much stucco, some of it mixed in with frescoes. Fantastic place.

Next I went to the National Museum. Lithuania, in contrast to Latvia and Estonia, was its own state before the 20th century. For over 500 years, from the early 13th century to the late 18th, this land was the Grand Duchy of Lithuania. It was mostly a monarchy, but lords had democratic votes on things. In the 15th century, Lithuania made a commonwealth with Poland and the two of them defeated the Teutonic Order: German crusaders who had much power elsewhere.

In the 18th century, like the rest of the Baltics, Lithuania was invaded by Tsarist Russia. From then on Lithuanian history is similar to Latvian and Estonian history.

Next I went to Gediminas Tower, which was once part of a castle on a hill high about Vilnius. The hill is rather like a giant green thimble in the landscape. Brilliant views of the Old Town from the top, and a small exhibition on the 1989 "Baltic Way", because the tower was its start point. 2½ million people held hands from Vilnius to Tallinn via Riga in a protest for freedom. They aimed for 1½ million - that was how many they needed to cover the distance (650km) - but in the footage you can see that in many places the line was several people thick. It was nearly half the population of the three countries that did it.

Next I wandered over to the Republic of Uzupis. Yes. There is a Vilnius neighbourhood that claims to be its own state. It's a community of artists and creative types. There's a very official looking sign at the entrance, in the style of the EU ones that do everything by symbol. It has a smiley face symbol, a Mona Lisa symbol, a 20km/h speed sign and a symbol of a car falling into the River Vilnia. In Uzupis, you have to be positive, you have to be creative, and you mustn't drive over 20 or you might end up in the river. (I saw many cars breaking this rule, though.)

Uzupis apparently has its own president, and I overheard a tour guide saying that they used to have an army of 12, but they disbanded it because Uzupis is a peaceful place. Now they have a guardian angel instead. There is, indeed, a statue of an angel in central Uzupis with a sign on the pedestal saying it was erected by the Republic of Uzupis.

They also have a flag and a constitution, which is displayed on a wall in several languages. It includes such things as, "Everyone has the right to die, but this is not an obligation," "Everyone has the right to be happy," "Everyone has the right to be unhappy," "A dog has the right to be a dog," "A cat is not obliged to love its owner, but must help in times of need," and "Everyone has the right to celebrate or not celebrate their birthday."

Finally, I went to the former Jewish ghettoes. A ghetto had existed for centuries - because Jews have always been persecuted - but in Nazi times there were two. The smaller of these, with up to 11,000 prisoners (that's the term the sign uses, so I'll stick with it) was only in operation from the 6th of September to the 24th of October 1941. This is because it was the place for the elderly and sick, and they were all killed that October. In total, 30,000 were killed in late 1941 - in the same manner as those from Riga, in a forest called Paneriai. On one of the buildings in the ghetto I found a sobering memorial in the form of several enlarged photographs of ordinary people. The photographs were found in the wreckages of the ghetto after the war. Most show children and young people. Some have been identified, some not, but all are presumed to have been killed.

The streets are the narrowest of laneways (restaurants have taken over some for their al fresco dining areas) and I only saw one open space: the former site of the main synagogue. The buildings there were destroyed in the war. I learned in Tallinn that almost all open areas in Old Towns, including most squares and parks, are only open because the buildings were bombed. Old Towns were not designed to have open spaces; they were designed to cram as much as possible into the space inside the town walls.

I went to the Centre For Tolerance, which is a museum about the Lithuanian Jews, or Litvaks. There's some art, some religious objects saved from the ruins of the synagogues (105 synagogues were destroyed in Vilnius), and a haunting exhibition telling the stories of the children who survived the Holocaust. They all (all the ones I read anyway – there were too many to read them all) survived by being hidden by non-Jewish Lithuanians. Some adopted them as their own children; others' situations were more fraught and they were moved around several times. I can't image what that does to one's mental health. And, of course, most of their families were killed.

There were also many photographs of children who did not survive; most of whom have not been identified, because when their families were killed too, who will claim those photographs? The museum looks after them.

There was also an exhibition on what happened to the surviving Lithuanian Jews under the Soviet Union. At first, of course, the Soviets were very keen to open mass graves and construct memorials because they wanted to discredit their enemy, the Nazis. But nationalism in the SSRs was, of course, banned, and pride in being Jewish and recognition of the horrors the Jews suffered were both seen as elements of nationalism. When Israel was established, some USSR Jews got to go there, but then the borders were quickly closed and those who'd registered to go but hadn't made it were persecuted. Monuments to victims of genocide in places like Paneriai were rebranded to simply say that they were "Soviet citizens" who had been victims of Nazism.

Also, many Jews being traditionally involved in more bourgeoisie professions, many of those who survived Nazism got deported to Siberia...

Has nothing changed?

<u>12th of June, 2:25pm:</u>

I am sitting listening to communist music and looking across a pretty water channel at five busts and one slightly broken statue of Lenin. I am at Gruto Parkas, which is a *real* Soviet theme park. Unlike VDNkh in Moscow, it doesn't deny what that means and it aims to tell the horrible truth about life under Soviet communism. It's kind of a "lest we forget" memorial: to help people understand what happened in the hope that it will never happen again.

I wish I knew what they were singing about. Music tells all. When I first came to this part of the park, the music that was playing sounded exactly like what I'd heard at the Chinese border. But the music's got more boring since then, and actually I'm freezing so I think I'll go and sit in the Soviet cafeteria.

<u>3:05pm:</u>

The communist theme park does not have free wifi.

Gruto Parkas is surrounded by a fence with control towers every so often, two of which blare Soviet music. Apparently the original plan of the owner was to have visitors arrive at the park in cattle trucks as if they were going to a Siberian gulag, but the idea was unpopular so he abandoned it. He sounds like a pretty eccentric person. He made lots of money from mushroom products after he "acquired the fortunes of his collective farm" at the downfall of communism. This is from a newspaper article displayed at the entrance, and I'm not sure what it means. How does one person acquire something that was previously public property - particularly when he was not, at that time, rich? Maybe he had more to do with the Soviets than he's telling us; or conversely supported the conversion to capitalism for reasons of personal ambition rather than collective freedom. There are many people like this. Anyway, he owns a lot of land here and he decided to build a Soviet theme park on it.

You might be thinking that a theme park usually requires more than sobering museums and old statues, and you'd be right. It also has a very large and awesome-looking children's playground and enough animals to open a zoo. Everything from owls to zebras. White peacocks to monkeys. Llamas to bears. This man is more than a little eccentric.

I entered through the fence past the first guard tower, saw the first few statues and a cattle (read: people) transportation train wagon and read a bit about the establishment of the park, and then I suddenly realised I could see llamas and a zebra. Weird.

There are hundreds of statues, busts and friezes set around a hollow concrete and metal-lined pathway that winds through a beautiful pine forest. Every so often, there's a pavilion which provides information on an aspect of Soviet rule. The first is on "elections". After the war, the Soviets were keen to show the world that Lithuania had "chosen" to join the USSR by having a series of elections: in which voter turnout was 99% and 95% of those people voted for the candidates of the Communist Party. They had trouble achieving this initially in Lithuania because the majority of people boycotted the elections, so they made "mobile polling booths" to go around to people's homes and intimidate them into voting. The officials also filled out many ballot papers themselves.

There were compulsory clubs and reading groups, even though most reading material had been banned – the idea was to get people to read propaganda. Every single kid was in a propaganda group too, from grade one.

One pavilion displayed newspaper clippings, with analyses of what they really meant. For example, having found that the Nazi occupation had greatly strengthened feelings of "national identity", the Soviets now had "to liquidate the consequences of German occupation in people's minds". In reality what they were liquidating had nothing to do with the Germans - it was the anti-Soviet resistance.

It was interesting to read the propaganda...

There were a couple of displays of awards given to people for various workplace competitions, which were used to drive productivity. No pay bonus, but I get a trophy! And there was art, some of it very good. One enormous painting of a factory by a river almost made me think that factories were beautiful! There was stained glass too, and sooo many statues, many of them of Lithuanian communists - a surprising number of whom had been killed by their own people during the Stalinist purges.

None of it was new to me. I'd seen it all hundreds of times on the streets of Russia, on proud display. Some of these statues are damaged because of the rough way people ripped them down in 1991 (many had their heads cut off when the park owner got them, but he stuck them back together). The ones in Russia aren't damaged, of course. That's the only difference.

There's one particularly big one of Lenin (accompanied by a photograph of it being toppled in Vilnius) which I didn't fully recognise until I got up close to it. Do you know why? Because it was so big that when I got close to it, I could only observe it from below. Suddenly I realised that this statue wasn't just *like* the many Lenins I'd seen in Russia: it was *exactly the same one* as they have on Lenin St in Yekaterinburg and in Irkutsk! I couldn't tell until I got up close because those things are on such big pedestals I'd only seen them from below!

I'm glad I got to go to that place today, because tomorrow night I'm leaving the former USSR. It'll be interesting to see if things were any different in the rest of the Iron Curtain countries. Probably not - they weren't much different in Mongolia. Gee, Mongolia did well not to be annexed by the USSR. Nearly all the other central Asian countries were. I finally saw a list of the 15 former SSRs today. Only 6 were European.

13th of June, 12:15pm:

I have just had an incredibly interesting, and haunting and alarming, visit to Vilnius's only surviving synagogue. An informative local Jewish lady showed me around. The only reason it survived the war is that the Nazis used it as a medical store.

My guide told me that only 4% of Lithuania's Jewish population survived the war, but that this was not due to the help of local good Samaritans as many claim. She said there were some such people who helped, but not many, and that after the war many people claimed that they had helped Jews when they hadn't. Of the 4% who survived, she said 2% were in Siberia and 2% were in the army.

Now, the Jewish population of Vilnius is about 1,500, and of Lithuania a little over 3,000. This synagogue holds small services twice a day and a big one on Saturdays, but it is struggling to survive as most of the local Jews have become secular, intermarried and/or assimilated. She mentioned assimilation a few times and how she doesn't want to do it, and how the Lithuanian Jews were always fairly good at not doing it, but that they're not anymore. She said there are some young people involved in the synagogue now, but that most of it revolves around the service leader. She said he sings prayers and leads the service and he's particularly good. He sings like an opera singer almost, and it's in the traditional way because he learnt it from his father. But now nobody has learnt it so without him, the synagogue would close. I wish I was in Vilnius tomorrow because it's Saturday and she invited me and the other tourists who were there to come to the Shabat service and hear the singing. She was very welcoming.

The alarming things she told me were that even the Nazis were surprised at how brutal the local population were to the Jews in the Baltic states and Poland. Anti-Semitism has always been high here and *it still is*. She said Lithuanian Jews don't have it directed at them too much because they don't have much of a Jewish look about them, and there are so few of them now that mainstream Lithuanians don't know what Jews look like. But they still learn that Jews are bad for some reason; and these anti-Semitic feelings come out when they are talking to a Jew whom they don't realise is a Jew. She told a story of a doctor she knows, a very friendly, likeable, well-respected surgeon. One time he heard her listening to music by a Jewish composer and he asked her to turn it off. When she asked him why he didn't like the music, he said, "I hate Jews. If I had a Jew on my surgery table, I am not sure that they would stay alive." But this man is not a Nazi or even a Lithuanian nationalist; he likes Russians when many Lithuanians don't, and apparently he even likes Arabs, but not Jews.

I just can't understand these sentiments at all. Not only to dislike someone just because of their ethnicity - that's wrong enough in itself - but to dislike them so much you want to kill them? Why? I don't understand! They are doing nothing to hurt you! In the Centre For Tolerance museum they had a statement from a Lithuanian man who'd been involved in the killings at Paneriai – he was either a policeman or he'd joined the German army – and he was casually describing how he'd shot so many Jews and he didn't even know why he'd done it! I don't understand.

I'm a very passive and impressionable person; I have some opinions but I'm always willing to listen to the other side and to try to understand why they think that way. Usually I can achieve that understanding; I can say, "OK, I disagree with them, but they think that way because of this, and that's fair enough." In Russia, for example, I tried to understand why they held onto all their Lenin statues. I thought it was a bit weird - and after what I've learned in the Baltics I think it's even more weird - but they said, "It's part of our history," so I said, "OK, fair enough." Sometimes I try to analyse them and wonder why their nation is like that, but I will never say, "They're stupid; they shouldn't do that." They have their reasons, and I do my best to understand them. I think a lot of it is just that they're proud to be Russian, and the Soviet era is part of that. Of course, I'm sure Germans don't think Nazism is a part of being German, but I think they're more educated about the horrible truth of what their former leaders did than the Russians are...

So, any standpoint I will try to understand, but racism is one I've never been able to comprehend. And this... wanting to kill people because of who they are? *Not* feeling regret and abhorrence about what happened here? I don't get it. I don't understand and I never will. And it terrifies me that there are people out there who are like that, and that all it took was one foreign invader who had a specific policy against Jews and a bunch of locals went, "Oh, you mean it's not illegal for us to kill them anymore? Awesome." They can't even claim the Nuremberg defence, because it wasn't their army who was doing it. I DO NOT UNDERSTAND!

I'm sure the majority of Lithuanians today aren't anti-Semitic, but if there are enough of them out there for this Jewish lady to have felt it - and quite regularly, by the sound of it - then it is a problem. And not only here; in other parts of Europe too. There were two other tourists at the synagogue who were from Hamburg, and they said that the police need to protect the synagogue there. WHAT? To be honest, I would understand if it were Muslims making the attacks, because that would mean it would be to do with Palestine, and I do hate what Israel does to Palestine so that's a standpoint I could understand (though not a course of action I could agree with). But it's not. It's the Europeans doing it. Have they learnt nothing from history? I don't get it.

<u>5:13pm:</u>
My train is passing through Paneriai. I can see the forest. It sends chills down my spine.

There's some kind of museum and memorial here, but I couldn't handle that. Is that bad? Am I turning a blind eye? I don't think I am - I'm certainly thinking about it a lot; I just don't want to see the dreaded site of it.

It's really not far from Vilnius. I think they marched here...

The Warsaw Rising

<u>14th of June, 9:05pm:</u>

I have just successfully completed cooking pasta in an electric kettle. It worked, but not as well as two nights ago when I cooked it in a deep fryer.

I suppose I am a bit weird.

Two nights ago it was because the hostel in Vilnius had the worst stocked kitchen I had ever seen; yet still they had advertised it as a "kitchen" and when I'd seen it when I checked in it looked like a kitchen, so I bought pasta. Didn't realise it had no cook top. No oven I was expecting, as I haven't seen an oven this entire trip, but no cook top? That is not a kitchen. The one where I stayed in Kuressaare had only a microwave and a kettle, but they said that in their information, and they said it was a kitchenette. They even said what was in the kitchenette, so I made sure I bought something that would cook in the microwave.

In this one, in Warsaw, I wasn't expecting a kitchen because the hostel was booked out so this is the hotel that's attached to it, and it said nothing on their website about there being a kitchen at all. So this evening I asked if I could cook in the hostel kitchen, which I'd seen this morning and I knew it had cook tops. But the receptionist said, "Oh, don't worry, there is a kitchen exactly the same in the hotel." So I walked to the hotel, which is two streets away, with my bags, and then back again because the door wouldn't work, and then back again and the door still wouldn't work: I only got in because a local man helped me. I was already hating the receptionist by this point. He was two streets away and he didn't even understand his own doors. So by the time I discovered there was no cook top, I wasn't walking back there again. *Screw you*, I thought, *I'll cook my pasta in your kettle. And maybe sometime you can learn the difference between a kitchen and a kitchenette.*

It worked – I was a bit surprised! A kettle is a lot smaller than a deep fryer, though, and it has no setting other than "boil", so it boiled over many times! Can you imagine a kettle boiling over? Bubbles were just pouring out of it – I had to hold it over the sink many times. But that never happens when it's just water, even if you overfill it. It must be something the food solids do to the water. See, I'm learning about physics here. It's been a very enlightening dinner time. And then I had to scrub out a kettle. Never done that before in my life...

Guess what! Tomorrow morning my friend Alma is coming!! Yay! She's flown from Japan just to travel with me for two weeks! And she got delayed – she's supposed to be here already. But I know from experience that when I'm travelling with somebody else, my journal never ever gets up to date until they leave again. So, I'd better get it up to date now. After making a cup of tea. I'll see whether the kettle has survived my anti-receptionist abuse...

9:35pm:

It's fine! I've done a scientific experiment, folks, and I have proved that it is perfectly fine to cook pasta in an electric kettle or a deep fryer. Err...

providing it's not one of those old ones with an element in there. Ooh dear. I wouldn't try it with one of those.

Yesterday, Alma flew from Japan to Munich. That was the easiest and cheapest airport she could get to. The plan was that she would take a night train from Prague to Warsaw at the same time as I was taking a night bus from Vilnius (Prague is in between Munich and Warsaw). My bus would get in at 6:15am and I would go to the central train station and meet her off her train at 7:45.

If it had gone to plan, it would have been brilliant. But for some unknown reason she had problems getting to Prague – her bus just didn't come. So I spent my last hour in Vilnius desperately trying to find her something else, unsuccessfully. Then I had to go and take my bus.

My bus was something else. I swear I heard an "Oooh" from the waiting crowd when it arrived. It was a huge double decker: the driver had to climb a ladder to access the luggage compartment, and inside you could order drinks and snacks and buy duty free products! Perhaps this was more for the daytime legs, because the thing is, this bus was making a more than 24 hour journey. You'll be gobsmacked when I tell you how many places it was going to, and how many countries. I think they had two drivers. They were behind a curtain so I couldn't be sure – I had all my dealings with the stewardess. She spoke three languages, and I couldn't even tell what the other two were.

There were actually two buses from that company going to Warsaw last night, and one or two from another company too. One was an express bus going to Warsaw and Berlin. "That's express?" you say? I don't think it even started from Vilnius – Riga, maybe – but it was an express. Wait a moment and you'll understand.

I wasn't too surprised to see this second bus, because when I'd booked there had been two buses I could choose from leaving Vilnius at 10:15pm: one said it would arrive in Warsaw at 5:15am and the other said 6:15am. I said, "I'd like an extra hour's sleep, please," and picked the 6:15 one.

This is the list of stops it was making, copied word for word from the sign behind the windscreen:

RIGA – PANEVĖŽYS – VILNIUS
- KAUNAS – MARIJAMPOLĖ
- SUWALKUI – AUGUSTOW – BIALYSTOK
- O.MAZOWIECVKI – WARSZAWA
- PIOTRKOW – KRAKOW – BRATISLAVA
- VIENNA – BUDAPEST – SZEGED – SOFIA

One bus. Non-stop. It had come from Latvia; I got on in Lithuania and got off in Poland; and then it went to Slovakia, Austria, Hungary and Bulgaria! That's seven countries!!! When I got off I had déjà vu, because the stewardess was standing at the door with her list again with a big queue of people in front of her - just as she'd been when I got on!

I arrived at Warsaw Zachodnia bus station late at 6:45am. I went inside, found a seat, logged onto the free wifi and remained there for some time, a: because I couldn't go anywhere until the currency exchange place opened at 8; and b: because I wanted to find out what was happening with Alma and whether she would be able to get here today or not. She eventually woke up, logged on and told me that she was still in Munich.

So I went to the hotel and then went out sightseeing: to the Chopin Museum and then the Palace of Culture and Science. This is Warsaw's version of Riga's "Stalin's birthday cake". The size is somewhere in between Riga's and Moscow's, but what looks different about this one is that it's got four big clockfaces on the top of the tower, giving it a striking resemblance to Big Ben! I don't know what the style is called, but I'd call it Soviet Gothic, and Big Ben is gothic ("gothic revival", according to Wikipedia). The lines and colours are very similar. They have, I must say, done a very very good job of removing all the Soviet references from the façade and fittings. I didn't see any wheat at all!

I enjoyed the buildings I passed as I walked around. I'd been told that Warsaw was ugly because it was bombed to hell in the war. Not true. Yes it was bombed to hell, but it's not ugly. It has many very lovely buildings. At first I thought, *I'm so glad these survived the bombing!* but now I've learned that they're almost all reconstructions. And I've learned that reconstructions are good. Just because a building was built in the mid-20th century doesn't mean it has to be ugly.

I did a walking tour of the Old Town. I thought I was sick of Old Towns, but I'm not. I knew going in that Warsaw's Old Town is almost entirely a reconstruction, but I don't care. It's so beautiful. The colours, the frescoes, the shapes, the cobblestones...

My guide was a young history graduate called Krysztoff. He told us that Poland first became a nation in 966, and that from the 16th century it had a nobles' parliament like Lithuania did. But its political system got a bit weak by the end of the 18th century, and there were heavyweights in the area wanting to flex their muscles (it just happens over and over again): Prussia, the Austro-Hungarian Empire and the Russian Empire. They invaded and partitioned Poland between the three of them, and it remained so divided for well over a century. It was reunified in 1918 because Prussia (now Germany) and Austria had just lost a war and Russia had just had a revolution and was now having a civil war. But it wasn't just that – Western powers actually made decisions about resurrecting countries. Czechoslovakia and Finland were two others that were reformed at the same time, and we know about the Baltics. But it was the war's winners who decided this should be done – Poland's independence day is Armistice Day.

Like the Baltic states, they had 21 years of independence between 1918 and 1939, and then WWII happened. Krysztoff told us that 85% of Warsaw's buildings were destroyed in WWII. The city was devastated. And yet somehow they managed to rebuild the entire Old Town by 1956. What? Did I hear correctly? Yes, they started as soon as they could and they finished (pretty much) by 1956. The memory of what the Old Town had looked like was still fresh in people's minds, and many who had lived there were architects who had great memory of architectural detail, so they did a pretty good job of making it look authentic. This new Old Town is now on the UNESCO World Heritage List - that's how much it looks the part.

"Where did they get the money from?" asked one tourist.

Krysztoff listed the following sources:

- the Polish Government
- local donations
- donations from the Polish diaspora
- reparation payments from Germany
- the Soviet Union

My university knowledge of the rebuilding of Europe after WWII was ringing around in my head, and there were two words that Krysztoff had not mentioned.

"Did they not get anything from the Marshall Plan?" I asked.

"No," he replied. "The Soviet Union decided that they didn't want that. We were not allowed to accept any money from the Marshall Plan – it was used in Western Europe, not in the east."

Poland, Germany and the Soviet Union funded all that? After having just been devastated by war themselves? And the Soviet Union was providing money all over Eastern Europe, just so they could avoid accepting anything from the USA? Wow. I'm sure they got the money by gulag prisoners, but still. I'm impressed.

They rebuilt hundreds more buildings outside the city wall, but in the Old Town itself, only three buildings had retained their structural integrity after 1944. And by that I don't mean their whole structure – they were still bombed to hell – but most of their walls were still standing. Only three buildings….

Europeans certainly threw a lot of fire power at each other over six years, and Poland was at the centre of it for some of that time, but bombings and gunfire are either targeted or random, right? They either throw everything they've got at one small area, or they throw bits everywhere. It's everywhere, but it's still bits. It's like a bushfire: it doesn't destroy *every* building, does it? One house gone, one standing, three gone, two standing – doesn't that make more sense? How can conventional bombs destroy 85% of a city?

They can't. Not in conventional warfare. But, for 63 days starting on the 1st of August 1944, there was the Warsaw Rising.

Krysztoff reminded me of Hitler and Stalin's horrible secret invasion plan attached to the Nazi-Soviet Non-Aggression Pact; how certain countries were allocated to either the Soviet Union or Germany's "sphere of influence" and Poland was to be split between the two. The way Krysztoff described it was that because it was a bigger country, it would be easier to defeat if both the Nazis and the Soviets attacked it at the same time: the Nazis from the west and the Soviets from the east.

Almost everybody in the West knows (maybe not all the young people, but everybody else) that WWII started when Hitler invaded Poland. Britain had given him an ultimatum telling him not to extend his "sphere of influence" any further or else. He ignored them and invaded Poland. Britain said, "OK, we declare war on you," and it all kicked off from there.

I was never told that Stalin invaded Poland at the same time. History is written by the winners. The losers get blamed for everything.

So the Nazis occupied one half of Poland for two years and the Soviets occupied the other half. Then Hitler decided he'd had enough of Stalin and took the Soviet half (or "liberated", depending on which museum you go to); then invaded the rest of the Soviets' "sphere of influence"; and then Russia itself.

When Russia was taking that territory back in 1944 the Polish were a bit worried because, though they wanted to be liberated from the Nazis, they thought that if the Soviets did the liberating they would never leave - they'd just become a new occupying army (all in all, a fair assessment). So the Polish army and many citizens decided they wanted to do whatever they could to liberate themselves. They knew they'd need the Soviets' help, so they waited until the Soviet army was at the edge of Warsaw to do it, but they just wanted to be on a stronger footing when they arrived. Plus, they were damn sick of those Nazis and they wanted to fight them. So, they began the Warsaw Rising. Many ordinary people fought. They even had 12-

year-old kids working as messengers. Everyone did their bit, and they fought hard.

But the Soviets never came. They were less than a kilometre away from the Old Town, just the other side of the river, but Stalin said, "Ha, let's stay here and watch the Poles fight," and he never sent his soldiers forward.

It took 63 days for the Warsaw Rising to be lost. In that time, 18,000 Polish soldiers, 15,000 German soldiers and 180,000 civilians were killed. The Nazis were particularly brutal, to both the people and their city. They executed many civilians, and they demolished almost every single building, just to punish Warsaw.

It's very heavy stuff. I'm going to the Warsaw Rising Museum tomorrow, so I'll tell you more then.

15th of June, 6:43pm:

15th of June, 6:43pm:

Alma arrived this morning! Yay! We checked in to our hostel and then went to do the Communist Walking Tour! We had the same guide, Krysztoff. He took us first to the Polish Communist Party HQ, which later became the Stock Exchange (ironic); and then to a monument of a dying revolutionary, which later became a monument of a dying soldier! They just changed the words on the plinth. But people think the artist put anti-communist themes in it anyway because it looks a bit like the very many religious statues of Mary Magdalen and dead Jesus. So they thought it was appropriate to claim the monument for Poland.

I've been meaning to mention the religious thing. In Gruto Parkas, I saw a copy of an underground illegal publication that was produced by the Catholic Church. Because Communism is opposed to religion, in Soviet times religious groups were among those who were resisting and doing risky things like producing underground newspapers. In Lithuania and Poland Catholicism is the main religion, so it was the Catholic church doing this. Pope John Paul II was from Poland, and he is revered here for helping to inspire Poles and give them hope during Soviet times. I saw part of a speech from him from the late 1970s at the Warsaw Rising Museum. In it, he spoke the truth about the Rising that the Soviets denied and criticised the Allies' lack of support. He was proud to be Polish and people loved him for it. I guess a pope coming from behind the Iron Curtain was a source of hope, too. But his speech was saturated in religious stuff too. and it is so surprising to me that the Catholic Church, which is best known to me as an impenetrable Establishment institution often protested against, was the one doing the protesting!!

Next, Krysztoff told us the real reason why they were able to rebuild Warsaw so quickly. The Soviets created a slogan - it was, "Poles will rebuild

166

Warsaw" or something like that - and it was a rallying cry to get everybody to do their bit, to put in everything they could to rebuild the city. But the real reason why they were doing it, and doing it so fast and so early after the war, was to distract those patriotic Poles from fighting Soviet rule.

Inspiringly patriotic though the Warsaw Rising story is, actually it did a lot to help the Soviets take over the country. The reason why the Soviets didn't help the insurgents is that it was in their interests to let them keep fighting until they lost, because it was precisely those insurgents, and that city, that would have most resisted Soviet rule. For the Soviets, it was much better to just let all the patriotic fighters die fighting the Germans. Taking over a country and a population that had previously been devastated by another army is, of course, much easier. They swoop in, rebuild the place and look like the good guys. The Poles could probably see through that, but they did want to rebuild the place and they had to co-operate with the Soviets for that.

Krysztoff explained that there was one building in the Old Town that wasn't rebuilt by 1956; in fact it wasn't even attempted until the 70s. This was the Royal Castle. The Soviets, for obvious reasons, considered this a symbol of Polish national history, monarchy and sovereignty, and to be "unnecessary" to rebuild. In the 70s the Poles finally raised the money and did it themselves.

A couple of stories on life under communism from Krysztoff's parents:

There was always a lack of supply to the shops. There would be one or two that were kept full just for appearances, but most were distinctly lacking. A lot of the time, they weren't even open. When a supermarket, for example, was open, there would be long queues to get inside. You might need to queue for up to three hours, only to get inside and find that there was nothing left. Krysztoff's mother had ways of getting around this, but his father wasn't so good at it. Almost every time he went to the supermarket, he would find the shelves empty of anything useful by the time he got inside. There would still be some stock, just not things you would actually want, e.g. mustard or vinegar. Krysztoff's father didn't want to go home empty handed, so every time he had this experience, he would buy a jar of mustard. By 1989, when Poland got back its independence, an entire shelf of the family's pantry was full of jars of mustard. Their way of celebrating the end of communism was to smash them all!

Clothing and furniture was available, but not very much of it and it was all the same stuff. Walking down the street, you could see many people wearing exactly the same clothes. Young people would alter their clothing by cutting holes, sewing or painting designs on them – anything to make themselves look different to everyone else.

Furniture was all the same too, and home furnishings like pictures, ornaments and so on. On my train from Ulaanbatar to Irkutsk, Sascha told Alex and I a USSR joke about a man who got very drunk one night, and then his friends put him on the train home. The man fell asleep on the train and missed his stop. He got out at a different stop, but he didn't realise it wasn't his stop. Actually he was in a completely different city, but he didn't realise because all the streets looked the same. So he went to his apartment on Lenin St (there's always a Lenin St), sat on his couch and fell asleep. He was awoken in the morning by a strange woman screaming at him to get out of her apartment. He screamed right back, because he genuinely believed it was his apartment. The street looked like his street, it had the same name as his street and the apartment block, which looked the same as his, was in the same position on this other Lenin St as the one on his Lenin St. Even inside the apartment, he still couldn't tell the difference because all the furnishings were the same...

Funny joke. I hadn't realised exactly how close to reality it was until Krysztoff told the story of his father, as a teenager, returning home from school one day and being distracted on the apartment block stairs by some people moving some furniture. He passed them and arrived at his apartment. He went inside, turned on the TV and sat on the couch watching it. A woman came and sat next to him on the couch and he suddenly realised that the woman was not his mother; she was the lady from downstairs. Then he realised that he hadn't gone up as many flights of stairs as he should have. He was in the wrong apartment, but he hadn't noticed because the entranceway looked the same, the lounge room looked the same, the TV was the same and the couch was the same – only the woman was different!

True story. Wow.

The tour finished at the Soviet skyscraper, which Alma immediately recognised as a phallic symbol because it has two extensions either side of the bottom of the tower. Krysztoff said, "Yes, people do call it 'Stalin's penis.'" Apparently it's still controversial – some people want to knock it down. It was built in only 2½ years as a show of power. The size of it shows power. The phallus shows power. The fact they built it when much of the rest of the city was still rubble shows power. The fact they brought Russian workers in to build it shows manpower. And the fact it only took them 2½ years? Wow. It was entirely meant to intimidate the locals. And you could only enjoy the culture and science it was offering if you were a party loyalist.

On celebration days, which happened fairly often – the 9th of May; the 22nd of July (the date the Polish puppet government was created in 1944);

and others – Communist leaders would gather on the platform at the base of the building to address the crowds below. Then, they would have marches. The building is about 200m away from Central Station, where I met Alma that morning. As soon as we emerged from the station, she said, "Whoah, this road is huge – that's a Soviet thing, isn't it?"

I hadn't noticed at all - I just thought it was a big city so it had a big road - but Alma is from Manhattan. If she thinks it's a big road then it must really be exceptional. Pondering this, I remembered a documentary I'd seen on Hitler's Berlin which revealed that he had plans to build, and had commenced building, huge tunnels beneath the main roads to redirect cars, so that the roads could be used just for parades. *Maybe it's an autocratic thing*, I thought.

Well, Alma had hit the nail on the head. Krysztoff said the road was designed for parades.

After lunch, Alma and I went to the Warsaw Rising Museum. It's very dramatic – there are sporadic sounds of gunfire and explosions, underlined by the constant sound of a beating heart. It goes into great detail on the horrors of the Nazi occupation, particularly in the treatment of the Jews. There are graphic photographs and videos. One TV screen is in a box saying, "Warning! Graphic scenes!" and it contains mostly still photographs of executions. But the one which disturbed me most, which was not in a censored box, was the video footage of hundreds of naked, skeletal bodies of Jews being dumped in mass graves. It was in central Warsaw, so they hadn't been gassed – I think they had starved. Unfortunately, that particular video had no explanation, just shot after shot of lifeless skeletal limbs hanging off the edges of carts, of lifeless babies and children being picked up and thrown on piles, of bodies being slid down a chute into a mass grave. It wasn't clear whether the burial was being supervised by the Nazis or the insurgents, but there was also a shot of some old bearded men watching it with bowed heads, so I think maybe it was the insurgents.

The insurgents had an incredible film crew recording everything. The best item in the museum's collection is newsreel footage, made by the insurgents for insurgent-controlled cinemas, detailing many key events. The newsreels were found in 1956, and soon disappeared – the Soviets got rid of them. But later, the original uncut films were discovered, and some of the original documentary team were still alive and they were able to remember what bits they'd used in the newsreels, and they re-recorded the commentary. They're amazing to watch.

There's also another video in 3D which is a computer-generated representation of what the city would have looked like after the war. There isn't a single building that is untouched. Many blocks have been levelled completely. It looks like a nuclear bomb went off.

The Soviets didn't help, but in other parts of the country the Polish Home Army was fighting with them. As soon as they didn't need them anymore the Soviets disarmed them, sometimes arrested them. After the war, the Soviets claimed that they had organised the Rising, and that the Home Army had been fighting alongside the Germans.

There's a blow-by-blow account of the uprising, with videos of people who were there explaining it. They were children at the time – there were so many children involved. Mainly as messengers, but there was one who died in battle and was posthumously awarded a medal at age 11. Being a messenger was really dangerous too. They made their own postal service, with stamps and everything, but the stamps were just for sorting purposes – the service was free. Many of the messengers died.

The children also worked as sewer guides, because often to get around people had to use the sewers.

At the start of the Rising, everyone was so happy. They had some success and they could finally fly their flags, listen to radios and sing their songs again – they could refuse to do what the Germans wanted them to.

They held out for 63 days, but eventually the insurgents had to surrender. There was no way they could win. They were captured and sent to POW camps in Germany. At least that meant they were finally recognised as combatants and afforded the rights associated with that – during the Rising neither the Soviets nor the Allies recognised them as legitimate fighters, so the Germans were not obliged to keep them alive or treat them well when they were taken prisoner.

The Germans evacuated the city. Only about 1,000 people stayed (in hiding), of a pre-Rising population of 900,000 and pre-war population of 1.5 million. Many of those people must have been killed, as the Germans proceeded to systematically destroy almost every single building.

It's wonderful that they rebuilt it so well because it's so beautiful, but it's also so tragic to walk around the Old Town, because you know that something so beautiful and so old was wilfully destroyed. Many of the buildings have their original building dates and their rebuilding dates displayed, e.g. a church that says, "1370, 1953". Yes the 1953 one is beautiful, but a beautiful church from 1370 was destroyed.

That evening we tried Polish food: I had a pancake with mushroom sauce followed by blueberry dumplings (pierogies). It was yum.

The next morning, we went to the Jewish Cemetery. It's a pretty emotive place when you read all the memorials and see the mass graves (the ones I'd seen on the videos the previous day) and the "symbolic graves" for

170

people whose bodies were never found. But it's also a very beautiful and romantic place because, like so many other eastern European cemeteries, it is in a forest. But it's much more mysterious and haunting than those other cemeteries because it's just been let go. For all of the pre-war graves I guess there was nobody to take care of them, because the people's relatives had all either died or emigrated, so the forest has taken over. In some places the undergrowth completely covers the graves, or the roots have toppled them. In others the trees are holding up tilting graves by growing around them. Forests are always beautiful, so it's impressive to see. So big and so green.

There are 100,000 graves there. The pre-war Jewish population of Warsaw was 33%.

There are many memorials that have been erected by relatives of Holocaust victims, many in the diaspora. This was the most poignant one I saw. It was on a symbolic grave:

> *For our grandparents Rabbi Yechiel Meyer and*
> *Nechama Blumenfield, our aunts Sara and Tola and*
> *whole Baum family Shlomo, Ruvka, Wolf Leon, who died*
> *in the terrible Holocaust of our people.*
> *We never met you, but we will never forget you.*
> *May you be at peace, may you be at rest, may you*
> *know we remember you.*

The milk bar

For lunch, we went to a "bar mylczeny": a milk bar. I don't know why they're called milk bars, because they do not serve ice cream or milkshakes. They are Soviet-style cafeterias. I'd been hearing about them since Russia but hadn't got around to eating in one yet. They're a positive socialist thing, designed to serve low cost food to people who need it. They seem to be particularly popular with families, pensioners and students. They are heavily subsidised by the government, the service is terrible and the food is basic at best, but they're very charming and endearingly retro.

We looked for one that had an English menu, but the English menu only served to confuse us all the more. When you have no idea what any of the food is and the menu has as little description as possible, then basically you're just looking at ingredients - and poorly translated ones at that.

The first item on the menu was "pasta with quark". This "quark" appeared in several other menu items also. The menu was in three languages: Polish, English and French. Not having had a single French lesson in my life, I turned to it for answers. I realised that all of the menu items that said "quark" in English said "fromage" in French. This was a very helpful discovery which enabled me to understand the menu... sort of.

I ordered the pasta with quark and the beetroot leaf soup. It cost me 10 zloty, which is a little over AUD$3. You pay the grumpy lady at the (very old) cash register, and she writes your order on a piece of receipt roll (apparently printing on a receipt roll was beyond the cash register). You take this to the even grumpier lady in the kitchen, which is accessed by a servery hatch. She takes food from the assortment of pots on the stove behind her and gives it to you. But my pasta didn't come from the stove, it came from the bench, so it was cold. She covered it in some sweetish cottage cheese I'd had in crepes in Russia, and another kind of cottage cheese that was runnier. That was it. It was pasta with cheese. Maybe the reason why the English menu only listed ingredients is that the food *was* ingredients.

The soup was very, very pink. I mixed it with the pasta and cheese, and that made it very nice. And the experience was fantastic (including the kitchen lady talking louder when Alma didn't understand what she was saying).

Then we wandered around the Old Town a bit. I had an absolutely enormous ice-cream. Then we took a train to Krakow (pronounced "Krakov").

There are many many things to see and do in Krakow, and daytrips outside. If Warsaw's Old Town is a delicious and generously-sized soft serve chocolate ice-cream in a waffle cone, then Krakow's is a sundae piled high with several different flavours – choc mint, boysenberry, raspberry sorbet, cappuccino, blackberry cheesecake, cookies 'n' cream and more, with whatever toppings you want and a cherry on top, made by a boutique ice cream café.

The Old Town is original, and it's enormous. Especially the main square – it's at least five times the size of Warsaw's, not including the Cloth Hall in the middle. Before coming to Poland I'd met a couple of people who'd been here, and they said that Warsaw was boring and Krakow was incredible. Upon arrival in Warsaw, I couldn't believe how wrong they were – I thought Warsaw was an amazing place, so interesting, so unique, and its buildings so beautiful (I was not expecting that in a city that had 85% of its buildings built in the 20th century). But Krakow really is incredible. Maybe those other travellers did it in the wrong order. If you have a boutique multi-flavour multi-topping sundae and *then* downgrade to a plain chocolate soft serve, even if it is in a waffle cone it's probably not very exciting for you.

On our first day we did a walking tour and then went to the Wieliczka (pronounced "Viyaleitchka") Salt Mine. The salt "block" is about 10km long and 400m deep, with 240km of tunnels over nine levels. It was created when an inland sea receded, leaving salt, and the Carpathian Mountains rose up, pushing it into a block. It was discovered in the 13th century and the mine has been operating since then, but people had been extracting salt from ground water for thousands of years before that – they think since 6,000 years ago, in the Neolithic Age. It seems to have been worked fairly consistently since then. The mine part was operating for 700 years, very profitably, particularly back when salt was the world's only known food preservative. Now all the purest salt is gone and global salt prices have fallen substantially, so they've stopped extracting rock salt and gone back to the salty ground water to get the salt produced by the mine today. Just like the "Neoliths", but with much better technology.

The mine is a never-ending labyrinth of grey tunnels, usually supported by log structures which in many cases are covered in salt crystals! Our guide said that metal won't last long down there, but wood will stay strong for centuries. There are also many enormous caverns: some with small lakes in them; some with chapels; some with sculptures or mining dioramas carved from salt; and one concert hall (the biggest chapel gets used for that as well – it has great acoustics, apparently). Also two gift shops, a restaurant, a post box, a banquet hall, a multimedia room, a museum, several toilets and a helping of free wifi.

There are thousands of salt carvings done by miners on their own time, and they're incredibly well done. Many are religious in nature because mining is dangerous work. There used to be some insane number like 4,000 chapels, but many have collapsed. The floors of the chapels are carved too, into beautiful shiny tiles. It's all salt. Apparently salt is as hard as marble, so it's a very good carving material. They're still doing it today.

The statues are particularly awesome, and so are the salt crystals. Throughout the mine, salt vapourises due to heat, ground water and/or condensation (particularly from our breath), and then re-crystallises later. In the museum we saw a wagon wheel that looked just like a pretzel and a broom head covered in the purest clear crystals that were at least 15mm deep.

There are too many where we are

The day we went to Auschwitz was one of the most depressing days of my entire life. It's traumatising just to hear about, let alone live through (for the precious few who managed to). But everyone should go there. Everyone. Every citizen of the world should go there and have a good hard think about all their prejudices.

There are so many visitors it's compulsory to take a tour if you arrive between 10 and 3, and though we tried to arrive before 10, we didn't manage it (Auschwitz is 1½ hours from Krakow). Taking a tour ended up being for the best, because our tour guide was really good and she really made us think. The reason we would've preferred not to take a tour is that we thought we wouldn't be able to experience the place properly if we were always surrounded by people and being herded around, but really, does one's "experience" of Auschwitz need to be enhanced in any way - to be made any stronger than the punch to the heart it already is? Did I want to stand alone in a gas chamber; did I need to spend time introspectively studying the piles and piles of shoes of thousands of murdered innocent

175

people? To stare for minutes at the children's clothes? No, I was quite happy to be rushed through there...

So we took a tour, in a group of 25, with headsets so we could still hear the guide as we filed past scores more groups of 25 with tour guides speaking in several different languages.

Our tour guide was aged about 50 and had been working there for 20 years, and she was exactly like a teacher – and a stern one at that. She didn't smile once – of course she didn't, how can you smile when you have subject matter like that – but she was a damn good teacher. She repeated every major point, she stated her facts simply, and she was always asking us questions which made us question our own prejudices.

The site we know as "Auschwitz" was actually made up of three camps: Auschwitz I, Birkenau or Auschwitz II, and a third camp known as Auschwitz III of which almost nothing remains. We visited the first two. Birkenau was the main death camp – there were six gas chambers there. They weren't even hidden, as it was built later in the war after the Nazis had perfected the most efficient way to kill Jews and Roma, and they didn't care who knew about it.

Auschwitz I was where they did their first experiments with gassing, in a small prison there which was used for local Polish arrestees - I can't say criminals because they were all arrested for political reasons and tried in under a minute - as well as camp inmates who had (not necessarily) broken the rules. The first gassing took over two days.

Auschwitz III had no gas chambers, so our guide said that prisoners from there who survived tended to be in better shape mentally.

First, we saw around Auschwitz I. Its buildings are all brick and two storeys tall, and it looks like a barracks, because it was – it had been a Polish Army facility. So it was all ready to go when it was opened in 1940 as a facility for political prisoners. It was not for Jews – the ghettoes were still operating then, and those that weren't had been "liquidated" in the manner I described in Latvia and Lithuania: by marching the people into the forest and shooting them. Genocide by gassing had not yet been invented in the history of humankind. So the prisoners of Auschwitz were:

- Polish insurgents
- Poles who were political prisoners for other reasons like that the Nazis wanted their land – the occupants of all the villages surrounding Auschwitz, for example, were kicked out, imprisoned and their homes demolished for building materials
- priests
- homosexuals

- after 1941, 15,000 Soviet POWs, of whom only 86 survived the war.

I would like to restate my earlier point that the Soviets were as bad as the Nazis in *almost* every way: those POW survivors, as soon as they were repatriated when the Red Army liberated Auschwitz, were sent straight to the gulags for "working with the enemy" by being imprisoned at Auschwitz...

The concentration camp was not a new concept, our guide explained. Forcing people to work while they were close to starvation was not a new concept; slave labour was not a new concept; torture and abuse of prisoners was not a new concept; racism and discrimination against large swathes of people was not a new concept – it had been going on since the beginning of time and it still goes on today. The Soviets had gulags; the Japanese had concentration camps for POWs in WWII; the British had them in the Boer War; the Australian and American governments had differential rules governing where to live, how to walk down the street, what pubs to go to and whether you could sit or stand on a bus according to whether you were black or white; the Australian government and many others still imprison asylum seekers – the list goes on. Our guide pointed out that the Nazis were not unique in any of this. What was unique was that they created this cruel and super-efficient method of murdering thousands of people in a day using only gas, and that they deliberately set out to kill all the Jews of Europe – not just relocate them, not just force them to work, but to murder them all. This, our guide explained, was unique in the history of humankind, and nobody was expecting it, not even the Jews.

The buildings of Auschwitz I now contain several exhibition rooms. The first one we saw showed the statistics. The number of people deported to Auschwitz from all over Nazi-occupied Europe - as far away as Narva, Oslo, Paris, Rome, Thessaloniki and Bucharest, and everywhere in between - was approximately 1.3 million.

Among them were:

- 1.1 million Jews
- 140-150,000 Poles
- 23,000 Roma
- 15,000 Soviet POWs
- 25,000 others

Of the 1.3 million, 1.1 million died, including approximately 90% of the Jews. This was not only in the gas chambers (only Jews and Roma were gassed). Those prisoners made to work were given a diet so low on calories that it was not possible for them to survive more than a few months. In another building we saw mug shot photographs of hundreds of prisoners - taken before the Nazis decided photographs were too expensive a means of identification and started tattooing prisoners instead. The photographs were labelled with the prisoners' arrival dates and death dates. The longest I saw was about four months. For some, it was mere weeks. Our guide explained that to survive, you did not simply need to be a strong worker. You had to be allocated an easier job, particularly one that was inside, and you *had* to have some way of getting extra food – the diet they gave you would kill you. It wasn't designed to keep prisoners alive, because they had thousands more they could bring to replace the dead ones.

Those who survived also needed to be incredibly strong mentally. Incredibly strong. The vast majority of them were men. In that first building our guide showed us a photograph of a group of people arriving at Auschwitz, the majority of them women and children under 10. From the age of the children we can immediately tell that this is the group being sent to the gas chambers. For every transport of Jews and Roma, as soon as the people got off the train they were immediately split into two groups, the men and the women. The children would stay with the women. Children from 14 up were eligible to be taken to work, but every child under that age was gassed immediately - apart from twins, on whom they wanted to do medical experiments to find out how to get Aryan women to bear more babies. If you are a woman arriving at a terrifying concentration camp with your children, you will stay with them, won't you? There were male Auschwitz survivors of all ages from 14 up (though no old men, of course), but all women who had young children were gassed, and that was pretty much every young woman from age 19 to 35. In the photographs of prisoners who weren't gassed immediately I saw some older women, but most were very young. They were the ones who didn't have children.

Looking at this photograph of mothers and children marching to their deaths, our guide said, "I am showing you this photograph so that you know that the majority of people who were gassed were women and children. The vast majority of Auschwitz survivors were men."

One of the Auschwitz I buildings is dedicated entirely to the possessions of the people who were murdered there. First, there's a pile of spectacles about the size of a large kitchen table. There's an entire room full of shoes. There's half a room (and these are big display rooms) full of pots, pans, bowls and other kitchen items. These people were told not that they were going to a concentration camp, and certainly not that they were going to be killed, but that they would be "resettled". This is what the Jews believed, and what the majority of civilians in the places they had left believed too. This is how our guide described it:

"The way people were thinking was not necessarily that the Jews are bad people. We have some living in our apartment building; they've been our neighbours for years and they are very nice people, but the thing is that there are just too many of them. There are too many where we are – if some of them could be sent away to somewhere else, it would be better for all of us."

She looked around the tour group. "Have you heard this before?" she asked.

She paused.

"Do you have groups of people like that in your country? When, sometimes, some of them are deported, do you object; do you try to stop it?"

She looked around the group again. Out of 25, only one nodded. It was me. But I did it very gingerly, because I know that I do not do enough for those people...

"*That* is how this started," our teacher guide said with finality, as she turned and led us to the next room.

Of the Jews and Roma who were brought to Auschwitz, some were coming from ghettoes and some from other camps, all over Europe. They were told simply that they would be resettled; that they would be given somewhere to live in some other place. They had no choice but to go and no idea where they were going, but they thought that they would start a new life there, and the Nazis needed them to think that because they wanted them to bring all their most valuable possessions. Each person was allocated one suitcase. Everything in them was stolen - the valuable things sold and the non-valuable things given to German charities. All the clothing they had taken off before their "shower", the same. And after they had all died, Jewish prisoners were made to cut the hair off the corpses (that was valuable too), to pull out any teeth that had gold fillings, and to do a cavity search for hidden gold or diamonds. A full cavity search of thousands of naked corpses. Only Jewish prisoners were made to do this. Then they cremated them and sifted through the ashes to look for any jewels that had been swallowed or gold fillings that had missed the first search.

What we were seeing in this building was whatever the Nazis hadn't had time to dispose of. For example, when the camp was liberated, several hundred kilograms of hair was found, mechanically packed into scores of large sacks with the contents and point of origin clearly labelled. They were destined for various textile factories in Germany. They knew exactly what they were getting...

179

The sacks have been emptied and the hair placed in a display case. The pile of hair is maybe 20m long, 2m wide and 1m high. In some places you can see braids, some so small they must have come from a little girl.

There are children's boots, children's clothing... and the suitcases: most clearly labelled with the person's name, point of origin and often birth date. For many reasons, these are the most humanising items in the museum because they give the victims' names. The Nazis didn't record their names. They recorded how many they killed, but they didn't record their names. The birth dates are particularly poignant. Not all of the items are from people who were gassed – suitcases, hair and clothes were taken from everyone - but the birth dates will clearly tell you if that person was a child. Our guide pointed out a suitcase belonging to a girl who was only one year old. I saw one for a boy who was four. Probably their parents gave them suitcases so the whole family could bring extra things with them. They were probably packed by their mothers, who died with them.

Then we saw the prison. I have mentioned that Polish political prisoners were tried here in under a minute. The difference between them and the Auschwitz prisoners was they got a trial. Some went on to become Auschwitz prisoners, but most were executed in the yard next door. They were instructed to turn around before being shot. Many refused.

I've also mentioned that Auschwitz prisoners who did or did not obey the rules were kept here as punishment. Sometimes this punishment was to be shut in a dark cell, but usually not alone. One time they shut 39 people in there. By morning, 20 had suffocated to death.

There were also "standing cells" of about one square metre where they would put five people.

There's a memorial in one of the normal cells to a priest who sacrificed his life to save another prisoner. Ten prisoners were randomly selected to be sentenced to death because another prisoner had escaped. This is what I mean when I say "did or did not obey the rules": a big deterrent to escape from Auschwitz was that everyone knew the other prisoners would be punished for it. Their families could be interned for it, too - if they were not of an ethnicity that required that all of their family members had already suffered that.

One of the men selected broke down and begged for his life. The priest stepped forward and said, "Take me instead." The sentence was death by starvation. The priest took too long to die, so they poisoned him.

The man he saved survived Auschwitz and dedicated his life to telling the story.

But our guide pointed out that such instances of solidarity and support among prisoners were fairly rare. For one thing, they spoke 21 languages, so it was likely that one may not be able to communicate with one's bunkmates. Secondly, the Nazis tried their best to pit them against each other. Each bunkhouse was overseen by a prisoner who had their own room and extra rations because they did exactly what the Nazis told them to, including betraying their fellows on a regular basis. Everyone else slept on three-tiered bunks which were very crowded, and in Birkenau in particular they were not well constructed, so sometimes one collapsed in the night. You would certainly want to be on the top bunk if that happened. Also, many people were sick and starving and they were not allowed to get up in the night to go to the toilet, which is another good reason to want the top bunk – to avoid having someone with diarrhoea above you. So people would fight each other to get to the top bunks, and the Nazis encouraged this.

The first gassing of a large number of Jews took place in 1941 in a building just outside the fence of Auschwitz I. It was not purpose built, so it was not as efficient as the ones constructed later at Birkenau. There were no change rooms – the victims were made to undress outside. "Their feeling as they entered this building was not fear, it was shame," our guide said. They were naked in front of hundreds of people. They did not know they were going to die.

The gas chamber is a large, dark room in a building built partially under a hill. The room is the size of a medium-sized dance hall or church. There are square holes in the ceiling through which the gas pellets were dropped. Unlike in some later gas chambers, there were no dummy shower heads.

In the very next room are the huge ovens of the crematorium.

A stone's throw from this building stands the Commandant's house, where he lived with his wife and children. Many wives and children lived at Auschwitz - apparently they thought it was a wonderful place to live because it was away from the front line. They liked it so much that when the first commandant got another posting somewhere else, his wife and children elected to stay at Auschwitz.

After a quick break, we took a shuttle bus to Birkenau, which is 3km away. Birkenau looks nothing like Auschwitz I. For one thing, it's much bigger. It has hundreds of small camp buildings, arranged in row after row after row either side of the railway tracks. On one side of the railway tracks are brick bunkhouse buildings which were built using materials taken from the homes of Poles who had formerly lived in the area. They were very poorly constructed using only one layer of bricks, so in many places supporting beams have been set up to protect the heritage site.

After the bricks ran out, they started building wooden bunkhouses which had been pre-fabricated in Germany – they were stables for the German army. The modern army didn't need so many stables anymore, so the Nazis thought housing people in stables was a great way to find a use for them.

Most of these buildings were burned down when the Nazis attempted to hide evidence of their crimes as they fled the approaching Soviets. All you can see now is hundreds of chimneys. The stables came with prefabricated heaters to keep the horses warm. The Nazis did not bother to light the heaters to keep the prisoners warm.

At the entrance to the camp is a large brick building with a tower. On the other side of that are the railway tracks – one line going through, and two branching off to either side of a long, low platform. I have seen this image in films. It's harrowing to see it in real life and to imagine thousands of people arriving there, climbing down from cramped cattle wagons to be led to their death...

The journey took days and days, sometimes a whole week, depending on where they were coming from. They were not allowed to leave the cattle wagons for that entire time. There was nowhere to sit or to sleep, and nowhere to go to the toilet. They must have been quite relieved to finally arrive and be able to get out - although at the same time they were disappointed to see that they had arrived at another camp, not at the promised "resettlement area". After days and days on a train, though, it made absolute sense that the first thing they should do was to have a shower. Of course they wanted to have a shower - wouldn't you? So they were split into gender-segregated groups. This was the first time families were separated.

Then, each group was split again. The men were split into those deemed fit to work and those not. Those deemed fit were led off to have a real shower, to have their heads shaved and their possessions taken, and then to be let in to the camp. This is what *everybody* thought would happen to them. So when, for example, a young man was separated from his ageing father or grandfather on the train platform (quite likely both, as the people were transported in whole family groups), they at first tried to resist being separated but were unable to so. As they were led away from each other they would call out, "I will see you in the camp!" They really thought they would. But we know what happened to the "unfit" men.

Meantime, the children were still with the women. All those who looked under 14 were put straight into the "unfit" line, no questions asked (apart from twins). But when a child looked as though they may be over 14, an officer would ask the mother, "How old is your child?"

These people had no idea that the big red brick building up ahead was a gas chamber and crematorium – they thought it was a bathroom. No-one had ever attempted genocide on this scale before; *no-one* was expecting it.

The families had already been split once. The women had already been separated from their husbands, fathers, brothers and uncles. Their priority was to keep their children with them. Also, they knew that the reason the Nazis were asking that question was that children over 14 would be sent to work in harsh conditions. Their mothers didn't want that. So, in many cases, if a son or daughter was 14, 15, 16, even 17, their mother would lie and say that they were 13. And so they would be sent to the gas chambers with her and their younger siblings.

The gas chambers of Birkenau survive only as crumpled ruins. The Nazis blew them up as they were leaving. One was destroyed earlier by a rebellion of the Jewish prisoners who were responsible for shaving, searching and cremating the bodies. They realised that less and less transports were coming and that they would soon be out of a job, which meant they would be killed. They hoped other prisoners would join their rebellion but they didn't, still hoping that they might survive. All the rebels were killed, but they went out fighting and they managed to burn down a gas chamber.

We didn't see the ruins of that one but we saw two which were either side of the train tracks - which means they were the most efficient, as they were right next to where the victims got off the train. They were purpose built. The size of the gas chamber can't be easily seen because of the rubble, but it can easily be seen that it was much smaller than the change room.

The change room was large enough for a couple of thousand people to get undressed. The people at the end would start filing in to the "bathroom", ready for their shower. More people would keep coming, and those already inside would say to them, "Hey, what are you doing? There isn't enough room for you in here - we won't be able to wash properly!" But the people coming in couldn't do anything about it because there were soldiers in the change room pushing them all into the "bathroom". The people already inside could do nothing either because they were already trapped. Collectively, they realised that this could not be a shower because the soldiers were pushing them in like sardines. They had not realised it before, but now they knew they were going to die. Many panicked; many prayed. The mothers were the most calm, holding their children and telling them they loved them.

Our guide said, "They were singing and screaming when the doors closed."

I do not know where she got this information. The soldiers must have described it, the sick bastards.

There's a memorial there, a sculpture, and the following message written in 22 languages: the 21 spoken by the victims and inmates, and English.

Forever let this place be a cry of despair
And a warning to humanity,
Where the Nazis murdered about one and a half
million men, women and children, mainly Jews, from
various countries of Europe.
Auschwitz-Birkenau
1940-1945

Within ten minutes, everyone would be dead. They would open the chamber after half an hour, aerate it and begin the desecration and cremation. That would take all day, which is why they were so keen to cram as many people as possible in there so they could kill them all in one day. And they still didn't think their "efficiency" was high enough...

A second memorial is located where some bodies were burned outside when the crematorium was full - what they needed to improve their "efficiency" was more ovens, not more gas chambers - and where crematorium ashes were dumped. Our guide told us that it was highly likely that there were diaries and personal possessions of prisoners buried in the area. Some have already been found, but they cannot disturb the area around the crematoriums for fear of disturbing the ashes and upsetting survivors and relatives. So, they will remain where they are, for now.

Next we saw through a brick bunkhouse, and then a stable one and a stable toilet building. There were two long concrete benches with two rows of bottom-sized holes in each. Beneath them was water, which was pretty impressive sanitation for the time. Survivors have said that Auschwitz had the best sanitation they had ever seen. The Nazis bothered with this for fear of disease – they were cramming together hundreds of thousands of people from all across Europe, and who know what they were spreading with them. The toilets still stank like hell and the diseases spread anyway, but perhaps they would have spread more without the sanitation.

Because the toilet stable stank so much, it was the only building the officers wouldn't go into, so the prisoners had some privacy there and they could socialise while waiting to go to the toilet. For many, this was where they waited to see the relatives they'd been separated from on the train platform. They knew about the gas chambers, but they also knew how huge the camp was - it was possible that their relatives survived somewhere.

They were in denial. You would be, wouldn't you, if your whole family had been pushed into that other line.

That was the end of the tour, so I hope I am nearing the end of this account because it's bloody depressing to have to relive the most depressing day of my trip every time I open my journal. But there are a few other things I want to mention: firstly the people, who they were and where they were from. The number of Jews in Europe at the time actually wasn't that large, but Hitler made it larger by making everyone who had even one Jewish grandparent "Jewish". They came from every country the Nazis occupied. The only occupied country whose Jews were largely able to escape extermination was Denmark, and only because Sweden opened its borders to fleeing Jews. They were boat people. Sweden saved their lives. No other European country did this – small numbers escaped elsewhere, but they had to get documents and permission. Sweden just let them all in, and this was the only thing that saved the lives of the Danish Jews. Our guide said that if the other free countries of Europe had opened their borders, the Holocaust may not have happened. There are many "ifs" in history...

The Jews of countries who were allies of Nazi Germany were mostly spared from transportation to Auschwitz initially, but Hitler had a tendency to turn on those countries and make them his enemies instead. In the case of Hungary, it was the other way around. With the Soviet Army making great gains against the Nazi army, the Hungarian government decided to negotiate with them in the hope of avoiding a Soviet invasion. The result was a Nazi invasion, and the immediate deportation of all the Hungarian Jews to Auschwitz. 400,000 people were deported in 56 days. The average percentage per transport to be immediately gassed was 75%, so that means about 300,000 Hungarians were murdered. They came in on over a hundred transports, so that means 40,000 per transport, 30,000 killed per transport, and given the time period it was two transports per day, so that's 60,000 deaths per day. That was the point when the crematoriums started overflowing. It was also the point when the Nazis were starting to lose the war, so why were they bothering to... oh Jesus, I don't get it - I'll never get it, so there's no point even trying to understand a Nazi...

And now to the Roma people. They are usually forgotten in Holocaust discussion, but actually they were the only group to be targeted as much as the Jews were by the Nazis. They were the only people apart from Jews to be gassed. But, though in the 1940s there were more Jews in Europe (under Hitler's definition) than Roma, now there are more Roma. There are up to 15 million of them - more than the population of many EU nations.

"That's 15 million people with no country," said our guide. "The Jews now have Israel, but the Roma have nowhere." They are also one of the most unpopular groups in European society. "If something like this were to happen today, targeting Roma people, where would they go?" our guide asked. "Would your country open its borders to 15 million Roma?"

That night, we wandered around Krakow rather listlessly, utterly harrowed by what we had seen. We took a very long time to find something to eat, because nothing inspired us. Alma seemed to be taking it harder than me - I guess my emotional blocking mechanism was working in overdrive - but it really hit me the next morning when I was taking a shower. I was naked in a windowless room. I imagined over a hundred others crammed into the same bathroom. The water threatened to suffocate me. I have always thought that suffocation would be the most terrifying way to die...

And it was *so* recent, and yes the world changed a lot in the 20th century, but it didn't change that much. People still hate Roma and Jews. People still elect idiots. People still jump on crazy bandwagons and subscribe to overpowering group mentalities.

In our tour group, there was a woman carrying a baby. They would have been killed, not so long ago. In the visitor centre toilets I saw a woman combing her hair. I thought of the museum room full of hairbrushes that belonged to thousands of women who used to stand in front of mirrors fixing their hair just like this woman was. It so easily could have been her. It was so recent. And the reason we can't understand it is we can't believe it, but it *did* happen, so... could it happen again?

That's why every citizen of the world should go to Auschwitz. So it won't happen again. It's harrowing to see, but everyone should see it. Just make sure you're not in a bad place mentally at the time and make sure you have easy access to plenty of chocolate afterwards.

The fog, the factory and the mountain

So. The day after Auschwitz, Thursday the 19th of June, in Krakow. After emerging from the shower I entered the hostel's breakfast room, which had one of the best hostel breakfasts I've ever encountered – several kinds of cheese, two kinds of cereal, filter coffee, bread, jam and chocolate spread. I am not a sweet tooth and I am a diabetic, so on every other morning we were there I went straight for the cheese. But that morning I had *five* pieces of bread smothered in *thick*, twice-applied layers of chocolate spread. And I needed it.

We were quite listless after the previous day – I'm gonna call it the Post-Auschwitz Fog. To anyone going to Krakow, I would recommend going to Auschwitz on your last day. There are very many things to do in Krakow, but even though we spent four days there, we missed a lot of them because the day after Auschwitz we were so damn foggy we barely managed to do anything.

The walking tour company had a Jewish tour, for example, which went through the pre-WWII Jewish quarter and the WWII ghetto and would have been fascinating to do, but there was no way we could face it in the Post-Auschwitz Fog. Instead we did the Street Art Tour, which was interesting but let's face it, in a city as fascinating as Krakow, a tour about street art is never going to be as good as a tour about Jews, communists or medieval

187

times. Still, it was something different, and we needed that to help us get out of the fog. Which it did, but it also absolutely knackered us because the route was longer than the other tours, and it was sunny and it involved climbing a hill, so by the end of it we were in a much better state mentally but a much worse state physically!

We went to the Jewish quarter, Kazimierz, which I instantly liked even better than the Old Town because it was more cultured and less pristine. Street art is allowed in Kazimierz but not in the Old Town, even though both are heritage listed, because Kazimierz's buildings are still run down. This makes them appear more real, less poncey, and certainly less tourist-ridden.

A surprising number of synagogues survived the war. We went inside one called Remuh Synagogue. It was quite small, but had lovely frescoes and a prayer book with English translations, which was interesting to read. There was an attached cemetery with many rectangular gravestones, which my guidebook said were Renaissance style. I still can't pick Renaissance style – I can pick Gothic and Baroque, but not Renaissance. I love Baroque: it's a little easier to identify a style when there are angels singing in your head.

The graves were in very neat rows, completely unlike the Jewish cemetery in Warsaw (they were all standing up, for one thing). We later found out that this was because the entire cemetery had been bulldozed by the Nazis and it had been reconstructed later.

The next day we went to the Oskar Schindler Museum, not realising that, while it is located inside Schindler's factory, it doesn't actually tell you very much about it. It's actually an Occupation museum, going into great detail on every aspect of the Nazi occupation of Poland from 1939-1945, and the impact on Krakow in particular. It does so very well, with photos, video, text and amazing reconstructions of places in Krakow at the time (the ghetto wall, for example). But there's only a small display on the enamelware factory and on who Schindler was.

He was a German entrepreneur who came in with the invaders and got the factory cheap because it'd been stripped from a Jewish company. The only reason he had Jews working for him initially was that they were cheap. He had to pay a fee to the Nazis per Jew – it sounds a bit like a slave hire fee – and he didn't have to pay the workers anything at all. But he didn't want them to die, and he spent all his income and his reserves on saving them. He even constructed housing for them after the ghetto was liquidated, so they wouldn't have to live in a concentration camp.

There are many interviews with Schindler's Jews in the museum. They all say it was a wonderful place to work and that the conditions were so much better than anywhere else, even though they had to work for 12 hours a day with no pay. That shows how awful the other places must have been. They got food, and it was much better food than anywhere else – Schindler got a lot of it on the black market.

Nobody had a choice but to work there, though – everybody was just allocated a job, the non-Jews too.

That somebody who was within the Nazi system can take a stand and say, "No!", risking everything he had to do it, really shows the kind of person we should all be. The Holocaust happened because ordinary people, both within the system and outside it - who in other circumstances probably would have been normal, decent human beings - got caught up in the group mentality, the propaganda and the fear and did not say no. If they had, it wouldn't have happened...

We should all take a leaf out of Schindler's book. No matter who you are, you *can* make a difference in the face of injustice.

Next we travelled to Zakopane, which is in the far south of Poland near the Tatra National Park or, more specifically, the Polish Tatras. The Slovakian border runs right through them and there are many more Slovakian Tatras too.

The following morning, we took a bus to the national park entrance and paid 5 zloty to get in. We were going to Lake Morskie Oko, but it was still 8km away, up a road that ordinary people and buses aren't allowed to drive on - but my guidebook had mentioned that it was possible to take a horse and carriage ride to the lake instead. This sounded like a good way to see the national park in style.

The rides were quite popular so there was a large queue of people waiting at the horse and carriage stop. I can't say "bus stop", but that's what it looked like. Alma asked the people in front of us if they were waiting for the horses, to check we were in the right place. I'm always very wary of doing that because I hate having to talk a foreign language at people, but fortunately in Poland everybody speaks English, especially these people. One had worked in New York, two had worked in England, and even the two children they had with them could speak English fluently. They were also among the friendliest people I have ever met, and we ended up becoming great mates and staying together all day!

There was a young couple called Gosha and Dominic – they were the two who'd lived in England; in fact they'd met there and had only recently moved back to Poland. There was a man called Marius who'd lived in New York and in England too – they were all very worldly people! He was maybe in his 40s and he had with him his two children, Yulia and Max. Yulia was about 14 and Max about 12. We never got around to asking their ages or how they were related to Gosha and Dominic, but they seemed to be family because they were all travelling together.

It took an hour for the open-air carriage to get up to the lake. It started to rain fairly heavily, and at some point we became aware that there was mist in front of us, but only in a very specific area. It turned out it was coming from the horses' bodies! The rain fell on them, and because they were so hot from climbing the mountain it evaporated immediately!

The rain had stopped by the time we got out, but we were bloody cold, so we accepted our newfound friends' offer to join then in the restaurant. We had sandwiches with us, but we bought some hot tea with rum. Then we walked to the lake, which was very pretty with mountains all around and bits of streaky snow. Unfortunately, there were so many people you almost had to fight for a spot at the front of the viewing platform to take a photo. It turns out that in Europe, national parks are just as crowded as beaches! On the road we went up with the horses, the stream of walkers never ever stopped. Walk along the lake a little way, though, and they do thin out.

We were very happy to be seeing the lake and the mountains in the sun because Alma and I are more than a little cursed when it comes to seeing mountains clearly, or even seeing them at all. The first time we travelled together, in Kyushu in Japan, we went up a live volcano called Mt Aso. Not only was it covered in cloud so thick we could barely see the other side of the road, it was also covered in poisonous gases. We sat in the visitor centre all day waiting from them to clear. They didn't. We saw no mountain.

A few months later, we went to Everest Base Camp. We had some beers we'd brought from Lhasa to drink looking out at Everest, but could we see Everest? Not in the slightest. Alma's fingers turned orange as we determinedly drank the beer in the rain and cold whilst looking out at cloud.

18 months later, Alma visited me in Tasmania. I took her up kunanyi / Mt Wellington. Could we see anything from the top? Hell no!

It's not me that's cursed, though, because I've been to clear mountains on my own plenty of times; I even went to Mt Aso a week after I went there with Alma and it was shining in bright sunshine with no poisonous gases anywhere. I thought it might be the combination of me and her together,

190

but she told me that earlier this year she went to see cherry blossoms at Mt Fuji, and that she saw many beautiful cherry blossoms, but no Mt Fuji. So it's not me that's cursed, it's her.

We were, therefore, overjoyed to see the lake and mountains in sunshine because it was a very new thing for us, but not 15 minutes later it started raining again and the mountains got covered in a blanketing mist! Cursed, I tell you.

We had a very pleasant walk, despite the rain. We climbed up to a second lake on a saddle further up. It wasn't high, but it was steep. Alma's been complaining about hills ever since.

Slovakian towns

The main thing to see in Slovakia is mountains, which is heaven for me with my passion for hiking, but not good for city girl Alma who doesn't like hills. That's fine, though, because I had changed my travel itinerary around. I'd only known she was coming since about St Petersburg, and I already had a travel plan before then which had me going from Zakopane to all the Slovakian Tatras and various other hiking places, then briefly to Hungary and then Vienna - bypassing Bratislava altogether. So when Alma told me she wanted to come and join me I asked her, "Do you like hiking?"

and she said, "Erm...no..."

and I said, "Actually if I go to the Slovakian mountains with you they'll be hopelessly cloudy and rainy!" So I changed my travel plan to quickly bisect Slovakia after Poland - making a beeline for Hungary, which Alma was more interested in - and to travel Slovakia alone later. I gave her a list of non-mountain-climbing Slovakian destinations we could visit in between Poland and Hungary, and she chose Spišské Podhradie and Levoca. They're close together but neither has a hostel so, after much discussion, including contemplating staying in a third place which did have a hostel but which sounded completely boring, we settled on a pension in Spišské Podhradie.

Then, when Alma was in a wifi café in Zakopane, she looked up how to get there and became very worried that it was quite "in the middle of nowhere". Staying in a small town didn't bother me, but I knew there are small towns in Tasmania with accommodation places way out in the fields or the bush somewhere that claim to be in that town when they aren't, so I appreciated her worry. She said she hadn't been able to find the bus stop on Google Maps, so we didn't know where we would arrive in the town. This could have been an issue, but it's usually a fair bet that in the absence of a bus station a bus will let you off right in the middle of the town. After discussing things a little more, I realised that actually Alma did know where the pension was in relation to the centre of town and that it wasn't far.

It became apparent eventually, after various discussions and mentions of "middle of nowhere" and also a fair few mentions of Bratislava, that actually Alma was more ill at ease with the simple fact of it being a small town. From the way she was talking, I was picturing it being a blip of a village with no restaurants or shops open - which would have been a problem, as we had no food with us. When we got there I was quite surprised to see that it was at least a medium-sized town with a good few thousand people living there, which would have been noticeable on Google Maps owing to the number of close together streets that would have been visible. I don't know, I didn't see the map, but Alma did and her conclusion was that it was tiny and in the middle of nowhere and that this would be a problem (she is from Manhattan, remember). And she kept mentioning Bratislava, Slovakia's capital, for some reason, which we were planning on visiting at the end of the trip. She said we should allow for at least two days there. I'd read the Bratislava entry in the travel guide and previously decided not to go there at all because it didn't sound very interesting. I wondered if she knew something I didn't. "Has someone recommended Bratislava to you?" I asked.

"No," she replied.

"Why do you want to go there so badly, then?" I asked. "Is there something in particular you want to see there?"

Her response, I tell you no lie (I don't exaggerate in this journal), was simply, "It's a city!!"

In her defence, she had also seen on Google Street View the train station of Spišské Podhradie, which caused a large portion of her worry. We saw it in real life the next morning, and it is probably the shadiest place I have seen on this entire trip. But we didn't arrive at the train station, we arrived by bus in the centre of town and it was only about 500m from our accommodation! Got there very easily, me marvelling at the charming pastel-coloured Slovakian town buildings and loving it, and Alma getting scared by the lack of people and the many abandoned buildings we passed. I didn't even notice the abandoned buildings! Because I'm not a big city person I am very trusting and I don't always notice when there are potentially dangerous things about, so she points them out for me, which keeps me safe. In return I say, "Yes you can climb this hill; it's not far to the top," and, "It's OK that there are hardly any people and most of the shops are closed – small towns are meant to be like that."

This isn't new for me because actually I've never had an Australian travel partner - not for overseas travel, anyway - but it's really cool travelling with someone from somewhere else because then I can learn about their home as well as about wherever we're travelling. So, for example, I learned that there are no public toilets in New York City, and that in Time Square there are people dressed up as Disney characters who fight with each other. And I was telling her about my amazing discovery of the heating systems in Mongolia, Russia and Soviet Bloc apartment buildings: how they're only turned on for half the year but for that time, they're always turned on and you can't change the temperature, and she looked at me funny and said, "Is that weird? My apartment building has that."

So anyway, Spišské Podhradie. We checked into our accommodation, which had cute kittens and our room had a private balcony with a perfect view of Spišs Castle (pronounced "Spish Castle"). Our first priority was to go out and get food, because I knew the restaurants wouldn't stay open long (it was a Sunday night). We started walking along the street, where the sky was starting to turn pink, and Alma said, "Maybe we should get take-out."

"Oh, and eat it watching the sunset?" I asked.

"No, because I don't wanna walk back in the dark."

It was so sweet how scared she was of the smallest town we visited on the whole trip! I was actually quite sick of eating out, so I went along with her suggestion thinking maybe we could just get something from a supermarket and save some money. We found one supermarket that had closed at 4:30pm! But on the main square - a beautiful place, the castle high on the hill behind it - we found another one that was open.

It was a very small supermarket, and we must have walked all the way around it at least four times trying to find something appropriate to eat. Our accommodation had no kitchen but it did have a kettle, so we got 2-minute noodles. Alma suggested putting them with pasta sauce to make them more interesting, but we couldn't find pasta sauce so we bought some packets of cup-a-soup to put with our noodles! My portion of the meal cost €1.65, including the beer. It was the weirdest meal I've had in a long time. We had to boil the water in the bathroom because that was where the only spare power point was, and cook the noodles/soup in my plastic container -

of which I only have one, so we couldn't eat together; we had to take it in turns!!

The next day, we went to Spiŝs Castle. It's the biggest ruined castle in Europe. It sits on a steep hill next to Spiŝské Podhradie and is surrounded by fields. It's visible for miles around and must have been a very strong fortification.

I'm not that into ruined castles because I find it hard to imagine what things must have been like, but this one had an excellent audio guide which told intriguing stories in a very amusing dramatic fashion with particularly entertaining sound effects. It was a hoot – and it helped us to understand a bit about the lords and knights who lived in the castle and their trials and tribulations. It said that the castle had mostly been a Hungarian stronghold, and that was how I learned that most of Slovakia used to be part of Hungary, and later the Austro-Hungarian Empire.

This was the day that we gave up on having sandwiches for lunch, because that beautiful Baltic rye bread was no longer available and so sandwiches had become boring. However, that day wasn't the best day to start our new "buy lunch as you go" plan because for some reason the only things available for consumption at the castle were ice creams, coffee and beer. However, the place that had the beer was also offering a Slovak sausage and something that seemed to be just bread and mustard. As this was apparently the only vegetarian food there apart from ice cream, I ordered it. "Is no sausage?" I asked the waitress and she replied in the affirmative, which is why I was very surprised when she served me a sausage.

This was how Alma came to eat two sausages for lunch, one of which was enormous, the other thinner and looking more like a frankfurter. Both had orange fat pouring out of them and she said both had gristle too, so that wasn't such a good lunch for her. All I had was three small bits of bread and mustard that had been supposed to be a side dish, so my lunch didn't work out either. Fortunately, the beer was excellent – the Slovaks are very good at dark beer.

That afternoon we took a bus to Levoca, where we stayed in another lovely place in the Old Town, which had fruit trees in its garden and the cherries were ripe! That evening we had dinner in a restaurant in an atmospheric stone cellar. Alma had pierogies (Polish dumplings with filling) and I had something which I can't remember what the translation was but it was basically a slab of grilled cheese – no bread, just cheese, but it came with potatoes and salad. It was nice, and it seemed to be a traditional meal. Alma loves trying local food specialties, so the next day, when we had lunch in an interesting diner-themed café, she ordered the same thing. It came out as breaded and fried cheddar-like cheese with chips and tartare sauce, and it really tasted like fish and chips! My Facebook status that day was: "Landlocked country? Lack of fish? No problem. Take a large hunk of cheese, cover it in batter or breadcrumbs, and deep fry. Serve with chips and tartare sauce."

In Levoca the old town walls are almost entirely intact, and the main sight in the Old Town is St Jakob's Church. It's got an enormous main altar and many smaller altars, all carved with intricate images - some from as far back as the 15th century - and some very old frescoes also. But you aren't allowed to take any photos, and the staff member was umm... This is where we learnt how terrible Slovakian customer service is. The staff member told us that we could only enter the church on a tour, which was in Slovak, but that she would give us an English explanation sheet that we could walk around with. We were glad of that because the people on the tour had to sit and sit and sit while she recited something she had clearly learned by heart and said every hour with no trace of expression or interest in her voice. Even when she used gestures, which was very rare, they looked choreographed. Worst tour guide I have even seen.

But we were quite happy wandering around with our little English explanation sheet, so much so that we didn't notice when the tour ended and everybody else left the church. We then found ourselves locked inside said church, fortunately not alone because there were some workmen refurbishing some things in there. Two other workmen were trying to get into the church and she'd locked them out. They called out to her and she wandered over slowly, unlocked the gate and calmly demanded our English explanation sheet back, not offering any apology for locking us into the church.

Then we went to the church shop, because since we hadn't been able to take photographs I wanted to buy some postcards instead. We were looking around the shop when the tour guide's equally sullen-looking colleague said, "Pay now please, I will have lunch now," and kicked us out!!

That afternoon, we took two buses and a train to Hungary, but before I leave eastern Slovakia I must mention the large number of Roma people we saw there. This is something I needed Alma to point out to me, as I had never seen a Roma person before and I simply assumed I was seeing large numbers of Indian immigrants. We had learned at Auschwitz that the Roma people are originally from India – I hadn't known that. It was many centuries ago so I didn't expect them to still look Indian, but the ones in eastern Slovakia really do. On the Spišs Castle audio guide we learned about a lord of the castle who had a soft spot for a certain Roma princess, and who had been asked by the Roma people for protection. He issued a decree granting it, instructing all his subjects to take care of the Roma and help them if they needed it, and offering them permanent protection within his kingdom. Their descendants still live there today, lots and lots of them – I think 50% of the people we saw on the street in Spišské Podhradie and Levoca were Roma, maybe more. Not in cafes and shops, mind, but on the streets. They are poorer than the Slovaks and apparently they are looked down upon by them...

The Blue Danube

The first place we went to in Hungary was Eger (pronounced "egg-air"), a small city in the north east which is known for its wine production. Unfortunately we had less than 24 hours there because I'd managed to stuff up our itinerary and lose a day, but fortunately there were only two main things we wanted to do there: soak in a historic Turkish bath and drink some wine, and we managed to do both.

Usually it would make sense to do the wine second, right? Given that people don't usually drink in the mornings, and also that it's not advisable to drink before going swimming. However, the bath didn't open until 3pm, so we had to do the wine first!!

I'm not sure exactly what the Valley of the Beautiful Women is called in Hungarian, but the English translations on all the signs leading to it say, "Nice Women Valley"! There's a little tourist train that takes you there from town. It's gorgeous.

The main tasting area is a small semi-circular depression in a hill, which has a semi-circular road going around it connecting a good two dozen wine cellars which are tunnelled into the hill. Each one has tables both outside and in and offers 100mL tasting glasses for 300-700 forints (US$1.50-$3.50) of bottled wines and 100-300 forints (50c-$1.50) for wines straight from the barrel, which are served from glass jugs.

Bull's Blood is the speciality of the region, and the story goes that the Hungarians of Eger held off a Turkish invasion because they were drinking this wine and the Turks thought they were drinking bull's blood. The Turks came back with a successful invasion later, though, hence the Turkish bath.

Also in the Nice Women Valley are some wine cellar shops, whose entrances look a little sketchy but are essentially the same thing: caverns going back into the hill, with various kinds of plastic receptacles hanging from their doors - from tiny barrel-shaped thingies to enormous four or five litre plastic bottles with handles on top. You can buy wine in these, or you can bring your own bottle. We had a look inside one cellar shop just as a lady was walking in with an empty 500mL Coke bottle. The man inside took it over to an enormous wooden vat at the back, filled the bottle, brought it back over and sold it to her for a very cheap price.

Sketchy indeed, especially the very dark, mould-covered cellar the shop was in, but it's just how they do cellar door sales! Earlier, we'd seen a group of about three people each carrying two of the enormous 4L bottles. It would be a very cheap way of catering for a party. Providing, of course, that the party guests were wild enough to drink absolutely all of it, because, as I learned the hard way at age 15, a plastic bottle will turn wine into vinegar in a very small number of days...

I wonder if the lady with the Coke bottle poured it into a nice carafe when she got home... or if she just drank it from the Coke bottle.

We went to the baths and then moved on to Budapest. We stayed in a charming building there that had a very pretty shop façade and one of those old iron lifts that sit in the middle of the stairwell. We were in the middle of downtown Pest, which unfortunately meant we were bang in the middle of the touristy area. Still, it meant that the next morning we had only a 200m walk to the start point of the free walking tour.

First, the guide told us a bit of Hungarian history. In the pension where we stayed in Eger, I saw a map on the wall which showed that in Hungarian, Hungary is called Magyarország. This surprised me somewhat, but I could see that the names for some of the surrounding countries were completely different to the English ones too, so I didn't think too much about it.

Our Budapest tour guide explained that many centuries ago, in the time of Atilla, the Huns occupied the area which is now Hungary. They lived there for a while, but then they left completely and went back to their home, which was in Asia.

Later, a completely different Asian tribe called the Magyars came and settled the area. The Europeans thought that the Huns were back. The rest of the world has been calling Hungary and its people by the wrong name ever since.

So Hungary was Hungary for a while, and then the Ottomans invaded and it was the Ottoman Empire for a while, and the Hungarians asked Austria for help in kicking the Ottomans out. They gave it but invaded themselves, so then it became part of the Austrian Empire. The reason why we, and the history books, know that empire as the Austro-Hungarian Empire is that, in 1848, the Hungarians had a revolution. The ruling Hapsburgs won out, but then Austria was weakened by a couple of military defeats elsewhere and the Hungarians kept up the pressure, so the Hapsburgs agreed to compromise with them and create a dual monarchy federation-type deal. This gave Hungary some of its own powers again whilst still being part of the Hapsburg Empire, which was renamed the Austro-Hungarian Empire.

That empire disintegrated after WWI, when they were on the losing side. Our Budapest tour guide said that because Austro-Hungary lost the war they were punished by having lots of land given to all their neighbouring countries. The thing is, though, that most of those neighbouring countries didn't exist before that, so was it Hungary's territory being ripped away or was it other peoples and nations they'd previously dominated gaining their independence? What my (later) Bratislava tour guide said was that the Slovaks and Czechs were able to gain independence and finally get their own country because the Austro-Hungarian Empire was no longer strong. It's the same story I'd heard in Poland and the Baltic States – the war weakened the big empires, allowing previously oppressed peoples to take control of their own lives!

My own political leanings cause me to err on the side of the Slovaks in this situation; however, the Western Allies didn't draw the new borderlines in a very sensible or careful way. Apparently Bratislava wasn't even very Slovak, but the Allies granted it to Czechoslovakia because they had requested a Danube port! In Hungary, people still call it by its Hungarian name, Pressburg. When we were checking out of our Budapest hostel and the receptionist asked me where we were going next, I said, "Bratislava," which is only 200km away, and he said, "I'm sorry, I don't know which city that is." He had to look it up! Many tourists travel straight from Budapest to Bratislava, but he still hadn't learned the international name for it...

But I'm getting ahead of myself. When a country's borders have been a certain way for a long time it is very hard to get people to let go of them, and the Armistice agreement did too much at once, I would say. Because, you see, it caused WWII. We know Germany was crippled by the reparations etc. and Hitler wanted to get it back on its feet, but the reason Hungary joined him is they wanted their land back.

The tour wandered around Pest a bit first, with its elegant 19th century buildings and ordered streets, and then we crossed the Chain Bridge to Buda, looking out at the lovely view of the hills of Buda, the Hapsburg palace on top, the towering church spires and, on the Pest side, the incredible Parliament building. Budapest really is a beautiful city - its buildings match up with the beautiful landscape of the river and the hills and it's just lovely.

As I was walking along the bridge marvelling at all these amazing things I was seeing, it happened. I knew it would. "It's happened!" I said to Alma.

"What has?" she asked.

And I started singing "The Blue Danube".

I have a chronic problem whereby whenever I go to a place that is associated with a particular song or tune, the song or tune jumps into my head uninvited and not remotely controlled by me, and it stays there for the duration of my time in that place and won't go away. I had intelligently anticipated having this problem in Moscow and put "Moscow" by Ghengis Khan onto my phone in preparation, but I did not think to put "The Blue Danube" on there.

The thing is, if you have a song in your head but you cannot listen to the full song, it can never sing itself out – the little bit you know will just keep going round and round like a cracked record. "The Blue Danube" was exciting at first because the river is beautiful, the symphony is tantalising and we were in Budapest, but after four days of the two of us involuntarily humming it non-stop, it got rather annoying.

On our last night in Budapest, Alma looked the piece up on YouTube. It was wonderful to hear it - I was stressed out at the time, and it calmed me right down! But it's ten minutes long, so my brain got confused and wasn't quite able to sing it out of my head. It left by the time I got to Bratislava though, which is ironic given that Bratislava is also on the Danube! But Bratislava just doesn't have the grace that Budapest does...

After the tour ended, we joined the guides for lunch in a cheap Hungarian restaurant! I think it was the Hungarian version of a Polish milk bar. It was certainly cheap and was mainly used by locals, but the food and service was way better than the milk bar! I had an incredible mushroom stew: it tasted a bit like stroganoff. It was served with a pile of small, spindly dumplings a bit like gnocchi. Alma couldn't finish her dumplings and she gave them to me, and by that time I had no stew or sauce left but they were delicious on their own too. I think they had been coated in butter. Yum yum!

Afterwards, we explored the sights of Castle Hill, including Matthias Church - incredible patterned spires and colourful tiles - and the Hospital of the Rocks. Buda, particularly Castle Hill, is built on an extensive network of caves. They have been used throughout history for various purposes including cellars, escape tunnels and bunkers. In WWII, it was decided to build a hospital in the caves so it would be protected from air raids. It's quite small - it was built to house only 60 patients - but during the siege of 1945 and the 1956 uprising, there were hundreds of patients crammed in there.

The museum is very proud of its wax mannequins. It really does bring the hospital to life when you can see a man bleeding everywhere with an expression of extreme pain on his face! They bill it as a "time travel" experience, and it is because they've still got all the original furnishings and original medical supplies, toilets and operating equipment!

In the kitchen, Alma noticed a box labelled "A gift from the American people". We'd only heard about the WWII part at that stage, and she thought it rather odd that America should be giving food to a country allied with the Nazis. She asked the guide and was told that the box dated from 1956, when the hospital reopened just for a few months during the Hungarian uprising against the Communists. It contained milk powder - there had been some kind of food drop, Berlin style.

"Ah, the Cold War," I said, rolling my eyes inwardly.

From the 1960s until the end of the Cold War, the hospital was given a new use as a nuclear bunker. Numerous sophisticated machines were installed to clean the air, along with huge storage drums for water and petrol (for generators). A husband-and-wife team took care of it, living there with their children. Apparently the children used to cycle around the corridors. They'd be great for that - so windy and undulating! The husband's job was to turn all the machines on at least once a week and keep them in perfect working order. The wife's job was the keep the hospital's linen laundered and the equipment clean. The plan was that in the event of a nuclear attack, a select group of doctors would have half an hour to rush to the bunker, and they would seal themselves in for 72 hours. Then they would go out to search for survivors and, if they were able to move and hence likely to survive, bring them back to the hospital for treatment.

The facility was top secret. They even had a secret pipe to the surface for filling up petrol. They'd pretend they were filling up something else on the surface.

To finish our day, we wandered around Castle Hill and the courtyards and promenades of its grand palace (there is no castle, only a palace). Walking around the palace building, we realised that there were several bullet holes which had been patched up rather visibly. I liked that, because the palace still looked grand and you could only see the bullet holes if you were looking for them, but it you did look for them you would find loads and then you could really appreciate how intense the fighting was. Castle Hill was the Nazis' last stronghold. It's possible to identify particular windows they must have been firing out of from the concentration of bullet holes around them.

The Nazis also had a bunker in the cave system of Castle Hill. It was quite near the hospital.

When we got to the front of the palace, which is perched high above the Danube with a fantastic viewing promenade running along its length, the sun was just starting to set. This always takes quite some time to happen, so we spent ages there ignoring our rumbling bellies and taking photos of sunset over the Danube. It wasn't setting over the Danube; it was setting behind the hills of Buda, but the buildings on the Danube looked wonderful and so did the river, and in that light the scenery was just to die for.

The next day we went to St Stephen's Basilica, which, as basilicas usually are, is enormous, with beautiful frescoes etc., though it's not very old: late 19th century. Its main drawcard is St Stephen's hand. Blimey, Catholics and their relics! We actually saw a severed, shrivelled hand, and it turned my stomach - which doesn't often happen. Saint bits and Mongolian goat guts are about all that'll do it...!

St Stephen was the guy who united Hungary, in the late 9th century. Years after his death, they dug him up and found that his left arm was well preserved. They hacked it off, cut it in three and gave the bits to three different churches. Of all the possible bits, I suppose the hand *is* the coolest – the other bits would just look like small logs.

The funniest thing about St Stephen's hand is, though it's in a glass box that's visible to anyone at any time, you can't really see it properly unless you turn the light on. And the only way you can turn the light on is if you put €2 in the slot. This gives you two minutes of light.

Fortunately, our guide the previous day had advised us that we didn't have to pay if we waited around for someone else to put money in the slot. Two huge tour groups did, with their tour guides, so after we'd fought our way through the tourists we got to see and photograph the disgusting severed hand for free! Just what I've always wanted. Alma was quite excited about it - she seems to collect relic experiences. She couldn't believe it when I told her I'd seen a severed saint's head in Ireland!

Then we did a Jewish walking tour. Initially Pest was the centre of commerce but all the Jews were forced to live in Buda, which was very annoying for them because there were no bridges. So, as soon as the area beyond Pest's walls was opened up for settlement, the Jews moved there and they created the Jewish Quarter. Nowadays, like in Krakow, it's the centre of nightlife in the city, and it's a bit run down and has a more charming, grungy feel to it than the rest of Pest.

When the Nazis invaded in 1944, they set up a ghetto within the Jewish Quarter, only in a much smaller area. They gave the people almost no food – the Red Cross had to run soup kitchens to feed them. It was winter time and heating was very minimal.

After the Soviets came in and opened the ghetto, they found the streets littered with bodies. There are mass graves behind the main synagogue where 2,000 people are buried. But what was unique about the Budapest ghetto is that it only operated for six weeks. As we know, the Nazis didn't invade Hungary until near the very end of the war. They installed a Hungarian Nazi party as the government, who resisted the creation of a ghetto. The German Nazis forced them to do it at the very end. At the same time, knowing that the Soviets were coming and that they were losing the war, they were transporting as many Jews as possible to Auschwitz because they knew it was their only chance to kill them... But those were the Jews from other parts of Hungary – the 400,000 in 56 days did not come from Budapest. The Budapest ghetto was never "liquidated" – the Soviets came before that could happen. And when they opened the gates of the ghetto, they found the streets strewn with people who'd mainly died of hunger or cold. TWO THOUSAND IN SIX WEEKS.

These days, of course, there are nowhere near as many Jews living in the Jewish Quarter as there used to be, but there are three surviving synagogues, two of which are still in operation. They're from three different branches of Judaism and they all have interesting architecture – the Orthodox one is art nouveau! And we saw some normal buildings and many very grungy ones. Our guide showed us one that is public housing now and it's really been let go. Now there are some Roma living there. Funny that in the absence of the Jews, another minority group has moved into the Jewish Quarter, but it's a poorer one.

Something the Jewish Quarter of Budapest is very well known for now is "ruin bars". I was picturing bars set up on romantic stone walls or in old cellars, but no no: these are modern ruins. Because of a lack of investment money during the communist period, many of the buildings in the district have become very run down. Even though people could restore them now, many of them (like the public housing one) are so run down their owners know they'll eventually be demolished, so they don't bother. Some concerned young citizens, not wanting this to happen, decided to find a use for the derelict buildings. At first they tried to make moonlight cinemas, but these didn't prove as popular as they'd hoped, so they happened upon the idea of bars. There are now lots of them throughout the district, and they're called "ruin bars". We went to the original one, Szimpla, which is quite an institution now. There are about four bars inside and so many things to look at, from old computer screens to shop dummies to an enormous cassette – anything that's old. Seats range from an exercise horse to a bath tub, and every square centimetre of wall is covered in graffiti. It's quite an experience. We had a nice night there!

The following day, we went to Visegrad as a day trip. I'd chosen it because my guidebook said it was on the Danube Bend and you could walk to a ruined castle on a hill which had a great view of said Bend. I've mentioned how much Alma dislikes climbing hills. When we got there and she saw how steep it was she said, "I think I'll sit in a café in the village." I attempted to encourage her to change her mind, and then I realised that she was wearing sandals, demonstrating that from the time she had got dressed that morning she had no intention of climbing the hill! I wasn't going to ask her to hike in sandals, so I let her go. And that is of course the only reason why it didn't rain and I had beautiful clear views from the top!

We took the ferry back to Budapest, two blissful hours sailing along the Danube... *da da daa daaa...* We thought they should've been playing "The Blue Danube" on the boat, but they weren't so we had to sing it instead.

The weather was perfect; the water was a beautiful blue green; we passed charming towns, much greenery and plenty of kayaks and people enjoying the beaches. Did you know the Danube has beaches? It has lots of them. And I saw from the top of the hill that in this region it has a sandy bottom. What a wonderful place to spend some time. And what a wonderful way to arrive in Budapest!

My friend heart

The next day we travelled to Bratislava, from whence Alma left on the 30th of June. We went for lunch before she left and I ordered "gnocchi with sheep's cheese". It turned out to be the little twirly dumplings I'd had in Hungary, translated as "gnocchi" on the menu. Having those with soft sheep's cheese and cream stirred through them is a staple of Slovak cuisine. It's pretty nice. A couple of days later I had them with cabbage stirred through instead – it tasted like a cross between barbecued onion and sauerkraut. It was surprisingly nice! We also had some of that wonderful Slovakian dark beer.

Amazingly, in the same café, right before Alma left, my friend Karra arrived! Not by coincidence – we were coincidentally in Europe at the same time, but we weren't coincidentally in a café in Bratislava at the same time:

that was planned. Karra is one of my friends from uni. I hadn't seen her for two years. We're both travelling Europe in completely different ways on completely different routes and we weren't sure if our paths would cross, but they did! And she arrived in Bratislava about two hours before Alma left it! How's that for timing.

So I didn't get any time to mourn the loss of Alma, but I think it's worked well as a way of easing me back into solo travel because Karra travels in a completely different way to me – she's not remotely interested in museums, palaces, concerts or indeed many tourist attractions at all. She sleeps until 10 or 11 most days and then whiles away the afternoon in cafes or parks soaking up the culture and planning her evening. "I organise my travels around my nightlife," she said! So, we each did our own thing during the days and then Karra took me to all the best bars in the evenings!

I'd planned my time in Bratislava to be restful, which I really needed after two weeks of rushing around with Alma. I also needed some time to update my journal (ha, still haven't completed that) and to plan the rest of my journey. I did do a free walking tour, though, to learn a bit about Slovakian, and Czechoslovakian, history.

The nations that are now Slovakia and the Czech Republic were both part of the Austro-Hungarian Empire for hundreds of years. When the empire was weakened by WWI, at the same time as the winning Allies were looking to diversify and decentralise power and politics in Europe whilst taking their former enemies down a peg or two, the Czechs and Slovaks saw their chance for freedom. They decided to embark on that journey together, for strength in numbers and because they got on well and had a lot in common (including up to 90% of their languages). And so Czechoslovakia was born in 1919.

It stuck around until 1939, when Hitler met with the leader of the Slovakian National Socialist Party and said, "If you don't split with the Czechs and align yourselves with us, we'll invade and split your country whichever way we want." So Slovakia became "independent" for the first time in 1939, although it wasn't really independence because the Nazis were telling them what to do. The Slovaks had an uprising in 1944, which was viewed with hope around the world, apparently, because it showed that even Hitler's allies didn't want him anymore. But the uprising was crushed and, as happened in Hungary, the Nazis took full control.

Slovakia and the Czech Republic were later "liberated" by the Soviets. My guide, Sonia, said that Slovakia had wanted to be independent again but the Czechs had wanted to reform the federation, so Czechoslovakia appeared again in 1945 and stuck around until 1993.

Sonia explained the reason why younger people tend to view the communist times differently to older people. I'd been hearing since Russia that some older people miss the communist days, and I'd heard in Mongolia that the reason they were able to come out of it in a stronger, more definitive way than Russia is that they have such a young population. Sonia said that things weren't all bad under communism because there was full employment and social security, and the transition to capitalism was particularly hard for older people because they suddenly had to compete for jobs - something they didn't necessarily do well at. There was almost no social security system to fall back on when they failed or when they got too old to work, and under communism they hadn't been able to save up any money because everyone had been paid so little, so they didn't have any savings to fall back on either. That's a pretty tough situation to be in, so I can understand why those people would look back on the communist era with rose-coloured glasses. Economically, it's a pretty tough change.

The tour ended at the Blue Church, an art nouveau church that looks exactly like a wedding cake, or maybe a marzipan creation. It's amazing. But there's a super ugly building opposite (complete with Soviet workers' relief) because the Soviets knocked down half the Old Town. Apparently they wanted Czechoslovakia to have one beautiful city – Prague - and one industrial city - Bratislava. The previous night, Karra and I went to a bar that was on the other side of a highway, and we were quite confused because we'd been walking through the Old Town and then suddenly there was an underpass with a busy highway running above it So I thought we'd left the Old Town, but when we got to the other side we found more cobbled streets, and the bar was in a charming small, old, pastel-coloured building.

Do you know what the Soviets did? They ploughed a highway right through the middle of the Old Town. Oh joy.

The second night, I and a Canadian woman from our dorm called Robin went on Karra's Pub Crawl. Karra had found a brochure on nightlife in Bratislava which listed several pubs and bars and gave them numbers on a map, and she had it all planned out. First we were going to number 8 and then number 13 or something like that, but we dropped the brochure's numbers pretty quickly and started using our own numbers, allocated by their chronological order in the pub crawl.

Karra and I had dinner first (so…many…dumplings and so…much…sheep's cheese…) and then went to Pub No. 1, which was some kind of student bar on the top floor of a new building in the Old Town. It had nice décor and colours and was pretty cheap. Robin met us there. Karra, who was checking the opening hours she'd written in the brochure for all the pubs she wanted to go to, noted that it was past 11 and that Pub 3 closed at midnight, so she proposed missing Pub 2 so we could get to Pub 3 on time.

"Sure, no worries, you're in charge," we said. She led us onto the streets of Bratislava, following the blue dot on Google Maps on her phone. In a moment of false confidence she declared, "I think the dot is wrong!" Some time later, she realised that the dot had been right and that we were in the wrong place. Talking and laughing and teasing Karra for getting us lost, we came to a street that was lined with really good street art. Karra found Pub 3 on that street, but it was closed. So we walked some more, still enjoying ourselves immensely even though we'd only been to one pub!

Karra lead us to what was meant to be Pub No. 4 or No. 5 on her list. Inside, the colour scheme was bright red with bits of black and there was metal music playing. It was definitely a place that had character. After we'd ordered our drinks and sat down, Karra realised that we were in the wrong pub. But that didn't matter - we had a lovely time in the metal pub! A drunk Slovak guy came and sat down next to us. He showed us two tickets he'd bought for a concert by a band called Hatebreed. They were his favourite band ever. He said he'd seen them once when he was 15, and he was now going to see them again, and he was so excited (he was now aged about 35). He said, "Hatebreed!" several times with a big grin on his face. We asked him if they were Slovakian and he said no, they were American. This means that the band members understand what their name means.

The man didn't have much English, but he was able to get quite a bit of information across by using gestures. This included pretending to fly (nay, soar) as he told us about stage diving, and grabbing hold of his nose and ripping it to the side as he told us about injuries he'd got while stage diving.

He'd bought the second ticket for his very good friend. He made a shape on the table with his hands and said, "My heart," and then he drew another one inside it and said, "My friend heart." Aww... They were going to see Hatebreed together...

We had to keep moving, because we were on a pub crawl, so we told him that we had to leave. He didn't like this, and at first he said, "Drink with meee!" in a whiny voice and then when we said no, he said, "Drink with me, motherfucker!" It's very interesting that even when people have only very basic English skills, they still all seem to know the word "motherfucker". I can only assume that this is from American movies...

A classical accompaniment

I arrived in Vienna late on the 2nd of July. The border was interesting – tiny blue sign, blink and you'll miss it - but from the other side you can still see Bratislava. It's always interesting to be looking at another country than the one you're in, but I realised with a start that that border used to be the Iron Curtain. From where I was, you could see past the Iron Curtain. I wondered how heavily guarded it used to be – very, presumably. So different now.

The next morning, I walked out of the apartment I was staying in with "The Blue Danube" in my head. I mean, it literally popped in there as I was putting my hand on the door to leave the apartment, because it knew I was going out into Vienna! I walked along the gorgeous fresco-ceilinged corridor and through the heavy door with lions on it, and onto the street. Turned into another street and saw my first gorgeous relief statue over a doorway: lions with gold. And there were beautiful cream-coloured Vienna buildings all around.

As I continued walking, the tune in my head suddenly swapped to "Do Re Mi". *Huh*, I thought. I hadn't been expecting that as *The Sound of Music* was set in Salzburg, but they did mention Vienna a few times in it, so I thought, *OK, fair enough then*, and I listened to it for a couple of minutes.

Then, as I emerged onto a broad street near the palace with a park and an incredible-looking building over to my left, something very funny happened. The *Inspector Rex* theme tune popped into my head. I can't control any of this, I promise you! It just happens! For the city I was in this was far more appropriate than *The Sound of Music*, so it took full control of my head and I laughed out loud. Several times! Do you know how stupid that song is? It's a song about a dog! I was in one of the most beautiful and graceful cities in the world; the centre of classical music, no less; the city with more well-known composers than almost any other, and what did I have in my head? A song about a dog. And evidently I'd watched *Inspector Rex* enough times to know the words to the theme tune by heart, so it was blaring from start to finish through my head! I was walking towards this incredible building I'd seen, which looked like a huge Greek temple with wings and had a large fountain out the front and a grand statue of a woman with gold on her head, and I was listening to a song about a dog! I was giggling incessantly as I walked along, completely by myself, in the beautiful city of Vienna, the whole situation being so bizarre that I could not stop laughing!

I took photos of the amazing building – it turned out it was the Austrian Parliament. Then I walked over to the palace, still listening to a song about a dog and still giggling, but fortunately by the time I got to the inner courtyard, with its incredible statues of Hercules fighting lions, my internal soundtrack had switched back to "The Blue Danube" again. I sighed with relief, and I wondered with a little trepidation which piece of music would win out. Which would play involuntarily in my head the most during my four days in Vienna: *The Sound of Music*, "The Blue Danube", or the *Inspector Rex* theme tune?

I am happy to report that the winner was "The Blue Danube". *The Sound of Music* never appeared again. *Inspector Rex* tried to. That day, he really tried – many times I could hear both *Inspector Rex* and "The Blue Danube". It was like a radio music panel where the DJ can be playing one track and then can turn a knob and play another track at the same time – I could hear the two pieces in my head at the same time! But fortunately I found that, while them being there was involuntary and not controlled by me whatsoever, in the event of there being two I found I was able to pick between them, and I picked "The Blue Danube" every time. So, *Inspector Rex* didn't bother me too much during my time in Vienna...

The following day I discovered that I was not crazy, because I realised that the reason the two of them had been popping into my head at the same time is that they have the same first bar. If you've watched *Inspector Rex* you may be aware that it starts slowly, with classical music, for just one

212

bar, and then the drumbeat starts, the dog jumps through the glass and they start singing a stupid song about him. I didn't realise, until I heard "The Blue Danube" oh so many times while I was in Vienna, that that first slow bar is the first bar of "The Blue Danube". So that would pop into my head, and then it could go either way, which is why I had Strauss and *Inspector Rex* competing in my head. Once I realised why this was, I realised that I only had to concentrate on the fourth "da", the strongest "da" in the opening of the main part of "The Blue Danube", which the *Inspector Rex* theme does not have. If I could just concentrate on getting that fourth "da" out, then the rest of "The Blue Danube" would flow on naturally and *Inspector Rex* would go away. So, "The Blue Danube" won the competition.

I went into the palace, which is called Hofburg. It contains the Sisi Museum. Sisi was Empress Elizabeth, who was married to Emperor Franz Josef I, the last long-serving monarch of the Hapsburg crown. He reigned for nearly 68 years. His successor had two before they kicked him out and established the Republic.

Sisi has her own museum because she was a very interesting woman who did some things empresses don't normally do, and to me they all sounded like things it was absolutely fair enough for her to do, but I guess because empresses don't normally do them, especially not in the 19th century, she was considered remarkable. The museum said, though, that people didn't think much of her when she was alive; that they either ignored her completely or criticised her for not being very empress-like, but after she died a kind of cult sprang up around her, with many people idolising her and wanting to know more about her. She died tragically – she was assassinated by an anarchist – which contributed to this. She was an interesting person, though, and a woman ahead of her time.

In the afternoon I discovered the fantastic Viennese pursuit of sitting in a café relaxing for hours on end. Wonderful. Highly recommend it. On my way café-wards I passed the State Opera Theatre, and to cross the road I had to go through an underpass, which contained shops and an entrance to the metro. I heard "The Blue Danube" coming from somewhere, and looking around discovered that it was coming from a public toilet! There were neon letters above the entrance saying "Opera WC". Inside, there was a large picture of the audience seats of the State Opera Theatre, through which was placed a turnstile gate and a vending machine saying, "€0.70". Classic...

Went out with Karra that night - always enjoyable. Tried Austrian dumplings. They were like really, really fat noodles. I appear to be taking a dumpling tour of Europe...

The next day, I went to Strauss's apartment. The Vienna Museum purchases as many apartments associated with famous composers as they

213

can – you can see Beethoven's, Mozart's and Schubert's too. I picked Strauss's because I'd discovered by this point that "The Blue Danube" is the unofficial anthem of Austria. It seemed appropriate. Unfortunately there wasn't much in the apartment, but there were two listening stations which I sat at for ages. One piece I particularly liked was called "Titch Tatch".

Emerging from Strauss's apartment building with "Titch Tatch" in my head, I walked to Kunst Haus Wien. I had to go along the Danube Canal to do this, which was the only time I saw anything Danube-related while I was in Vienna. The river itself is way in the north of the city and I never got anywhere near it. Ironic, right?

Kunst Haus Wien is a museum of an Austrian artist called Friedensreich Hundertwasser. He designed the building also and it's pretty insane. Lots of colours and cool shapes, and the floors undulate because Hundertwasser believed flat floors were oppressive and destroyed one's natural sense of balance. He was all about nature and he said a straight line was the only unnatural line, so there isn't really a straight line in the whole place.

There are also special tree nooks that are kind of like balconies in the building, and trees on top of it. A block away he designed an apartment building called Hundertwasserhaus, which is basically a building crossed with a tree. When he died he asked people to plant a tree on his grave so he could live on as a tree. At the entrance to the museum there's a picture of him with the description: "Friedensreich Hundertwasser 1928-2000". It's next to a picture of a tree with the words, "Friedensreich Hundertwasser 2000-2012".

In the museum café, I decided to try two Viennese things: Wiener Melange and Sacher Torte. The former was the only thing on the coffee menu that had "Wiener" in it. (I'm aware that sentence sounded weird, but I assure you that Wiener means Viennese, not penis.) I therefore assumed it would be what we know as Vienna Coffee – the stuff with the pyramid of whipped cream on it. It wasn't. It tasted like a weak cappuccino. I was disappointed. I later found out that Melange is the main Vienna coffee, not the creamy one. Its recipe is basically the same as a cappuccino. Minus the chocolate of course, but real cappuccinos don't have chocolate anyway – I think I've only had a chocolate-dusted cappuccino once in Europe. I was able to find the whipped cream coffee only once, in a café I went to the following day. I guess maybe the Viennese invented it but they don't drink it very much, which is fair enough. They'd all be fat if they did. (PS: the one I tried was *delicious*.)

The other thing I tried in the Kunst Haus Wien café was Sacher Torte, the famous Viennese chocolate cake. I found it most surprising. The icing was really strongly cocoa-ey, but then there was this sweet stuff beneath it that

214

tasted like jam, and then there was the cake – my mouth didn't know what was going on! I later found out that the jam was apricot and that it's traditionally placed right below the icing.

I met up with Karra, and we had a picnic dinner by the pond in front of the amazing Karlskirche, a church that's incredible from the outside as well as the inside. It has two pillars outside which look rather like minarets, but they have Biblical scenes on them – they're not Islamic. Muslims never invaded Vienna. The Turks did try, and they left behind coffee beans – that's how the Viennese discovered coffee!

The reason we were there is there's an outdoor screen that plays free movies every night in July. There's one at the Town Hall that plays concert and opera recordings, too!

The next morning I did the free walking tour. The guide's name was Charles, and he was the first one I've had who wasn't under 30 – he was about 50, but just as energetic as all the others. He taught me various interesting things, including:

- the reason Vienna has so many famous composers is that the Hapsburgs encouraged the arts by giving grants and tax breaks to composers. None of Vienna's most famous composers were actually born there.
- Adolf Hitler applied to study at a famous Viennese art school twice and was knocked back by a Jewish professor. Charles said that Hitler wasn't anti-Semitic when he arrived in Vienna but that he was when he left. This was not only because of that bad experience, but because he absorbed a "typical Viennese anti-Semitism." I wish he'd just become an artist; then he might've bothered the world a lot less! Or he might've failed at being an artist (apparently he wasn't any good) and still got angry and fought with the world.
- after WWII Vienna was divided into four occupation zones just the same as Berlin was – British, American, French and Russian. I didn't get to find out why, unlike in Berlin, this ended peacefully in 1955 and the city was not used as a pawn in the Cold War.

In the evening I went to a concert, because you have to go to a concert in Vienna, and it has to be a classical concert. I chose Mozart's *Requiem*, which was playing at Karlskirche. Tickets were I think €36 for seats in the front half of the church, €29 for seats in the back, or €12 to stand. I chose to stand, even after the ticket vendor offered me an €18 student price for a back seat, because "standing tickets" sounded like an interesting Viennese institution I thought I should check out.

I arrived early and claimed a good place leaning against a pillar. A steady stream of other concert goers filed in, most to the seats but there were also about ten or twelve others with standing tickets. When it got close to the performance start time, an usher came and took away five of these people, who were a family, and found them seats. I assumed they'd paid to upgrade their tickets, but then the usher came back and took another three. Only three or four of us remained. The usher returned again, asked for our tickets and said, "OK, let's go."

He led us to seats in the 36 Euro section for free! Ha! I guess they had a few seats left and decided to be nice to us. So I didn't fully get to experience the Viennese standing ticket phenomenon, but I experienced that it's not always as harsh as it sounds.

The church was gorgeous, of course, because it was baroque *insert sound of angels singing here* *then replace it with much deeper, stronger, louder singing of Mozart's *Requiem*.* There was a small orchestra and a choir doing it, and the acoustics in the church were so good they didn't use any microphones at all. They performed the entire symphony from beginning to end. There were brief breaks between movements, but no applause. There was applause at the end, and then it was all over very quickly – you can't do an encore of Mozart's *Requiem*, unfortunately!

Karra met me outside the church, and we went out for the last time. She took a train to Slovenia early the next morning.

What does "flughafen" mean?

On my way out of Vienna, a very strange and interesting thing happened. That night, I'd booked to take a night train back to eastern Slovakia - leaving from Bratislava, so I had to get from Vienna back to Bratislava. According to the Slovakian public transport website there are many ways of doing this, and, being a good public transport website, it lists absolutely all of them. There seemed to be more buses than trains, but they were leaving from a couple of different places, and the one I selected wasn't the one I'd arrived at. It was leaving from somewhere called "Flughafen Wien", which was on my Vienna train map at what I thought was the end of one of the subway lines. I assumed it was a bus station, since a lot of buses were going from there.

When I got to the metro station and studied the train map a bit closer, I realised that it wasn't on a subway line but on some other train line, and that it was further away than I thought. But I could clearly see which metro station I had to change at to find the line, and it looked fairly simple. It was also the station that the airport trains left from.

At the ticket machine, I looked for a "transfer ticket" option but there wasn't one. *Maybe it's all included*, I thought. I'm not so ignorant as to realise that this was wishful thinking, but I thought that if I had to buy another ticket, this would become clear at the transfer station.

At the transfer station, I could see no ticket windows but I could see a "departures" screen saying that the next train to Flughafen Wien was leaving in two minutes, so I quickly rushed to the platform just hoping that my subway ticket would get me through.

Finding a seat on the clearly-not-a-subway-train, I was aware that there were many people with lots of baggage. *Maybe Flughafen Wien is on the way to the airport*, I thought. Then I remembered that the destination of this train *was* Flughafen Wien. *Maybe changing trains at Flughafen Wien is a cheaper way to get to the airport?* I wondered. Then I thought, *Shit, what does "flughafen" mean?*

Craning my neck wasn't enough to see the train's map, so I unbuckled my pack (I fitted in very well with all these airport people) and got up to have a look.

The line continued, but Flughafen Wien was clearly marked as a station about halfway along it, with a nice big aeroplane symbol right next to it.

This is how I learned that "flughafen", in German, means "airport"!!

I was pretty sure a subway ticket wouldn't get me to the airport. I began looking around for a ticket inspector. I couldn't see one. I have fare evaded a handful of times on this trip simply because of not understanding ticket rules and ticket purchase procedures. I began hoping that this would be one of those times, because an airport train is sure to be expensive. I never would've picked that bus if I'd known. The airport was also, of course, bloody miles away and I was worried about the time. Fortunately I'd left central Vienna with time to spare, but more time on the train meant more time for a ticket inspector to catch me. I hoped that because it was Sunday there wouldn't be any, but if there was, I thought I'd just tell them that I hadn't realised until I got on the train that it was an airport train (which was true) and that I had thought I was going to a bus station on the normal train network (also true). Would they have believed me, though? I could've shown them my Bratislava-Poprad train ticket, I suppose. "I'm not going to the airport to take a plane, I promise!" Trust me to go to an airport to take a bus. It's what comes of internet-based travel planning, I suppose.

Well the good news is that there was no ticket inspector, nor a ticket gate at the other end, and the airport seemed to be the only place in Austria to have an open supermarket on a Sunday! Found the bus just fine, and made it back to Bratislava. But it wasn't over yet...

I had booked a night train, or at least what I thought was a night train, online. It said that the train would leave Bratislava at 19:55 and get to Poprad at 06:35. Its terminus would be at Košice. The geography of these places goes something like this:

So when I arrived at Bratislava Station and, checking the departures board, saw that the 19:55 train would terminate at Žilina, not Košice, I was a little concerned. I looked around and saw two ticket windows marked "complex bookings". One of these ticket windows had a sign with a German flag on it that said, "Hier sprechen wir Deutsch." The other had a sign with a British flag that said, "We speak English here." I went up to that one.

I explained my dilemma and the lady said, "This train terminate Žilina. It go to Košice only on Fridays."

"But I booked it through to Poprad!" I said. "I checked two websites and they both said this was a night train that would get me to Poprad at 6:35am!"

"No, no," the lady said, "The only night train leave Bratislava 11:40pm, arrive Poprad 4:30."

I knew about that one. I also knew I didn't want to arrive in Poprad at 4:30am, particularly since I wasn't staying there. I was staying in Ždiar, and I knew the first bus there didn't leave Poprad until 7:35.

The conversation went back and forth between me and this lady for a while, me putting my head in my hands frequently and explaining to her what a huge inconvenience this was to me because I'd booked accommodation in Ždiar the following night, but if I'd known about this I would have gone to Žilina first. I was ranting and complaining but also trying to get information out of her about what I should do. She was not forthcoming with this: either she didn't want to help because Slovakian customer service is terrible, or she was unable to help because her English actually wasn't that great, even though she was sitting behind a ticket window that said, "We speak English."

I decided I'd have to take the 11:40pm train, and then the lady said she needed a paper copy of my ticket (I didn't have one - I was just showing her a pdf on my phone). She said I should go next door to the customer centre to print it because she couldn't do that for some reason. I went there, and they refused! They gave me a phone number and said I had to call it for some reason, and I said, "Well, can I borrow your phone? I only have an international phone!" And they said no! So I went back to the first lady and said, "Whatever, just transfer my ticket to the 11:40 train please,"

and she said, "Not without a paper ticket."

As you can imagine, I was very stressed by this time and my Western "I am your customer so you must help me" hackles were way up. This lady wasn't helping me at all, so I yelled at her (very rare for me) and she nearly slammed her window shut on me, but then she said, "Your ticket will get you on the 11:40 train, though."

I said, "What? Are you sure?"

and she said, "Yes. But actually maybe you should take 7:55 train because there is one sleeper carriage on there. It will stop in Žilina for four hours and you can sleep."

This is 20 minutes in. 20 minutes in she tells me this. I remember thinking when I bought the ticket that it might do that, because the distance between Bratislava and Poprad is only a bit over 300km. But she waited 20 minutes into her conversation with a very distressed and confused backpacker before telling me that. I don't know if something was lost in translation, or if she thought I already knew, but right back at the start, when she first told me that my train terminated at Žilina and that the only night train was at 11:40, I clearly said, "What do you think I should do?"

There was your window, lady. There's where you say, "Oh, just ask the conductor to switch to the night carriage..."

I finally got my train, which was late and had been baking in the sun all day, so it was hot inside. It was the hottest day I've experienced all trip, and I had to go to Vienna Airport, carry my bags across Bratislava and have an argument with a ticket lady. By the time I got into the stuffy train carriage I had sweat pouring off me.

Unusually, my booking had given me a seat reservation: carriage 10, seat 15. I was in a seat compartment by myself. The ticket inspector came, I asked her if she spoke English and she said, "A little." It turned out my pdf ticket had a QR code and she had a ticket scanner, so she could bring up my whole booking and knew all about it - unlike the other lady, who hadn't even looked. But she was still surprised when I asked her if I could sleep on the train. It was possible, there was a sleeper carriage, but clearly sleeping on the train was not the default option for people who'd booked to leave Bratislava at 19:55 and arrive in Poprad at 06:35. If it was, presumably my booking would've allocated me to carriage 1, not carriage 10.

The inspector rang someone, presumably her colleague in the sleeper carriage, and then said, "Yes, it's fine. Go ten or eleven carriages that way."

So I picked up all my stuff again and walked the entire length of the train. I saw sitting car after sitting car, and finally the restaurant car, and I was running out of train. Then, at the very end, I opened the door to a carriage that was different.

There was a conductor, more of a provodnik, in fact, sitting on his bed in the first compartment, who jumped up as I came in. He checked a list which had three things written on it. I later wondered if that was how many people were in the carriage, because I didn't see anybody all night. This sleeper carriage is a wonderful service, but they're obviously not promoting it if ticket vendors don't even mention it until 20 minutes into an argument. It was a wonderful, quiet, magical place, and the provodnik man was so helpful. He gave me a clean, fresh compartment which had all the beds already made, and he gave me water, a wafer snack and a towel, which I particularly appreciated as I was covered in sweat. I had the compartment all to myself.

I didn't sleep well, as it was very hot and I was coming down with something, but I felt the train stop, and then my carriage got shunted around a bit until it came to a rest. Unfortunately as I wasn't feeling well I wasn't able to look around properly or take photos, but I did go to the toilet in the night, which was at the end of the carriage, and I could see that where the engine had previously been there was now nothing. I appeared to be in an entirely unattached carriage looking out at a rail yard. It was very interesting.

So that was the story of how I spent a night in a rail yard. In the morning I felt the carriage start to move again, and after a little while of trying to go back to sleep and failing, I used my foot to lift the curtain and I saw mountains! Yay!

When I got up, the provodnik brought me a cup of tea. No extra charge.

The train arrived in Poprad at about 6:50am, 15 minutes late - as is typical in Slovakia! I happily discovered that the bus station (where my bus to Ždiar would leave from) was right next door, and that next to the bus station was a supermarket. I stocked up on fruit, veg, garlic and orange juice, as I was feeling quite unwell by this stage and had realised it may have been because I'd been eating too many dumplings and not enough vegetables.

A bit before 9am, I arrived at the Ginger Monkey Hostel in Ždiar. Behind the reception desk was a very helpful young woman called Carolyne who let me have a shower straight away and offered me breakfast even though my paid accommodation wouldn't start for several hours. I'd already had breakfast but I loved the shower. Then I attempted to sleep on the couch, at which point Carolyne said, "I have found one free bed because someone didn't show up last night." So I went to bed at about 9:45am, and I really needed it! That day I spent watching movies in the friendly mountain hostel and trying to get well.

Climbing waterfalls

The next day, one of the hostel's very many friendly backpackers, a Belgian called Jeremy, mentioned over breakfast that he'd like to go rafting that day. I said, "Count me in, please!" as rafting was one of the things I really wanted to do there. Jeremy recruited five people and the hostel organised a taxi transfer and rafting trip for us. Apart from him, we were all Australians: me, Michael from Sydney and Esther and Rohana from Canberra.

The rafting is done on the river that forms the Polish-Slovakian border, with the borderline running down the middle of the river.

We were driven to the rafting start point, which was about an hour from Ždiar, given life jackets and helmets and told to pick up the inflatable boat and carry it across the road and down the bank into the river. It was very strange giving way to cars and bikes with a boat...

We could see Poland on the other side of the river and there were many other boats of a more traditional kind, some from Poland and some from Slovakia. They were made up of four or five squarish canoes tied together, with pine fronds tied to the front to prevent water from splashing inside the raft. Tourists were sitting in these rafts in chairs while two boatmen stood and used punting poles to propel them along. Our boat was inflatable and we only had one boatman, who was responsible for steering while we propelled ourselves with paddles. The river was fairly fast-moving so we didn't have to paddle very much – mostly we just relaxed and let the river take us.

Occasionally there were small rapids, which were fun!

I enjoyed getting to know the other backpackers, and it was pretty interesting to be rafting along a national border! We never knew where the borderline was exactly, but I'm sure many times it went right down the middle of our boat. At one point we saw some ducks and someone idly said, "I wonder where ducks go…"

and I said, "These ones are going to Poland!"

About halfway along I realised that, in my desire not to get any important things wet when, back at the taxi, we had been prioritising what to take with us in the waterproof bucket and what to leave in the taxi, I had left my passport there. This meant that I was crossing a national border, repeatedly, without my passport. It was quite a rush!

That evening, everyone from the hostel went to a local restaurant/pub to watch the first semi-final of the World Cup. I'm not into soccer or other sports, and I was quite relieved to hear the World Cup was nearly over, but I thought it'd be enjoyable to hang out with the hostel people and have a cultural experience of watching soccer in a pub. Where I was sitting I had my back to the TV, but I didn't mind at all! The game was quite boring (even the hardcore fans said so) because Germany beat Brazil 7-1. But I had a lovely night chatting to Jeremy, Esther, Rohana and another Australian woman called Nadja (pronounced "Nadia"). Jeremy, Nadja and I tried a local beverage called "Tatra Tea". It was not tea but a kind of liqueur produced in many flavours. I tried coconut, milk, berry and citrus. It was yum.

The following day was the first day I felt well enough to do a serious hike, and it was also the day it started pouring with rain. There was no point climbing any mountains because there would be no view, so I did a short river hike. I was frustrated but it was nice at the end, when the clouds cleared and I could see the mountains. In the evening I enjoyed hanging out at the hostel, and many people went to see the second semi-final but even the die-hard fans said it was boring: nil-all without many shots on goal. I retired early, and when an American guy came back to my dorm later I asked him who won, and he said, "I don't know, it was still nil-all at full time and I gave up." Later Esther and Rohana came back and we asked them who won, and they said, "We don't know, it was still nil-all after extra time so we gave up!" We didn't find out the score until the morning. Absurdly, it had jumped to 4-2 at the penalty shoot-out. Strange game.

I had discovered that the following day the weather would be fine, even sunny, in Slovensky Raj National Park. This was a bit of a distance away, but worth it to finally get to do a decent walk on my fourth day in the Tatra mountains, even though I'd have to leave the Tatra mountains to achieve it! I planned the walk and put the word out a little bit, because all the people staying in that hostel were awesome so I decided I'd like to walk with some of them. Danielle, one of the managers, put the word out a lot, so we ended up with a group of eight: an Israeli couple, Jeremy, Michael, Esther, Rohana, Nadja and me. We took a bus and then a train to a village called Spišské Tomasovče. The accent makes the "s" a "sh", and I should point out that the accent in Ždiar makes the "z" a "jz", or whatever the z version of a "sh" is. The "j" in Slovensky Raj is of course pronounced as a "y", making it "Slovensky Rai", which means "Slovak Paradise"!

We walked through the village, up and over a hill into a gorge which was called (when translated) Monastery Gorge. The reason I'd wanted to go there is I'd heard there were ladders and metal grids/platforms aiding your passage around the place. In many sections we were required to go out around a cliff face where there was no riverbank, and small metal platforms were protruding from the cliff face for people to step on! There was a chain to hang onto, and I enjoyed hanging onto it and leaning out over the river – it was very exciting! The metal platforms were grids, so you could see what was beneath your feet at all times, which was fast-moving water up to ten metres below!

Unfortunately, for three reasons which I will henceforth state:

- not taking a map with us
- me not reading the written instructions properly
- a "helpful" stranger saying, "Oh, it's that way!" when it wasn't

we missed a turning and missed the best part of the walk, which was some kind of ascent up a waterfall followed by monastery ruins. We knew we'd done something wrong because we emerged at a completely different place, near a town called Hrabušiče, but we didn't know what we'd missed and we'd had a great time going around cliffs - plus going the wrong way had made the track longer so we were really tired and not remotely interested in turning around and going back.

Nadja and I met a Czech man on the way to the bus stop who said, "You missed the cascades? You missed the best part of the park! You must come back another day, because that is really the best part! I can't believe you didn't take a map!" I got angry with him because I thought it was quite mean to harp on to people who've come all the way from Australia and most likely cannot come back another time about the amazing things you saw and they didn't. I'd been feeling really happy up until that point; I knew we'd gone the wrong way but I'd enjoyed the gorge and the company, and this man quite literally ruined my entire day. I became obsessed with trying to figure out what went wrong and what we missed, which depressed me more the more I found out, and I actually began to consider taking that annoying man's advice and coming back on another day. Nadja was stoical and said, "It's OK, we still had a really good walk." She and I made plans to do a Tatra mountain hike the following day, but I began to look at hire cars for the day after that - that's how desperate I was to do the walk again and climb that waterfall! I looked at pictures online and it looked so amazing...

The next morning, I awoke to pouring rain again. It didn't look like the Tatra hike would be possible. I wondered if I could go to Slovensky Raj again instead – oh, but I'd got up a bit later and had already missed the bus...

Over breakfast, I met a Taiwanese man called David and an English man who lives in Taiwan called Richard. They'd arrived in Ždiar in the rain the previous day, and they asked me what I had done. I told them that I'd found somewhere that wasn't raining but that it was a bit far, and that we'd done a hike but missed the best part.

David and Richard began asking each other what they should do that day, and Richard said, "At some point we have to go to Slovensky Raj; there's a really famous hike there where you climb ladders up waterfalls."

My ears pricked up, an idea forming in the back of my mind. "That's where I was yesterday: Slovensky Raj," I said. "The weather was a lot better there, but we missed the waterfalls."

"Well if the weather's better there, maybe we should go there today. If you want to do the waterfall walk, David."

I said, "Oh my god, if you go today, can I come with you?"

They'd already let slip that they had a hire car, so I was practically licking their boots at this point.

David said yes, so Richard said, "OK, shall we leave in half an hour? We have space for one more in the car too, if you want to bring someone."

I convinced Nadja to come. It was so awesome to be in a car. We went to the information centre in Hrabušice, where Richard bought a map. I'd learned the previous day that you should always have a map... When he was looking at the map and discussing the different walks with the information centre lady, I realised that actually the walk he was talking about, which he said was the most famous one, Sucha Bela Gorge, was different to the one we'd done. It seemed there were multiple places in

Slovensky Raj where you could climb ladders up waterfalls. Richard said Sucha Bela was the one everyone raved about and that it had the tallest waterfall: 30 metres. I was unsure at first, but I went with Richard's recommendation and I am so glad I did. Sucha Bela Gorge was more spectacular than I ever could have imagined.

I later found out that Richard has written six books on hiking in Taiwan, so he really knows what he is talking about when it comes to walks!

The gorge was awesome from the moment we set foot in it. There was no build up. It was just awesome the entire way. I'd come to climb the waterfalls, but I was nowhere near them yet and I was already taking ten times more photos than I had the previous day. The gorge was gob-smackingly beautiful, and the path went right up it. The creek was only shallow and a lot of the time there was no path: we just walked along the creek bed. In places where the gorge narrowed and the creek became deeper, there were horizontal wooden ladders erected right over the top of it, on which we balanced between two rock faces with the water flowing beneath us. The gorge was green and wet and lovely. And then we came to the waterfalls....

The bottom fall of the first waterfall and its first ladder were impressive enough. But after you climb that ladder, it just keeps going. It seemed to be about three times as tall as was visible from the base. The top two thirds (about three shorter falls) run through a curving vertical canyon. It isn't possible to see the whole waterfall at once – but that's half the fun. I kept finishing one ladder thinking it was over, only to find another ladder, and then another. On every part except the first waterfall at the bottom, you have rock on more than three sides of you as you're going up. You're climbing through a kind of open-sided tunnel carved by the waterfall, with the sound of crashing water ringing in your ears and never knowing what's next, because the top of a ladder is always blind until you clamber over it. And the view below is inconceivable until you can view it...

And then I looked down, and WOW! From the top, it almost looked like a corkscrew!

I did the entire thing with an enormous grin on my face. Halfway up I said to Richard, who was behind me, "This is one of the most incredible experiences of my life; thank you so much!"

It really was. And it kept going! There were three more waterfalls after that - not as big as the first but still amazing. And so many more horizontal ladders, creek bed walking and climbing through chasms... It continued for over two hours!

At the top, we reached the tiny spring which is the source of the creek, in a much gentler, rounder valley, with green leaves on the trees and brown leaves on the ground. It was so quiet and so beautiful.

By far one of the best hikes I have ever done and one of the best days of my whole trip. And it just goes to show that everything happens for a reason, because if I hadn't stuffed up the walk the previous day I never would've asked to go with David and Richard, and then I never would've discovered that amazing place...

That night, Carolyne made Slovak nettle soup with cream and cut up potatoes and eggs in it. It was very tasty. Some of the backpackers had numb hands from picking the nettles! Then some of us played "Scattegories". It was fun. The Ginger Monkey Hostel is the best hostel I have ever stayed at. Friendly staff encourage friendly backpackers - plus being a small place up in the mountains where there isn't much else to do, people tend to hang out at the hostel and/or go out with the other guests. Only a certain quality of people are interested in going to the mountains anyway - there's no riff raff! And the staff are so generous with everything: lending hiking equipment free of charge, randomly cooking dinner – they're genuinely lovely, helpful people.

I was sad to leave after five nights, but I had to move on. Nadja decided to come with me, so that lessened the blow! Nadja is one of those people who just travels where the wind takes her; she never plans anything. She was also checking out that day and had said many times that she didn't want to extend again, but she still didn't decide where she was going to go until the morning of the day she was going there!

In Žilina, I had arranged to couch surf with a woman called Veronika, who graciously agreed to host two of us instead of one. Her husband Miro drove us to their residence, in a Soviet apartment block 3km from the city centre, with Veronika's grandmother in the back as they had just been to a family function. There were many cakes left over from the function, some of which we got to try. One looked a lot like a sweet pizza, but the base was much softer. It had sweet cheese and sultanas on it.

Veronika also gave us many slices of sheep's cheese, and introduced us to thyme tea made from wild thyme she had picked herself and dried – it was incredible. She also helped us plan a walk the next day and gave us a map. Couch surfing is awesome.

We got up early the next morning for the 8 o'clock bus to Mala Fatra National Park, because our walk started with a cable car ride and Veronika said too many people would take the later bus and there'd be a queue for the cable car. When we were on the cable car, we saw some hikers below us with their heads down, bums up and hands rifling through bushes. They were picking blueberries.

Nadja had done a lot more European hiking than I had, and she'd been saying just the previous night that she'd done a walk in France where she could smell rosemary and thyme the whole way. We'd been talking about it in relation to Veronika's thyme tea. Veronika is an ordinary young woman who lives in a Soviet apartment block, but she goes out to pick wild herbs and mushrooms fairly regularly. They are just there – they're everywhere. She picks fruit sometimes, too. She showed us some dried apples she had, and some dried mushrooms from a previous year's haul. You have to be able to tell good mushrooms from poisonous mushrooms, but she can, so she has access to this incredible natural grocery selection.

Nadja and I walked along a mountain ridgeline looking at resplendent views and enjoying walking through an open alpine landscape. There were no trees because it was too high, but the small bushes, the small plants... would you ever expect to go hiking in a foreign country on the opposite side of the world and recognise the plants? Well I did. There was rhubarb, there were raspberries (not ripe yet, sadly), there were blueberries... I think I even found parsley, and there were other herby things that looked familiar. They were growing wild, though! This is Europe: this is where they come from! I was walking high up on some mountain tops in a national park, and I felt like I was in somebody's garden!

The blueberries at that elevation weren't ripe yet, but we found some ripe ones in a pine forest as we were descending from the ridge, and we stayed there eating them for nearly an hour – our mouths and fingertips turned purple!

We were killing time a bit because we knew Veronika and her friends were coming to meet us at the hut further down, and we were still too early. She called it a hut, but actually it was a pub. There's always a pub or café in the middle of a hike in Europe. It's so much of an institution that these pubs have ink stamps available so you can collect stamps of all the national park pubs you've been to! The stamps record the elevation of the pub as well - this one was nine hundred and something metres.

Nadja and I got ourselves a beer and sat at an outdoor table, where we were soon joined by Veronika and her friend Danka. They were a bit red in the face, having just climbed a very steep hill. They bought three beers in anticipation of the arrival of Danka's boyfriend Peter. He'd left much later, but apparently it only takes him 40 minutes to climb the hill as he lives locally and does it almost every day. Danka and Veronika told us that it'd taken them 1 ½ hours to climb to the pub.

The five of us sat there for well over an hour drinking – Veronika even convinced us to have some Borovička (pronounced "Borovitchka"), which is strong-tasting spirit made with juniper berries. Fortunately, one is not expected to "shot" it.

We then had to descend an extremely steep hill, and our Slovak friends had no intention of doing this via the road or the normal track. They were going straight down the hill in the shortest way possible: through the forest on a very vaguely defined track which was at an angle of between 45 and 70 degrees.

It didn't end up being the shortest way for me, because I was moving at a snail's pace as I was afraid of falling headlong down the hill. I'd bought a pair of cheap walking poles in Poland; this was the first day I got to use them. Oh my - I really needed them going down that hill! Peter lent his to Nadja and proceeded to swagger down the hill without them, as cool as you like, saying that he only needed them going up.

He told me that he tries to do this walk every single day. Up and back, every single day. The others had obviously done it a fair few times too. When I asked them why they wanted to go to that pub and not one which was easier to get to, they said, "It's more fun. It's good exercise and it's more interesting to go down after having alcohol."

It wasn't the alcohol that made it difficult for me; it was the steepness. My toes started hurting because they were jammed up against the front of my shoes the whole way. I tried to make my own zig zag to make the track less steep, but it didn't always work. I discovered that walking down the channels which were still filled with autumn leaves was much easier. I had no idea what was lurking beneath the leaves, but that there was matter there at all meant the leaves could provide me with much more support than any other part of the hill, and if I fell - which I did - I had a soft landing.

At the bottom of the hill we found Miro, with his car, at Peter's house. Peter has two pet deer! They're both babies. He's only had them for a month and he said that technically it's very illegal, but a hunter found them abandoned in the forest, and he just wants to keep them alive. They're different breeds; one is very small, the size of a medium-sized dog, and the other is big. She's called Litza and she was bounding around the garden in an erratic, non-surefooted fawn way, and chewing my backpack and walking poles. I got to pat her a lot. It was brilliant.

Back at Veronika and Miro's apartment, Veronika made us a scrambled egg dish using some mushrooms that she and Nadja had picked. Nadja looked the names up and one of them was a pecorino. I picked one ordinary white mushroom - of which we'd seen a few, but Veronika kept saying, "Those ones are boring - I don't want them." I ended up wishing I'd picked them all because I don't care if mushrooms are boring - they're still mushrooms! But by the time I had that thought they were all way back up the hill, so I only picked one. I was going to cook it for breakfast the next morning but I forgot, so I just tried a little bit of it raw. It just tasted like a normal white mushroom. Fine by me! But the fact that Veronika has access to so many wild, non-poisonous mushrooms that she can pick and choose between them is pretty cool.

The next morning, Veronika went to work and Nadja and I had breakfast with Miro (we gave him Vegemite) before saying goodbye and going into town. Even a small city like Žilina has a lovely cobbled square. We had lunch at an al fresco table there of deep-fried cheese, chips and tartare sauce. This time the cheese was camembert – we were each given an entire wheel of camembert breaded and fried! I don't think I'll miss Slovak food. The sheep cheese is nice, but it's so rich and there are so few vegetables! It's always an experience, though.

From the café, Nadja went to a hitch-hiking point Veronika had shown her to try to catch a lift to Bratislava, and I went to the bus station to catch a bus to the Czech Republic. It was great travelling with her; she's awesome and I hope I can see her again in Australia.[2]

---

[2] I did! She lives in Sydney but she's visited Hobart a couple of times since then.

A nation without a nation

I arrived in Brno, Moravia, on the evening on the 14th of July, and I found the Centre For Experimental Theatre very easily – it was in the Old Town. Why was I looking for the Centre For Experimental Theatre, you ask? Because my couch surfing host, Zuzana, was at that moment inside the theatre listening to a Scottish author read his works. She'd invited me to join her, but I hadn't been able to get a bus in time. So I sat in the theatre bar and ordered a Kozel, which cost me 38 Czech crowns for a 500mL tankard. This is somewhere around the AUD$2 mark.

The theatre let out at 8:30pm and Zuzana arrived, but there was nowhere for her friends to sit so we went to a small bar a couple of streets away. There was nowhere to sit there either, so we sat on some steps at the end of the cobbled lane. Nearby there was a piano, just sitting there in the lane with somebody playing it. Zuzana and her friends told me this was part of a new initiative by Brno City to put pianos around the place. They also told me that they go to the theatre to hear authors read every single night in summer, and that they then go to a bar to have only two beers and discuss the author's works.

Europe is so cultured. Young people in their early 20s go every evening to listen to authors read stuff, often in a foreign language (that night it was Scottish poetry) and then they sit next to someone playing an outdoor piano to have a discussion about it. The authors go on regular tours of the Czech Republic, Slovakia and Poland reading their works, and there are people in those countries to listen to them. Zuzana is from Košice, so if she doesn't catch a particular author in Brno, she'll go to see them in Košice instead. And she and her friends won't get drunk, they'll just have two beers whilst talking about poetry. My jaw drops at how cultured Europeans are.

Zuzana's friends' names were Tereza, Tereza and Endo. They didn't talk about poetry that night because they were too busy asking me questions about Australia and the Trans-Mongolian Railway. They all spoke perfect English, as did Veronika's friends.

We had one beer in the piano laneway, which was a sweetish, sourish ale which Endo declared was most definitely not a "typical" Czech beer. Then we walked to another pub, along more gorgeous cobbled streets lined with squarish pastel buildings somewhat similar to Vienna's - apparently Brno is sometimes called a "suburb of Vienna". Zuzana told me a bit about the history of Brno. It was mostly built by Germans, who lived there until the end of WWII, when they were all expelled - apparently quite cruelly.

At the second bar, which had a lovely outdoor beer garden from which I could view the pastel buildings in the street lights, we ordered a beer recommended by Endo. He said it was much more typical of Czech beer, but that it was from a small brewery so it wasn't mass produced. To me it tasted like a pretty standard lager. One of the Terezas ordered tea, and when we paid I was flabbergasted to discover that in the Czech Republic, tea is more expensive than beer!

Walking back to Zuzana's apartment, she told me that she lived in "the ghetto". She said many Brno residents would not want to cross the borders of the district we had just stepped into. There's an old arms factory there – Brno used to be famous for arms – and Zuzana said the district was originally built for the workers. She said there were various minority groups living there over the years, but now it is home to many Roma people.

She pointed out an abandoned apartment building across the road from her own and said that there were many deteriorating apartment buildings around but that that was a good thing, because as soon as they are restored the owners put the rent up and the poorest people have to move out. She said artists were looking at taking over spaces in this district and that she wished they wouldn't. If they make it trendy, prices will go up and all the poor people will have to move out. She also said that she has never felt unsafe in the district as it is now and that she likes living there.

The main reason I'd gone to Brno was to visit the Museum of Romany Culture, which was only one block away from Zuzana and her boyfriend's apartment. In the morning it didn't open until 10 and they had to leave at 9, so I wandered for an hour first - just around that district. I saw the abandoned arms factory, many Roma people and many interesting buildings - some in good condition, some in varying stages of decay. All beautiful European buildings with lovely pastel colours and stucco decorations.

The Romany Museum was very comprehensive. I didn't know anything about Roma people before I went there. Or at least I thought I didn't, not realising that I had been subjected to various pop culture representations of them, mainly during my childhood: all of them outdated and some racist. Their ethnic origin is Indian, and the museum said anthropologists had traced them to a particular caste, but that for hundreds of years the Romany people themselves hadn't known where they were from. The term "gypsy" derives from "Egypt", as to garner favour among Europeans the Roma at one time claimed to be Egyptian Christians fleeing persecution from the Muslims who had taken control there.

234

They entered Europe via Turkey in the 11th century – 1000 years ago. They were craftsmen, and they made money by selling their wares as they moved from town to town. They did live in "gypsy caravans" - some right up until the mid-20th century, when the communist government forced them to settle down. Others settled down much earlier, some by force and some by choice, but they of course required the permission of a region's government to settle. In many cases some Roma would try to settle somewhere only to be moved on.

For the first century or so, Roma people lived alongside white Europeans and were well treated - in some cases because they had been given protection based on the "fleeing Egyptians" story, but also because they had useful skills and products that people needed. But in the 16th century, the attitude of white Europeans and their governments to the Roma became outwardly hostile. The Hapsburg monarchy issued a decree saying that anyone was allowed to kill any Romany freely. In other cases the government did the killing, with standing arrest warrants for all Roma found anywhere on their territory.

When apprehended, the men would immediately be executed. The women and children would have their ears cut off and be branded, so as to identify them if they were ever caught again. They were then escorted out of the territory with a warning that if they ever came back, they would be executed immediately. The museum said that throughout the 16th and 17th centuries, one by one European governments banished the Roma, with no thought as to where they would go if they had also been banished from everywhere else.

Ironically the Hapsburgs later, in the 19th century, had need of the Roma because their own population was ravaged by war, and they had not enough farmers and thus not enough taxpayers. So the Roma were encouraged to settle and become farmers in the Hapsburg Empire. They were also encouraged to assimilate - and forced to by the forced removal of children. There were multiple stolen generations...

Many Slovakian Roma settled down, but many Czech Roma remained nomadic: making a living running travelling shows and circuses, for example. Roma musicians were also very well-known and highly regarded. I realised as I read this that I had seen some in Bratislava busking. The museum also detailed a move from skilled to unskilled work as skilled craftsmen's labour became mechanised. It said many Roma women had become cleaners. I had seen several that morning in "the ghetto" - walking around with mops and brooms and cleaning apartment buildings, some with their children.

The most extreme "culling" of Roma was of course done by the Nazis. Before the establishment of the extermination camps they lived in "gypsy camps", the equivalent of Jewish ghettoes, which were set up in discrete areas. These camps were "liquidated" as the Jewish ghettoes were and their inhabitants sent to Auschwitz, most to their deaths. Only 583 returned: of the entire pre-war Czech Roma population, only 583 survived. The Roma living in the Czech Republic today are largely of Slovakian origin, as since Slovakia co-operated with and appeased the Nazis (up until the uprising, at least) its minorities were spared extermination. Not spared persecution entirely of course, but spared transportation to the death camps. Slovakian Roma were later resettled into the Czech lands after they were reunified with Slovakia under the communist government, which sought to redistribute people around Czechoslovakia based on labour needs. This was a forced resettlement – again - and it ended the nomadic Roma lifestyle in this region.

The museum ended with some positive things about Romany culture, including a burgeoning film industry and a founding role in Flamenco music and dance. It said that in the 1980s the Roma got a flag and a national anthem and joined the United Nations.

There was one last room on Roma issues in the media today, which clearly showed that there are still severe problems and hardships faced by Roma around Europe. I discussed this a little bit with Nadja, because I had told her I was going to Brno to see the Romany Museum, and she said she'd seen a special exhibition on Roma in Sweden detailing, among other things, the stolen generations and forced sterilisation. The Nazis did that – they did it to Jewish women too.

Nadja said, "The Roma situation seems very similar to the Aboriginal situation in Australia," and I agreed with her. Stolen generations; institutionalised racism; entrenched social issues affecting education and job prospects; historical persecution and murder… "any citizen may kill any Roma"… Yes, those exact things have been suffered by Australian

Aborigines since 1788. And even a government back-track, possibly guilt-induced, which leads the Slovakian government now to provide the Roma with allegedly greater social security payments than Slovaks get. We heard Veronika complaining about this...

I guess the difference for the Roma is they don't have land rights - so where do they belong; where will they turn if they are exiled again?

Spring water and beer

I didn't have time to do much else in Brno because I had to take a five-hour bus ride to Český Krumlov, so I just wandered around the Old Town briefly, taking photos of beautiful buildings. Brno is a nice city – I could've done with some more time there.

Český Krumlov is super touristy but for good reason: its Old Town is even more beautiful than Tallinn's, and that's saying something. It's in a steep valley, so you can see the whole town from certain places, and it is so beautiful. I also amazed myself looking at the decorations on the outside of the 15th-17th century houses, many of which were highly detailed frescoes of saints and the like.

I took the free walking tour with a young tour guide called Jan (Yahn). He told us that Český Krumlov Castle was built in the 13th century and that different noble families ran it over the years. The last was the Schwarzenbergs. In 1947 it was nationalised, and the law passed in the early 1990s which gave back properties which had been confiscated by the communist government only covered properties which had been confiscated after 1948, so the castle is still owned by the government. Now the Schwarzenbergs are fighting to get it back. Personally, I like the Mongolian idea of re-privatising everything by sharing it equally among everyone much better...

Yesterday (the 16th of July) I took a train to Pilsen, or Plzen. My couch surfing host, Tereza, met me at the station, which it was immediately obvious to me had been built or renovated by the Soviets because it had station decorations I hadn't seen since St Petersburg. Tereza is 30 years old, works as a Sony corporate travel agent and speaks Czech, English, Slovak, German and Spanish, and is learning French. Her English ability is the highest I've encountered since I met Sascha and Alex – I don't have to modify the way I speak with her. I can speak fast again! I have to concentrate to do it, though – I've got so used to speaking slowly and simply and with bad grammar! I noticed Nadja was doing it too.

Next morning I got up early because I had a fun day planned which involved excursioning out of Plzen. It was an amazing day. I got to drink mineral spring water all morning and beer all afternoon.

First I went to Marianske Lazne, which is a spa town. There are over 100 mineral springs bubbling up in the area; 8 or so in the town centre. Some are quite mild and some are pretty strong-tasting. As with any spa town, Marianske Lazne was very popular among the elite at one time, and so it has very many grand buildings, most of them hotels. Elite mineral water lovers built grand pavilions around most of the spring taps - and a grandiose undercover promenade called the Colonnade, which has some nice statues and frescoes. But, as with most places I've been to in the Czech Republic, there are always a few unrestored, deteriorating buildings around the town, which for me just adds to the character of the place.

I walked from spring to spring happily sipping from my regular water bottle, but I found it quite interesting to see what receptacles others were using to collect the spring water. I saw one old man filling six or eight huge 1.5L plastic bottles, all of which had clearly been used many times before – perhaps he was prescribed large amounts of the stuff for some condition. There was a sign in one of the pavilions listing medicinal properties of the waters, which were different for each spring. It said doctors can prescribe 1½ to 2 litres per day as a treatment!

Other people only wanted a cup of spring water at a time. I saw only two normal plastic cups and very many re-used yogurt cups, some with a small plastic bag inside them. The Marianske Lazne tradition, though, is to buy a ceramic mug which, for some reason, has a spout on it - so that when people are drinking out of it they look like they are drinking from a teapot. It looks very odd…

After drinking mineral water all morning and already having to pee several times, I took a bus to the nearby village of Chodova Plana, which has the Chodovar Brewery and a beer spa. "Beer spa? What the hell is that?" you ask. Well it's exactly what it says on the tin, though not a spa exactly but more of a bath. It's a beer bath. Honestly, the Czechs have so much cheap beer that they can bathe in it! Apparently it's very good for the skin! The price of the bath includes two 300mL glasses of beer – perhaps it's good for the inside of the body as well as the outside?

I paid my money and went downstairs – it was in a lovely brick arched cellar. I was given a sheet, not a towel, and taken to the change room. The staff spoke no English so they spoke to me in German. We are near the German border here and many German companies have outsourced to Bohemia, so if someone speaks a foreign language it is most likely to be German. The first thing they did was tell me to remove "alles" my items of clothing, which rendered my carrying of swimming gear all around Marianske Lazne entirely pointless! The "spa" is actually several one-person metal baths in a cellar, which are all curtained off, so you get into them naked. I was led into my own curtained bath area dressed only in my sheet, given a beer and left alone.The liquid in the bath was covered in a thick foam head. I slid into it, and the head stuck to all parts of my body that were outside the bath. The liquid was dark – I couldn't see through it. It certainly looked different to the glass of lager they had served me, and I wondered if it was dark beer. I gingerly lowered my mouth into it and tasted it. It tasted watered down. I couldn't tell what type of beer it was. I found to my surprise, though, that I liked the taste of the froth! It had small green streaks in it which looked like seaweed, but which my guidebook had warned me would be hops. They were nice and the froth was nice; two things I never expected to enjoy consuming on their own.

Yes. Yes, I know. One is not supposed to consume one's bath. But it was a beer bath!

I lay there relaxing until my beer glass was empty. I wondered when the lady would come to give me another one. Meantime I amused/satisfied myself with consuming bits of hops-head…

The lady didn't come, and my eyes turned to the beer tap that was sitting temptingly at the end of my bath. I didn't intend to consume beer from it as I knew it wouldn't be cold, but I wanted to see what it looked like pouring into the bath. The bath had been filled before I got there, so I hadn't seen it. I turned the tap on in the tiniest of tiny ways. It made a hissing noise, and small droplets of froth fell into the bath.

I was sure I wasn't meant to be doing this, but I wondered whether the noise of it would call the lady so she could get me my second glass. I was too scared to turn the tap on all the way - I just turned it on a tiny gentle way several times. During this, some drops fell on my hand, and I tasted them. They tasted good. I allowed more drops to fall on my hand.

I realised that the beer was not warm – it wasn't chilly but it wasn't warm, and in comparison to the warm bath it did feel a little bit chilly! I realised that the bath was actually heated by hot water, which I could also see an outlet for - not by the beer.

Realising that the beer from the tap was not warm, and in the absence of a Czech and German-speaking lady to refill my glass, I decided to take matters into my own hands. The beer was quite frothy, so I put just a little bit, about 50mL, into my glass. This I did about four times, because it tasted amazing. It tasted like an ale: the colour was dark amber and beautiful, and it was way better than the lager they'd given me! And, happily, it didn't have bits of hops floating in it – they must've added that directly to the tub.

I lay back and enjoyed a smooth, frothy ale poured from a tap at my feet for several minutes. Then the lady came back, waving her hands horizontally to tell me that my bath was over. All she could see in my glass by that stage was thick creamy froth, but it certainly looked different to the froth from the lager she had given me. She pointed to the tap and said, "Nicht drinken!" I shook my head, like, "No no no, I wasn't doing that!" and I pointed towards the bar, reminding her that I was due another beer. She said or did something to indicate that I would be served that later.

Then she left, allowing me to rise from the bath and wrap myself in the sheet. But there was no bath mat or anything so, as I normally do when there is no bath mat (as has happened very many times on this trip), I simply grabbed the sheet and wrapped myself in it whilst I was still standing in the bath, which was now draining. Then the lady came back in and was obviously distressed by this, and she started grabbing the sheet at my legs trying to prevent it from getting wet (which it wasn't, as the bath was draining). She started talking in German and gesturing that I should get out of the bath immediately, so I stepped one foot out and she reacted negatively to that as well. Leaving my other foot in the bath, I realised that she was shaking one of her feet to show me what to do. I shook that foot before putting it on the ground, and to this she reacted positively. So now I know. The way millions of eastern European people deal with the lack of bath mats is simply to shake their feet before they get out. Now I know...

I tried to go back to the change room but was led by the other staff lady, who was carrying five 300mL tankards of beer, into another cellar which had several relaxation beds in it. These had a towel for the head to rest on

241

and a pink polar fleece blanket for the rest of the body, which the lady wrapped me in on top of my sheet. Here I received my second beer. I had to lift my head to drink it, but lying there with it held to my chest was the most relaxing part of my beer spa experience. There was gentle music playing and I was lying looking up at a brick ceiling, warm in a blanket and drinking beer. Fabulous.

Then the same lady came to tell me that my beer spa experience was over, and she spoke the first English words either of them had said the whole time: "No shower." It's just as well she said that in English, as I have no idea what it would be in German. "Oh," I said. "Shower is bad?"

The lady nodded her head.

"OK," I said. It must be something to do with the skincare.

I grabbed the towel from the relaxation bed, because I only had a sheet and I had put my head into the bath, so I needed to dry my hair. As I stepped into the corridor, the other lady came towards me saying, "No no! No shower!" and she took the towel off me. It is so important to the skin restorative properties of beer that you don't wash it off, that the ladies will actually confiscate your towel to prevent you from doing so! No concern for the fact that I had multitudes of hop fragments stuck in my pubes...

The ending was quite hilarious, and overall the beer spa was awesome - it was so relaxing!

Tereza met me at Plzen Station and we went for dinner at a pizzeria, and then to a chain pub called "The Pub" which has beer taps *on the tables* where you can pour your own beer! So you never have to wait for the barman to serve you or for them to judge whether you've had enough already – you just help yourself right there at the table! Moreover, there is a projector screen on the wall which records how much beer your table has poured and drunk compared to the other tables! I asked Tereza if the Czech Republic has responsible service of alcohol laws and she said, "What's that?"

The following day, I had time to see Plzen. It was a day quite filled with beer. I went to the Brewery Museum in the morning, which explained the origins of beer (accidentally fermented bread in Mesopotamia – I'd heard that story) and details of its production and popularity, particularly in Plzen. The "pilsener" beer was invented quite late, in 1842, after Plzen's beer quality dropped so low the city authorities were dramatically pouring barrels out in front of the town hall, declaring it unfit to drink. They tightened brewing regulations and sent a man to Bavaria to better learn how it was done. He brought back a Bavarian brew master who used a new technique, the bottom-fermented lagering process. He invented a new beer called "Pilsner Urquell", which means "the grand source of Plzen" or something like that (in German, not Czech!). The rest is history.

After the museum I went on a tour of Underground Plzen! It is accessed via the ice store of the old brewery cellars. They were able to keep ice there all year round (it must have been a lot of ice). As it melted, cool water flowed into the brewery cellars where beer was being fermented and matured. I know that lagers need cooler temperatures to ferment than ales, and I had thought that the reason why lager became popular so many centuries later than ale was that it required refrigeration technology. Not so. It helps, sure, but they didn't have it in 1842 – they just used ice. Even after refrigeration technology was invented, the Pilsner Urquell brewery continued to use ice as well, until 1987!

I'd been wanting to do an underground tour since Poland. They pop up in a few places but I hadn't been able to get to any yet, so I was quite excited. The tunnels were really cool. In and out, up and down, through narrow openings, gazing up and down wells, passing cramped chambers (the cellars of houses and businesses above). They had been carved out by hand – in one you could see the sandstone bedrock and how haphazardly carved it was. Other areas had brick reinforcing and others had newer concrete. One tunnel even had cast iron arches! It was all cut out by hand in medieval times. They wore hoods stuffed with hay and grass to protect their heads!

The cellars and passages were used for:

- underground pubs (a way of dealing with noisy patrons – out of earshot, out of mind)
- fermentation and storage of beer (special stone benches had been built or carved to hold barrels)
- wells
- rubbish pits
- food storage

And people hid underground in times of siege and war, and moved around the city underground when it was too dangerous on the surface. Plzen was so well fortified it wasn't invaded until 1618, though there had been many earlier attempts.

Next it was time to head over to Pilsner Urquell for a brewery tour. I had been uneasy about doing this at a big mainstream brewery, but Tereza recommended it. She said that you could taste beer straight from the barrel and that it was a great tour. The barrel tasting convinced me.

The guide was really good and so was the tour, but the best bit was going through the cellar system. We could see our breath in the air. I say cellar "system" because it's enormous. There are dozens and dozens of tall arched cellars hewn from the rock, arranged along corridors which are a good 50m long. It's cold and humid: you can see mist in the air, and the floor is slippery with water on its way to the drainage channels.

This is where the beer was traditionally brewed and matured until 1987, but it is no more. Now they have big electrically-cooled tanks above the ground. However, they still maintain the traditional barrel fermentation and maturing technique for tourists! First we saw a handful of large barrels (the size of a round spa) turned on one end with no lid, the beer visible inside them. That's where it's fermented, and then it's matured in more huge oak barrels. These are sealed and turned on their sides, and in each enormous cellar (at least 20m in length) there are two rows of them, lying on stone or brick "barrel benches" either side of a lower walkway. When you stand on this walkway, your head only comes halfway up the barrels. Above you is mist and ahead of you are sooo many barrels! It's magical! And the walls and ceiling are white - they've been sprayed with lime, and you can see how wet they are.

About halfway along the row of barrels there was one which had two taps on it. There stood an old man, a brewery employee, who was filling up the plastic glasses we had each been given. Straight from the barrel... We drank our beers in an adjacent cellar on the other side of the long corridor, where smaller barrels had been set up as standing tables. The tour guide said that it was possible to hire these cellars, and that the hire fee included unlimited access to the barrel beer for a timed period!

The guide was drinking a beer also: a 300mL one (to my 500mL). This surprised me, given that I have been a guide in a brewery with a zero-alcohol policy, as per Australian health and safety regulations. It makes sense for public safety too – it's better for tourists to know their guide has full control of their faculties, right? I asked her about it and she said, "That is why I have only a small one, but we are encouraged to drink the beer because it is polite to drink with people – if I did not drink, people would find it strange and they might think there was something wrong with the beer."!!

I found it strange that she *was* drinking, and also that they were feeding tourists alcoholic beverages in a place that had a very slippery floor. But perhaps Australians are too obsessed with safety. I don't think that we should make beer cheaper than tea and water, but I do think we should let our hair down and live a little, and drinking fresh, unfiltered, unpasteurised beer in a cold and misty cellar is awesome.

Man over beast and man over man

I travelled to Prague that evening. Karra warned me that Prague was hell on weekends and Tereza, who used to live there, confirmed it – apparently you literally cannot move for tourists in all the key sites. Therefore I decided to do my two planned day trips first, and explore Prague from Monday. So today I have come to the town of Kutná Hora, which contains the famous Church of Bones. This didn't take long to see, so I could've returned to Prague early but, mindful of said sardine tourists, I have elected to remain in Kutná Hora for the afternoon, which is quiet and peaceful, and am presently sitting at an al fresco table in a small pastel-adorned square, sipping a beer.

The Sedle Ossuary, the "Bone Church", is quite weird. It's quite small, but the bones of 40,000 people are in there. The cemetery was partially destroyed by the Hussite invasion in the 15th century and the bones were moved inside the church by a monk, who piled them into pyramids. The bones came to be used as ornamentation in the church, and then in the 18th century the Schwarzenberg family (the same family who owned the castle in Český Krumlov) acquired it, and they really went nuts on it. It already had bony baroque fittings, but the Schwarzenbergs made a bone chandelier and a bone representation of their coat of arms, among other things. Their coat of arms has an image of a raven picking at a dead Turk's eye, so they made a raven out of bones, and the Turk's head was rather easy to construct: a skull.

It's really weird. And, I think, disrespectful of the dead - especially when it's full of tourists taking photos. But apparently it's meant to remind us of our own mortality, and thus make us repent and fear God or something...

It's still an hour and 20 minutes until my bus. What shall I write about? Beer being cheaper than water? The absence of bath towels? The complete opposite of communism? Tereza told me that she will have to work until she is 77: that is the retirement age for people of her age group. She said there is compulsory superannuation but it is paid to the government, and when you retire you can only get about €400 a month - regardless of how much you put in. She also said that everyone has to pay health insurance, even if they are out of the country for long periods. She said she can't go home until her work is finished and she usually works nine hours per day including only a half hour lunch break. The number of public holidays in the Czech Republic is less than those in France or Austria.

"Huh," I said. "I'd have thought a former communist country would do better: that there would be some lingering idea of social equality."

"No," she said, "because after communism ended we wanted to do the opposite: to show the West that we are not like that." So they actually made a system that is more harsh than in the West! And corrupt officials siphon off the top of it...

"But hey, at least we have cheap beer!" Tereza said. She explained that beer is literally cheaper than water, because no restaurant or bar will give you free tap water. "So that's why Czechs drink so much beer," she said.

And a hospitality worker will only earn €300 a month, so you have to remember to tip them.

Tricky. Nice place to holiday; not a nice place to work. Oh, and unemployment benefits only last for six months – I heard that in Slovakia too. Just like in America. But they're in Europe - why didn't they copy the Brits instead?

20th of July, 4:19pm:

Today I went to Konopiště Castle. Its most recent occupant was Franz Ferdinand: a man very famous for his death in Sarajevo in 1914, which kicked off WWI. I was surprised to realise that I can even name his killer, Gavrilo Princip, because it is written in the history books in bold print. What I hadn't known was that his wife was assassinated along with him. I find this particularly sad given that they left three children behind. Interestingly, the couple married for love, and the only way the royal family would accept the marriage was if the couple signed documents stating that their children would not inherit the throne of Austria or any Hapsburg property. They insisted upon this because Franz Ferdinand's fiancée was a lowly countess! He had only become Crown Prince of Austria after his cousin Prince Rudolph died, and didn't have a good relationship with his uncle, Emperor Franz Josef.

Now to the weird stuff. Franz Ferdinand shot almost 300,000 animals in his lifetime. He made hunting trophies out of 100,000 of them and plastered them all over his house. There's a gallery lined with hundreds of pairs of antlers; hanging ducks and turkeys; mounted heads of boars, antelope, bison and foxes; and badger families! He killed whole families of badgers and mounted them together! There are tiger skins from when he went hunting in India, and there are full stuffed bears standing with their mouths open as if they are about to attack you! They've done that with a lot of the taxidermy: opened their mouths and pulled their faces into a snarl. You wouldn't want to wander around there at night.

There's also an antler chandelier and a glass cabinet full of deer teeth, and on the walls of the staircase by the entrance - arranged above nice normal religious statues and coat hooks - there are rows and rows of owls' heads! The owls' faces are really expressive, the poor little things. It's utterly creepy and weird.

The primary reason for my revulsion was concern for the animal's welfare, which some would not agree with me on, but chew on this: the man killed almost 300,000 animals. That means that almost every single animal he saw, he shot on sight. What kind of macabre killing obsession; what kind of sick desires must he have had? If put in charge of, say, the

Third Reich, an American slave plantation, or a European kingdom during the Reformation, what, or who, would he have been killing then? Society should be very worried about people with tendencies like that.

He even had a toy rifle range in his basement, with clockwork targets for practise! There are antler chairs down there - chairs made of antlers! - and yet more heads and another bear. Strange, strange man. But this next thing may be viewed as a: just as strange, b: more strange or c: *oh, that explains everything*. In addition to hunting trophies, Franz Ferdinand collected images and statues of St George and the dragon. He had 2,500 of them, and 900 are displayed in one gallery off the gardens, which you can go into. I looked around at the images and statues and thought, *Oh... I see*.

It's exactly the same thing. It's man pacifying beast and then brutally killing it. St George is always pictured killing the dragon as a brave hero. I know the Hapsburgs loved the man over beast thing – the statues around the palace in Vienna attest to that. They were meant to scare people; they were an ultimate projection of strength...

So there's the "We are the strongest so don't mess with us" idea, which is borne out by the fact that St George is always (testified by the 900 images I saw today) depicted above the dragon, overpowering it. If he's alone he's standing on top of it and if he's on a horse, the horse is on top of it. And usually he's slamming his lance right into its head. That dragon has been overpowered...

But the other thing I noticed, in every one of the images and statues I saw, is that the dragon is always quite small. Compared to George, it's no more than the size of a pony. I viewed this as a caricaturisation of winners versus losers: the hero being portrayed as larger than his enemy. Franz Ferdinand definitely thought of himself as a winner.

In one of the statues, the dragon had breasts. Was it a she? Was she trying to feed her young? I'd like to know more about this dragon...

I was walking around the exhibition with a revolted expression on my face, thinking, *What was wrong with this man?* I was also thinking, when I was walking thru the opulent rooms upstairs, that I can understand where Gavrilo Princip was coming from. Not against Franz Ferdinand specifically, but against all aristocrats. Many like Princip were sizing up similar targets in that time period. The common people had had enough. That's not to say that I condone killing him - I don't think anyone should kill anyone ever, really - but I understand where he was coming from. Something had to be done to bring that system to an end. And that's where communism came from.

Princip wasn't a communist; he was a Serbian nationalist, but my point is that ordinary people took extreme measures (assassinations and revolutions) to fight power and privilege.

22nd of July, 3:30pm:
To the gracious, yet sadly tourist-ridden, city of Prague. Yesterday I mostly just wandered around, firstly to Municipal House: a grand art nouveau building which doesn't seem very municipal anymore because it houses theatres and restaurants. Next to it is a grand gothic tower, a former entrance gate to the Old Town, which is at the same time strikingly different to Municipal House and also remarkably similar.

Tourists began swimming around me at that point, as I headed through some cobbled laneways to the Old Town Square. I arrived just as the Astronomical Clock began to chime, and was gobsmacked to see that there were about one thousand tourists standing in front of it watching its hourly show. I couldn't see much and it ended quickly, but I went back later. The show is just the Twelve Apostles moving past some windows and four of the clock's statues engaging in some clockwork shuddering. Death rings a bell, but other than that it's pretty lame. And yet 1,000 people assemble there every hour. When I arrived I found it easy to get a good spot, but when I tried to leave I found myself trapped by bodies.

The hourly show may be a let down, but the clock itself is very cool. It's enormous - it has two faces and neither of them tell the time; they tell the day of the year, the signs of the zodiac and the position of the sun and moon. Time might be in there somewhere as well - my tour guide later said something about Bohemian numbers, but I couldn't read them. It's all pretty confusing. But it dates from the 15th century! Incredible!

I then proceeded to Charles Bridge, the crowds with me all the way (and this was Monday – I can't believe what it must've been like on the weekend). I started to feel claustrophobic and wanted to get away, but then I found two incredible buskers whom I was so impressed with I sat down under one of the statues and ate my lunch listening to them! It was one violinist and one accordionist, and when I arrived the violinist was playing the first violin part and the accordionist all the other strings parts of the "Winter" movement of Vivaldi's *The Four Seasons*. I love that piece so I stayed and listened, and didn't leave until they'd been through their entire repertoire and played it again! Sadly, their repertoire was only about 5 tunes... But I learned that the Charles Bridge is nice if you have good buskers to listen to.

The statues on the bridge are all covered in spider's webs. That's interesting. Do the Czechs not like to disturb them, like the Japanese and my dad? The St George statues at Konopiště were covered in them too.

Finally reaching the end of the bridge I walked to the John Lennon Wall, which sadly has now been hijacked by regular graffiti artists, most of them foreign. But it used to be (since 1980) covered in political messages and Beatles lyrics, and the communist police never quite managed to keep it clean.

Today, I tried to go to the Cubist Museum but found it closed, so I went to the Communist Museum. When I got inside, at first I thought, *Oh damn, why have I done this again? I've already seen so much communist stuff!* But it was good to learn about the Czechoslovak experience, which was different. They tried to introduce reforms in 1968 and were stopped by an invasion - not only from Russia, but from all their bordering Soviet bloc states. Soviet soldiers kept occupying the place until 1989.

I'd heard about the end of communism in all the countries I've been to, and how it was a peaceful revolution in most cases – well, it was in Estonia; there weren't many dead in Latvia and Lithuania; and the so-called Velvet Revolution in Czechoslovakia had a death toll of zero, but there were many people beaten up by police with truncheons and fists.

I'd learned that it had happened in all the countries I visited in a similar time period, between 1988 and 1991, and it seemed quite obvious that they had spurred each other on: that a strong popular movement in one country had inspired people in their neighbouring states to do the same. And they did, and all the countries I've visited were released from the Soviet communist yoke within about three years.

But the focus of my trip, and indeed of most world media and education systems' references to "communism" and "the end of communism", is very much *Soviet* communism. That ended in the early 90s, but we often forget that there were, and are still, other brands of communism concocted by other dictators largely unconnected to the Soviets. I use the term "communism" very loosely here, of course, and refer to the many dictatorships still in existence which came to power through communist revolutions, but which nowadays do not follow anything close to Marxist ideals.

When I first went to China, way back in 2007, I did not write as negatively as I do today about the society and the polity, but I did lament the complete absence of communist social benefits there and the re-introduction of capitalist class privilege. This has been done, but the so-called "Chinese Communist Party" is still in power, unlike the Soviet one, and they're the ones who have screwed up the China of today.

The Prague Communist Museum pointed out something which I had never before realised - I hadn't connected the dots. The late 80s and early 90s saw a snowballing of anti-Communist popular movements in different countries, right? This is what they said:

"An apt saying is that the disintegration of communist power lasted in Poland for ten years, in East Germany ten weeks and in Czechoslovakia ten days. Neo-Stalinists, who in 1969 gained complete control over KSČ [Czechoslovakian Communist Party] and for twenty years held power with unwavering callousness, may have been considering the Chinese solution."

The Chinese solution?

"For this purpose they had the centre of the city...intersected by an arterial road so that tanks could get to Wenceslas Square, a traditional place for demonstrations, as quickly as possible. However, without the support of the Soviet Union [thankyou, Gorbachev] they did not decide on the massacre of protesters."

Oh yeah. The Chinese solution. The Tiananmen Square massacre. It happened at around the same time. The Chinese people revolted at around the same time.

The police could have shot dead the protestors in Wenceslas Square, but they didn't – they just used their truncheons instead. And that is why central and eastern European countries are free today for me to visit and enjoy their hospitality, while China is still under the control of the so-called "Communist Party" and is a difficult place to spend time...

In the kitchen of the Ginger Monkey Hostel in Ždiar, I had a conversation with David about why China is the way it is. I am quick to criticise "mainland" China, but I am also quick to differentiate between it and Hong Kong and Macau, where I have also visited and had a lovely time, and did not find the people to be whatsoever rude, pushy or even "rip-offy" like those in mainland China are. Modern Taiwan was, of course, founded by refugees from the mainland who fled the communist revolution, so many of its people have relatives still in mainland China. David is one of them. He said he has two uncles - brothers - who no longer speak because they fought over the same cup during the Cultural Revolution. The situation under communism was so depraved that people had to fight each other – even their own family - for basic things. The government had confiscated people's crockery for the army, so these two brothers were fighting over just one cup. The result has been a damaging "every man for himself" mentality I observed in mainland China. Even though the Cultural Revolution was some time ago, its impact remains in the mentality of the people. This is the fault of the "communist" dictatorship which still continues today.

The Prague Communist Museum also had a small exhibition on North Korea, and it very strongly stated: this is still going on, we must not forget, this is *still* happening. There were photos of malnourished skeletal babies and toddlers. There was a picture taken by satellite of Korea at night, with South Korea all lit up and North Korea completely black except for Pyongyang. There is a great shortage of food, money and electricity, and yet the dictatorship prioritises what is there for its own ends. Electricity is used to light up monarchistic monuments. The dictator has insane amounts of food, luxury homes and cars, while his people are starving. Every year they spend millions of dollars on military parades and on arena spectaculars performed by children, who are hit if they don't perform correctly and who acquire bladder damage from the lack of toilet breaks. This is their education: unwavering allegiance to the dictator. It's worse than it ever was in Czechoslovakia, and it's still continuing *now*...

Last night in my dorm, I met a young woman from Ecuador. She noted that I was a diabetic and likened its normalcy in my life to the normalcy of violence in South America. "You test your blood sugar and inject every day," she said. "Other people find that strange and they ask you how you manage it, but to you it's normal. Well to me, it's normal to always hold my possessions in front of me and never get too close to strangers on the street," she said. "People in other countries find it strange, but to me it is normal like diabetes is normal to you, and I deal with it and I'm OK."

She said she didn't like the fact that Jewish Holocaust stories are bandied about all the time, which at first got my hackles up because I've been to Auschwitz, but she said, "What about the horrors the Soviets did to people? What about the ethnic cleansing that happened much more recently in Bosnia – why does nobody talk about that? Nobody ever makes movies about that."

She said she has a Slovenian friend who has Bosnian classmates who remember their families being massacred, and they are so young. That was so recent. When I was marvelling at the amazing reconstruction of Old Town Warsaw after WWII, someone I met found a picture in a travel guide of a beautiful town in Bosnia-Herzegovina which had been reconstructed *post-1993*. Why do we never hear about, or talk about, that?

I am reminded once again of a belief that I have had great difficulty giving up ever since September 11 happened. The belief that the current age was different. The belief that wars and persecution were a thing of the past. The belief that things are better now. We have the United Nations, the EU and anti-discrimination acts, right? Humanity is better now. Well it may be in some discrete places in some discrete circumstances, but it will only continue as long as those positive circumstances hold. Overall, war is not over, racism is not over, persecution is not over, power-grabbing is not over, and the 20th century did nothing to reverse humanity's natural tendencies toward all of those things. They're minimised now in some societies, sure, because people are rich and fat and happy. But just how long would it take for them to come back? If you had a government which was taking away the very cups in your home, wouldn't you be fighting against your fellow humans for everything - and not caring how they fared?

On the 25th of July, I finally had to rip the SYD to PEK airline tag off my backpack and get a new one. The looooong overland part of my journey was over. Google says it's 8,000km from Beijing to Prague, but that's as the crow flies. The Trans-Mongolian is 8,000km, so I'd already done that distance by the 27th of May. Who knows how far I've travelled since then. It's 2,500km from Hobart to Cairns, but on the trip I did covering that distance, our van's odometer said over 10,000km by the end of it. You travel in and out and all over the place.

Applying the same mathematics (X times 4 – I can't believe I just said that – I hate algebra), I may have travelled 32,000km between Beijing and Prague. It's almost the entire eastern hemisphere. I've been on a few exciting trips in my time, but that was the longest unbroken line across the world map, and the diversity of landscape, cultures and people I met was just fantastic.

I was amazed by how much I learned, about so many things - from superstitions to home-smoked fish; from the music of ice to the rebuilding of razed cities; from gers to Kruschevki; from Gorbachev to Hitler. Before taking this journey, I didn't even know how to tell where Europe began and Asia ended, or that they were two parts of the same continent...

Watching the earth's surface change through a train carriage window never ceased to entertain me. Seeing the architecture change, the people, the cultures. Learning about the past and how it still shapes the present. Observing that we humans are all just the same as each other, no matter if we travel by car or horse; if we eat rice or bread; if we sing or chant to our gods; if we live in a bustling city or on a peaceful grassy steppe without any roads.

Crossing one fifth of the world's surface taught me most of all that we are all the same. We must strive to end repression and hatred; we must understand and respect all the peoples of the world. If we do, they just might share with us a little of their world - their food and their music; their culture and their humour; their beautiful places and their cosy homes - so that we might have a wonderful time together, and move forward richer, more fulfilled, and with a far greater understanding of our world...

Acknowledgements

Thank you to my father, Barrie Dallas, for his assistance with editing.

Thank you to those who provided advice and encouragement, including June Dallas, Siobhan Dallas, Steve Whittle, Heather Holland, Kathy Gausden, Robyn Armstrong, Elizabeth Fleetwood and Jamie Maslin.

Thank you to the tour guides and drivers who showed me their wonderful places.

Thank you to the hosts, who made me feel welcome and gave me somewhere to rest my head.

Thank you to the friends I met along the way.

Where possible I contacted those mentioned by name in this book to ask their permission. Thank you so much to those who gave it. In some cases it wasn't possible to ask as I didn't have everybody's contact details, but I've only said nice things about the people I mentioned by name (apart from Stalin and Hitler, obviously), so I hope that is ok!

My Trans-Mongolian rail journey was arranged by Passport Travel, Melbourne – not only the railway tickets but also tours, connections and accommodation in Mongolia and Russia, and flights and visas. They are experts in their field and provide a great service.

My post-St Petersburg travels were arranged by me with the assistance of a Lonely Planet guidebook and the internet.

I have a whole box full of other travel journals and several digital ones as well, so stay tuned for another book! Please follow me at:

https://www.facebook.com/carriestravelbooks
https://www.instagram.com/carriestravelbooks/
https://www.pinterest.com.au/carriestravelbooks/
https://www.linkedin.com/in/carrie-riseley/
https://twitter.com/CazTravelBooks

Thank you to Sandra and Ken Negro, both since deceased, who gave me my first travel journal notebook when I was 18, just before my first trip to Japan. I loved writing in it and have kept it up on every journey since.

Images list

About the author

   Carrie grew up in Tasmania, Australia but spent her youth living in Melbourne, England and Japan. She has travelled to 46 countries to date, and kept a travel journal for every single one. Because this book was written in the moment as she was travelling, you'll feel like you were there too. You'll marvel as she marveled, wonder as she wondered, and learn as she learned.

   Carrie lives in Hobart, Tasmania.

Printed in Great Britain
by Amazon